Sustainable Graphic Design

Sustainable Graphic Design

Principles and Practices

Peter Claver Fine

Bloomsbury Academic
An imprint of Bloomsbury Publishing Plc

B L O O M S B U R Y
LONDON · OXFORD · NEW YORK · NEW DELHI · SYDNEY

Bloomsbury Academic

An imprint of Bloomsbury Publishing Plc

50 Bedford Square	1385 Broadway
London	New York
WC1B 3DP	NY 10018
UK	USA

www.bloomsbury.com

BLOOMSBURY and the Diana logo are trademarks of Bloomsbury Publishing Plc

First published 2016

British Library Cataloguing-in-Publication Data
A catalogue record for this book is available from the British Library.

ISBN: HB: 978-0-8578-5062-1
PB: 978-0-8578-5063-8

Library of Congress Cataloging-in-Publication Data
Fine, Peter Claver, author.
Sustainable graphic design : principles and practices / Peter Claver Fine.
pages cm
ISBN 978-0-8578-5062-1 (hardback) -- ISBN 978-0-8578-5063-8 (paperback)
1. Graphic arts--Technique. 2. Product life cycle--Environmental aspects.
3. Commercial products--Environmental aspects. I. Title.
NC1000.F55 2016
740--dc23
2015034244

Typeset by Lachina
Printed and bound in China

Table of Contents

Acknowledgments

This book is the culmination of many years of study, research, and teaching beginning long before I commenced writing it and retains many vestiges of and debts to my design and art teachers over a lifetime.

First, thanks to my mother, who first showed me her drawings from college and always kept art in view around the house. Also, thanks to my father, who as a novelist introduced me to the role of an author and whose book covers were likely the first graphic design that held meaning for me personally. Also much gratitude to Robert Strobridge (Stro), who demonstrated to me firsthand as a child the work of a socially engaged artist and who was certainly the first person I knew who worked as a graphic designer. Much thanks must go to my high school art teachers, Joe Ferrara and Eileen Gardner of Shorewood High School and Carolyn White of the Art Satellite program at the Milwaukee Art Museum. Special thanks to all my university professors, especially Gregg Berryman at California State University, Chico, who first taught me design history, along with many of my studio courses in design. I would also like to thank my first art directors who kindly paid me to learn, both Larry Lewis and Laura Kling. Finally, I would like to thank my graduate committee at the University of Arizona, especially my graduate advisor Ellen McMahon, who encouraged me in my pursuit of a critical stance toward design, and Paul Ivey, whose guidance was crucial in this respect.

All of my teachers afforded me a great deal of creative and personal freedom to pursue my own ideas and take risks, something I try to allow my students as well. I owe a great debt of gratitude to my students who over the years have taken part in classes and coursework designed to elicit more sustainable design education and practice and whose work appears in this book. I would not have been able to raise my own expectations without first encouraging the same in them. Special thanks to Ramey Newell for photos of fellow students' work.

Several people helped greatly in the development of this book. Eric Benson, a friend as well as a peer in the small circle of design educators who are pursuing and implementing sustainable pedagogy, and also Yvette Perullo, Aaris Sherin, and Liz Resnick, who offered support, advice, and friendship in the same manner. My truest colleague Sarah Hagelin read, re-read, and edited numerous versions of this manuscript over the years and has aided and encouraged me greatly and over many hurdles. Ryan Cull also read portions of this manuscript, and finally many thanks to Josh Michels, who first introduced me to the ridiculous notion of green design many years ago.

The Introduction contains content originally included in "Sustainable Design Education Rethought: The Case for Eco-Modernism," which I co-authored with Eric Benson and was published in *Design Principles and Practices*. Chapter six appeared first as an editorial in the *Design Studies Forum* online journal. Twenty-one key factors for analyzing green claims first appeared as an article on *Re-nourish*. Some concepts appearing in the book were first worked out through presentations I gave at AIGA Design Educators conferences, including one with Eric Benson. Many thanks to my editors at Bloomsbury Academic, especially Tristan Palmer, who elicited the book initially under Berg Publishers, also Simon Cowell, and lastly Rebecca Barden, who saw it through to the end.

—Peter Claver Fine

Introduction

Sustainable Graphic Design: Principles and Practice is intended for advanced students of graphic design who are engaged in, or preparing to begin, complex research or thesis projects, especially when collaborating with other design students and disciplines. It assumes a keen interest in the activity of designing, along with an already established fascination with the basic skills and forms employed by graphic designers. It will offer particular advantages to students who have already experienced some of the limitations of graphic design and wish to take the process further in hopes of expressing the true promise of graphic design as an agent of positive change. In short, this book is for students who are both realists and optimists either by nature or through hard-won experience. The book springs forth from this ethos and was a reaction to a formidable design problem: how to reorient the researching, learning, and teaching of graphic design as sustainable.

The book provides a broad introduction to both design history and sustainability from sources both near to and far from design. It is especially concerned with how a clear and basic appreciation of the history of design allows us to understand how we might design for the future. Although this may seem apparent, it is the author's position that graphic design education often lacks a critical context. The weight of history informing how we learn design often limits the degree of historical and critical context provided to the average student. The book therefore questions how a design education can include more critical, historically sound, contemporary content as a means to address sustainability.

Design deals largely with how common and everyday items get made and used, which makes contemporary issues facing design and the larger society central to the book. It is not simply concerned with how the average person might affect positive change but rather how the self-identified designer, who at the moment may still be a student, can seek to design images, objects, and experiences that will have a life beyond the point where the design of the thing has ostensibly ended.

The book, through the text and the case studies, exhibits for students what must be designed if we are to design for good. This is important because it isn't necessarily clear *what* today's students are to design for now and in the future given the immediate and constant threat of ecological damage and the danger of ecological catastrophe. The design students may not yet be equipped to deal with ecological concerns due to the high degree of design specialization required of even beginning students. There are, of course, several key areas of sustainability that the design students may begin to reasonably conceive of designing for, including but not limited to, material issues of waste, energy, food, water, and shelter, but also an infinite number of cultural and economic issues. That said, the case studies shown here reveal that sustainable graphic design is an exercise in interdisciplinary work that deals with both material concerns and rich cultural content. Design students will find that their specialization in design is not a given and should not be taken for granted by them or others in its power to set agendas, guide discourse, and refine outcomes among a broad range of specialists and issues.

This book developed in much the same way that designers must approach sustainability. That is, an author seeks to define and resolve complex problems often without the aid or impetus of a client. In doing so, designers must then recognize not only their agency as authors deciding what to respond to and how to proceed but also the agency of the people and communities affected. For design students, it is therefore imperative that they move beyond the assignment and engage with issues and problems outside the walls of the classroom. This will also mean helping others in realizing the potential of design and of designers in facilitating sustainability.

Each case study has been carefully considered and selected for facility in exposing students to the varied and complex methods for leveraging the influence of graphic design to engage with sustainability. Case studies also were chosen for the ways they specifically address materials and materiality. Most importantly, each has been proven over time to generate reproducible results. The case studies are learning and design tools developed through serious thought and research by students and their instructors, who began with little or nothing except a desire to make a difference. In every case, those involved have embraced their own ignorance of the subject and are willing to now share whatever expertise they have accumulated. In short, any effort at sustainable design is by definition rooted in generosity and risk-taking. The case studies do not attend to what "in theory" many might assume must be addressed, but emanate from a direct engagement with the many tangled and thorny issues of sustainability. What results, then, is what can be addressed in practical terms through the teaching and practice of design. This eliminates many false assumptions born from the false dichotomy of what constitutes green design versus all other design. Each reader is encouraged to add to and expand on what is meant by sustainable design. Prescriptions for what others must do or accomplish are left to others.

The importance of graphic design to the question of what is sustainable is its influence on how things actually get produced and consumed. This is in part what Tony Fry terms the "prefigurative ability of design." What graphic design further promises is a means to defining the rhetorical power of sustainability as it continues to unfold. This is like a very long length of carpet rolled out, and ever forward, repeating a pattern that is already determined. Each case study also represents the emergence of new methods and methodologies, as they are currently being explored and established by students working in close cooperation with their instructors and communities.

In large part, the book intends to encourage students to further define sustainability through the creation of case studies of their own in which they not only research questions but also develop new tools and methods to achieve their goals. This assumes a foundation in a basic graphic design skill set and an interest in using it to engage with critical content beyond market-based imperatives assumed by many

to be the primary purview of the designer. Furthermore, the book defines *sustainability* as not only vital to the future of design but as a design problem in general that is now being outlined by design students, along with young and emerging designers. Therefore, design education and sustainable design are not separate or even parallel tracks but a single undertaking. So the importance of graphic design to the question of what is sustainable is not only its influence on how things actually get produced and consumed but how design is taught, what is taught, what is then learned, and what can be applied with some degree of reproducible success. The student reading this book will realize very quickly that this involves several things at once, none of which operate discretely from the others.

What the Case Studies Tell Us

The case studies in this book are the primary means and models for describing sustainability to the graphic design student. They represent less a specific methodology than an approach informed by a philosophy and based in the discipline of graphic design and a certain degree of success learned through trial and error.

Each chapter deals with a specific area of influence for the graphic designer, with the first being based in traditional graphic design for print. The following four chapters feature case studies that—although they exhibit work clearly identifiable as graphic design—also demonstrate how graphic design overlaps with many other disciplines and spheres within design and without. In short, they reveal the ways that graphic design mediates many of our everyday interactions with complexity. This is true whether we are interacting as designers or not. It tells us as graphic designers that our work is central to the way very mundane things define large systems and, therefore, problems of sustainability while still remaining largely invisible.

The case studies reveal how the graphic designer can clarify for everyday audiences, users, other designers, suppliers, vendors, and experts in different fields how graphic design can speak to and about sustainability in ways that otherwise may fail to be articulated. These case studies therefore make plain the need for graphic designers to put aside a prescriptive approach to graphic design outcomes and focus on highly critical and conceptual designs.

Sustainable Graphic Design: Principles and Practices views the role of graphic design not only as a means to an end but as a critical discourse unto itself. Considering the scope of graphic design's relationship to the history of design as well as consumption exposes how these emerged simultaneously. This is vital to sustainability because graphic design reveals our very basic relationship to consumption by virtue of the multitude of designed images and texts we encounter in our daily lives and then often discard. Despite graphic design's ubiquity, there is little appreciation for what happens to graphic design artifacts after their useful life has ended. Their omnipresence within the waste stream is even more distressing, seeming to implicate the graphic designer as an agent of destruction. Because all design results in some form of visual or material culture, it has to do with *things*—which things we value and which things we discard. This book is an attempt to understand what we as graphic designers value and how that affects the total health of our natural environment. It strives to bring to graphic design the same level of engagement with environmental issues that was long ago established in other design fields and to inspire and enable graphic designers to question their assumptions about this role, its limitations, and its potential. To remain relevant, graphic designers must understand their role and esteem it. This book asks not only what designers are doing about the environment but how graphic design can shape the way we think about sustainability.

Chapter One

The case studies in this chapter demonstrate the fundamental ways in which graphic design for print affects all of our perceptions of sustainability. At the heart of this is the act of crafting messages using words and images. This activity sets graphic design apart from the singular acts of writing or producing images. It is not simply a method for explaining a text or illustrating that text. It is an intimate process wherein the designer marries words and images to create new meaning.

These case studies reveal how graphic design is a process well suited to dealing with the complexity of sustainability through a host of methods, including both material and visual culture. In contrast to this complexity, the relative simplicity apparent in all good design is seen here to exist through the basic media of print.

Typically viewed as based in the visual, graphic design is often overlooked and then mistakenly lumped together with a wide variety of visual media. These case studies begin the process of showing that graphic design must be seen to be what it is, to be seen as design and its products as design artifacts. This is true regardless of whether many people conceive of them generally as branding, advertising, marketing, broadcast media, or style. Otherwise, we dilute the power of graphic design and design in general. In order to fully comprehend their role as designers within sustainability, graphic designers must recognize the specific products of the activity called designing. These demonstrate how a more critically oriented approach to graphic design is vital to success and that in order to develop this as a default, designers will need to take on not only the role of author but of researcher and tool maker as well.

This first chapter establishes collaboration as an important basis for sustainable design, as it will remain throughout the book. An interdisciplinary approach to graphic design is a proven basis for successful collaborations. In this first chapter, the rhetoric of sustainability is shown to be in play, especially in cases of greenwashing, where corporations seek to obfuscate their practices and avoid transparency. This tells the graphic designer the importance of harnessing the power of print and other forms to reveal best practices. Reversing the practice of greenwashing (i.e., manipulating words and images simultaneously) reveals how ideas emerge as effective graphic communication involving the many difficult and complex issues of sustainability. This reveals the role of persuasion in design as a mutual discourse between designer and viewer dependent on existing cultural references, both visual and verbal, but which must begin to outline new modes for incorporating sustainability.

Chapter one also introduces contemporary design initiatives such as systems design, service design, co-design, and design entrepreneurship within a user-centered approach to global concerns, especially relating to ethics. All of these emerging streams within graphic design will be shown throughout the book to be in sync with sustainability and employed to reduce the abstraction associated with production and consumption rather than perpetuating global systems of waste and degradation. This broad and global perspective highlights social patterns that link design to complex social, cultural, and economic systems. This demonstrates the relevance of design thinking as the means to analyze and synthesize complex information while navigating technology and social groups. The degree to which users mediate their lives via technology mirrors the designers' own complex relationship to the technologies they employ and their complicity in systems that are harmful; this is explored in relation to e-waste. In recognizing this, designers learn how the consumption of technology matters, from raw material extraction through product after-life and their effect on environmental concerns and economic gains.

Chapter one also begins to examine how the learning of sustainable graphic design unfolds beyond the typical four walls of the classroom within learning spaces and research sites that engage the instructor as an equal participant in the process of learning. This space is used to devise and model research questions and strategies that will result in thesis and other independent projects for students. Because this learning is in part situated beyond the classroom, the public sphere becomes a key element appearing throughout the book. The need and the desire of the students in making their work public directly results in detailed research that then must compete within the public sphere, requiring a dramatic increase in the students' commitment to the outcomes they create. The potential of design as an advocate for public good is seen in public arenas such as retail sites, where consumers are kept at a great distance from larger systems that they participate in daily. In order to educate, advocate, and persuade, graphic designers must assume more agency over the process and outcomes of their work.

Chapter Two

The case studies featured in this chapter on process include research, information and systems, as well as proofs and tools. Often these all thread through the designer's unique process as a complex methodology focused on creating new ways of developing knowledge and innovative outcomes. Information design is not seen here as an end in itself but as a visually persuasive and powerful process of investigation unto itself that makes visible the workings of systems we often take for granted. Design becomes a process of research wherein form-giving is determined by which details can be sifted and refined to create the most visually compelling revelation of the facts. This demonstrates the power of design to discover and anticipate simultaneously

that coalesces in an original product or service. This design entrepreneurship occurs through design's direct engagement with production and consumption, which seeks to define the users' needs along multiple lines of thought and modes of making.

This diverse and iterative approach given to intense and ongoing research for sustainable design drives and defines a question that may result in any number of outcomes beyond what we define as graphic design. By influencing what, how, and why we consume, designers can greatly influence the very definition of sustainable. These case studies also demonstrate the need for designers to create original tools, new methods, and processes for designing sustainably. These tools are designed to intuit the user's own experience. In addition, these projects touch on the design of systems that provide not only a service but an outlet for the consumer's desire to act as an individual to the benefit of their social group. This parallels the emergence of design thinking as a broader and far more critical engagement with design problems that have previously been seen as beyond the designer's purview.

Chapter Three

The case studies in chapter three deal with sustainability through package design, recognizing the package as a vessel not just of things but ideas. Here the package embodies not only material concerns, as vast and weighty as these are, but serves also as a vehicle for transporting new sustainable design concepts. The life of myriad products and packages can be tracked over time and distance, carrying with them and demonstrating the promise of design as an agent of change. Each step teaches students the necessity of developing better processes and builds an appreciation for a measured approach to achieving sustainability. These case studies exemplify the way design students must now be educated in how to best inform consumers in the ways the material concerns of the designer must become theirs as well. With packaging currently occupying as much as 30 percent of landfills, these projects model a holistic approach to graphic design as a means to reducing waste and maximizing materials.

Additionally, packages normally relegated to the waste heap have the potential to work to persuade consumers to make better use of their economic and material resources. The close reading required to decipher the life of a package reveals the large project of designing sustainably while also attempting to persuade producers and consumers of the need for socially conscious design. Through a sustainable redesign, the totality of the product can be expressed through the package. The total experience of a package and its product is not then constrained by the limitations of the final design but possesses a life beyond itself—through reuse, recycling, remaking, and reclamation of valuable waste material, all as a tangible reminder of the consumers' relationships to their essential needs. In reality, the line between a package and product is thinly drawn.

A tension exists in the ephemeral quality of the materials and the properties of the product as they address fundamental needs and as users experience a design from the sourcing of the product to reuse of the package. Users then can understand how their lives and health are tied to the products' origins and life cycle. Transparency is key in this dynamic, with the product wearing its heart on its sleeve in the form of the package. By including key components of the product and package life-cycle analysis (LCA) on or in the package, users are able to view what they are actually ingesting and encountering. This occurs in terms of product, messages, and acculturation. The very ubiquity and mundane quality of these packages tends to hide them in plain sight. These case studies highlight the student's primary role as designer, acting as mediator between production and consumption and creating a dialogue with consumers by visualizing for them the need to move beyond consuming blindly.

Chapter Four

The case studies in chapter four focus on graphic design projects within the built and natural environments and in the overlap between the two. They are situated beyond the printed page or surface of a screen, immediately challenging the notion of what graphic design is and therefore what it can be. The context for these projects is provided in the text, covering the long and complicated history of the rhetorical weight of land, space, city, waste, and nature, especially as featured in the US American imagination. This is not meant to imply that the virtual spaces that we occupy are not also vital to our understanding of where sustainable design is to evolve.

These case studies are by traditional standards environmental design projects, which are largely regarded as a narrow subset of graphic design. They have grown beyond this definition or any limited definition by virtue of their emphasis on sustainability. Their nonprescriptive approach allows students to move past basic information design, way-finding, or exhibition design. These case studies offer proofs of what constitutes sustainable design, pushing boundaries physically and materially, implying that sustainable graphic design is by its very nature interdisciplinary. They also demonstrate the importance of material experimentation in acquiring an appreciation of craft. The *how* of how things get made and the importance of understanding the ways in which material specification affect what and how we design are at the root of learning to design sustainably.

These case studies emphasize the omnipresence of ordinary, ephemeral materials that are easily discarded and readily wasted. Similarly, the second project considers wasted spaces and how designers can work to revitalize postindustrial spaces that bridge the natural and the built environments. The sheer quantity of these mundane castaways and their prevalence in our daily lives reinforces the necessity not only of sustainable design but also of designers who are trained to educate and persuade communities to act.

In these case studies, the solution emerges from the specific constraints of the project. So many new issues arise out of the morass of problems associated with unsustainable practices that a nonprescriptive approach should be maintained. This means that a healthy portion of research must precede and then dovetail with the design process. Adding to this is the necessity of designing with new or unexpected materials or processes, which may be impossible to anticipate in order to address material issues of use and waste. As a result, these case studies involve experimentation with a wide variety of materials, as well as the design of tools and methods for dealing with them. This is covered in detail in chapter two.

Chapter four more fully describes the process of collaborative design. Collaboration is not simply one element or portion of these case studies but is integrated from the bottom up. Design-research groups are at the basis of these, as well as specialists and groups situated to speak specifically to the issues being addressed by these projects. Communities that are directly affected by the issues and ultimately the users are involved as co-designers. This truly interdisciplinary approach assumes equal knowledge among designers and users and the promise of design as a universal pursuit. This is covered in more detail in chapter five. This involves a much broader approach than the pairing or mixing of professionals in different fields that one would typically associate with cross-disciplinary work. These design-research groups allow both individual students and communities to develop specific skills that they can carry forward as they develop their design skill sets.

In each case, a more subjective approach to designing is allowed to emerge. The highly personal nature of design ethics and sustainability highlight how a personal vision and passion for a subject can motivate a designer beyond esoteric pursuits. Simultaneously, these allow for the designer to embrace the unknown and the discomfort of working among others without the same devotion to one's particular mode of working and in new and unknown spaces. These case studies demonstrate how graphic design can serve to visualize the complex systems we design in and through and then live out as individuals. Through these projects, the students can come to find their place within design but also as citizen designers working to cultivate a personal vision while providing meaningful solutions for the benefit of others.

Chapter Five

The case studies in chapter five bring together elements of all previous chapters in service of social design. These projects occur in and for communities that are set apart from the largely designed world most designers occupy. These communities typically participate with little or no autonomy in existing systems of design; the case studies here reassert instead design's universality. These projects close the distance between the students and the users, who as co-designers become acquainted with self-supportive creative production and authorship. The communities then act as agents for their own work, defining the design goods they make and their value. This process redesigns the way the makers conceive of their own worth as latent designers, initiating both designed goods and services and economic systems scaled to meet the specific needs of their communities. This process resists an object versus subject relationship between design and users and evolves through multiple voices

working through mutual engagement. The results are a variety of design artifacts, sustainable design entrepreneurship, and genuine cultural capital grounded in the actual life and culture of the makers.

A true understanding of both the producers and the consumers and their empowerment clarifies graphic design's role in creating meaning. These projects also facilitate the development of students' particular voice and visual language, supporting their creative process and increasing their understanding of cultural context, while exposing them to the social, cultural, and environmental repercussions of design practice. They then see how their skills apply to real-world situations for the long-term care of the planet, and glean new insights into their potential cultural and environmental agency as visual communicators and global citizens. Furthermore, they see how their design skills are applicable not only to specific types of aesthetic problems but to systematic issues as well. The task then is not designing only for aesthetic pleasure or abstract notions but for specific communities and out of real necessity.

Chapter Six

Chapter six deals with the classroom as a shared learning space where students and teachers develop sustainable work and practices while striving to restructure design education to work at a human scale. Design education at a human scale stands in contrast to the ideologically weighted and industrially scaled model of design education common to the twentieth century. It rejects a static representation of design based in an ideology of the ideal and the notion that to reject this ideal is to transgress design standards.

This shared space of the classroom mimics small-scale technologies for creative production. The projects reject machine aesthetics in favor of technologies appropriate to the growth of the creative potential of individuals, small groups, and communities. The role of designer is seen as instigating creativity in and for others through forms designed to mediate the users' experience rather than acting as agents of consumption. This recognizes the complex and ambiguous relationship of design and designers to technology, consumption, and the authentic.

Teaching is not simply the job of instructing a group but is instead about the activity of learning and based in an ethos innate to the teacher. This implies the rejection of dogma and an embracing of the potential for failure where individual student success is subsumed within the collaborative environment. Teaching human-centered design helps design students to form themselves not in relationship to brands but as products of their own making through design, reaching their maximum performance level and prepared to design for themselves as well as for others. In this project, the school as an institution ceases treating students as a consumable and the studio becomes a research lab for incubating ideas and students to reach that potential. In this scenario, the student is able to generate the creative capital necessary for a sustainable design practice, and therefore we cease wasting human capital in the form of teachers and students.

Why the Past Will Matter in the Future

In the early nineteenth century came an explosion of new fonts with the arrival of wood type. Wood type came to dominate metal type by combining old and new technologies with a cheap, malleable, and readily available supply of material. In a relatively short period of time, hundreds of ornamental and eclectic fonts were designed in response to the increasing demand for advertising, posters, novels, periodicals, newspapers, and signage. This explosion was fueled by the rapid expansion of industrial capitalism, a growing middle class, and widespread literacy based in the popular press. By almost anyone's estimation, this was a good development, but the results and the reviews were mixed. Much of the work was poorly designed and manufactured. Much of it was based on vernacular forms rather than those passed down through the book arts. Metal type, on the other hand, had seemed to reach its apex at the end of the eighteenth century, eschewing most ornamentation and any traces of the hand-drawn. Additionally, its manufacture was precise and its aesthetic was highly refined and standardized.

Technology, as it often does, made possible new creative access to more people and with more avenues for expression. In the 1980s and early 1990s, this process was duplicated almost exactly when access to a Mac was all that was required to make almost anyone a type designer. What followed was a plethora of new fonts, many of which were poorly designed, having no roots in typographic traditions and conventions. Today, typography company Émigré's fonts are held up in design history texts as examples of some of the best work from the revolutionary advent of digital typography. Technologies emanating from that period continue to influence our lives both personally and professionally, engendering new avenues for creative expression in web, interactivity, and motion design. Don't be surprised if the future happens to you. It might be good to plan on it.

In planning for the future, it's important to understand the past. This is especially true with design. It is easy to forget that many of the important figures in design history believed and acted as if design was a tool for change and began their careers in response to some overwhelming problems. William Morris and his cohorts in the Arts and Crafts movement were reformers who believed they could offset the negative fallout from industrialization through the design of well-crafted objects and images. El Lissitzky and the other Constructivists left behind their roles as fine artists to pursue design as an integral part of a total revolution of society. The Bauhaus was established on the rubble of the First World War. Despite the near-total collapse of Germany, the Bauhaus hoped to establish design as a cornerstone of a new society. Although all of these movements experienced failure and success, they all contributed to the foundation of what is now regarded as the profession of design. The legacy they left can help designers today understand how to contribute to a new movement in sustainable design.

How to Begin

Following are six components the design student can apply now in designing for the future. It may seem obvious that there is something to be learned from the past in designing for the future, but to help in that, the student should know six basic things from design history:

- **A reform-minded approach to design.** The first component is reform as an integral part of design's role in society. Perhaps considered quaint in the present age, it can be revived if reimagined for the twenty-first century. The fact that the designers mentioned previously also produced work for commercial distribution might help bring things into perspective. Morris operated a comprehensive design studio in addition to seeking societal reform and establishing new models of design education. The Bauhaus was established as a means to revive the decimated postwar economy in Germany by designing goods for consumption. Even the Constructivists, who were helping to define what a socialist society would look like, still designed advertising and mass-produced goods to be marketed within the new economic system.

- **A holistic approach to designing.** The second component is a holistic approach to design that is interdisciplinary and media neutral. Beginning with Morris's attempts to break down class barriers by raising the applied arts up to the level of the high arts, all of the movements in modern design rejected disciplinary boundaries. They saw collaboration as essential to reforming how art and society functioned for the benefit of all.

- **An international spirit.** The third component recognizes globalization. All of the avant-garde movements in design and art were international in spirit at a time when nationalism was in its heyday and violently asserting its agenda. Art Nouveau, which was in part an extension of the Arts and Crafts movement, resonated well beyond France, taking root as the Jugend Movement in Germany, the Secessionist Movement in Vienna, and the Liberty Movement in Italy, among others. Members of various groups exhibited together, exchanged correspondence, and held meetings. This model was carried on among other often-competing art and design movements and finally coalesced with the Bauhaus. We need to recapture that legacy in order to reorient design practices to deal with environmental problems within a global context.

- **A rejection of assumptions.** The fourth component is rejecting assumptions about what design is, or rather what it has become. Revolutionary movements in design and art all began with a rejection of basic assumptions about creative practice. The old linear model of consumption driving more and more production, resulting in increasingly more waste, is doomed to repeat the same mistakes. There is nothing inherently linear or destructive about the design process, nor is it necessary to link it with driving consumption alone. In fact, the basic principles of modernist design fit very well with sustainability. These principles emerged initially with the Arts and Crafts movement in England in the late nineteenth century and were driving forces in all the movements in modern design well into the twentieth century. Interestingly, the things that the Arts and Crafts movement reacted to were the ill effects produced by rapid industrialization. Today, we face similar threats to our personal health, the health of our total environment, and the profession of design.

- **A commitment to fundamentals.** The fifth component is remaining grounded in proven design fundamentals and processes. Two fundamental principles emerged out of the philosophy of the Arts and Crafts movement that still resonate today and inform sustainable design. They are truth to materials and truth to process. The materials designers work with are the very substance of design practice; they determine environmental impacts and hold the answers to how to make concrete changes. Truth to materials and to process arose out of a reaction to the shoddy craftsmanship that resulted from industrialization. Cheap and nasty was the order of the day. Goods were produced quickly and in large numbers with no concern for craftsmanship or for whether the materials were appropriate or of good quality. Today, design faces similar concerns when considering the materials specified. At this stage in the design process, established professionals can influence what will be used to produce goods and whether this choice is sustainable. The appropriate material is even more a concern today than it was a hundred or more years ago.

Another aspect of truth to materials and process was the belief that design solutions reside in and emerge from the materials at hand. Given the new experimental and sustainable materials being pioneered, such as corn-based plastics and plastics derived from fermentation, we can appreciate just how significant these solutions are. Designers need to embrace new materials, because the solutions sought are hidden just below their surfaces and will emerge as designers work with and through them. Though the Arts and Crafts movement largely disregarded new materials, the Art Nouveau movement that followed quickly on its heels and extended to several countries absorbed much of what Arts and Crafts invoked while embracing new materials, processes, and mechanization. This was passed on to subsequent movements in art and design. It remains today as a legacy and a challenge for us to fulfill.

- **An appreciation of the value of things.** The sixth component emphasizes the high content value of mundane artifacts, materials, and processes. A point of interest about William Morris and his critique of mass-produced goods was his concern that shoddy materials, processes, and designed objects led to the spiritual degradation of a culture. Today, many people see solutions to environmental problems in a holistic light that includes spiritual and material solutions (Walker 2006: 61–70). The belief that poorly designed objects and images have a negative impact on people because they are aesthetically, and perhaps metaphysically, inferior gives credence to a holistic approach to design for sustainability. Nothing is so insignificant that it doesn't deserve to be designed well. Designers should be working to make others aware of the significance of the everyday things that surround them and that may be poisoning them. Design should seek a new aesthetic for sustainable design. This aesthetic will emerge out of new materials based in fundamental design process and will equate beautiful with sustainable, ugly with unsustainable, and can result in the final expression of modernist design to help in finding a new aesthetic beyond the machine, consumption, and waste.

The meaning of objects and the purpose of making have existed since the beginning of human culture. The legacy of the distant past resonates in objects and images often in the most mundane of items and activities. The little things that surround us matter, from the spaces between letterforms to the ultimate pinnacle of the tallest building. Today, the multiplicity of designed objects that once seemed to exist only as wallpaper have begun to move to the foreground. The conceit that little things don't matter and that anyone can continue to produce and consume without thought is contradicted by the tiny bits of plastic that will never completely degrade but remain within our bodies even beyond the grave. Therefore, much consideration must be given to designing material objects with intent and inspiration, as well as to the materials with which they are made. The object must speak to the user as a conscientious and ethical person whose object of desire is not simply the thing itself but the life of the object and how it will benefit the whole of society.

We need now to end what Brook Stevens in 1954 came to call "planned obsolescence" (Adamson 2003: 129–130) and which was shortly vilified by Vance Packard in *The Waste Makers* (1960) and first described as early as the 1920s by Ernest Elmo Calkins, severally as "Consumer Engineering: Styling the Goods and Forced Obsolescence" (Ewen 1988: 45–47, 51–52). The association of style and novelty with personal identity and status is what has brought society to the very edge of what can be disposed of sustainably. This initiates the discussion of how to remedy the problem while maintaining the important role of material culture to creating meaning. The very definition of the word "NEW!" needs to be redefined not as something bought, as described by Stuart Ewen in *All Consuming Images*, but as something truly innovative that will continue to renew not only itself but *ourselves*. What Victor Papanek described more than forty years ago as "our Kleenex culture" (Papanek 1972: 96–106) was recently brought to life in the exhibition *Design for the Other 90%* (Smith 2007) at the Cooper-Hewitt Smithsonian Design Museum. It details specific solutions to local problems brought about by living downstream of the developed world. Design that addresses the problems resulting from a throwaway society using the detritus that overflows from the developing world.

Avoiding Past Pitfalls

Designers need to aware of certain things when thinking about what sustainable design might look like. Specifically, they must avoid some of the theoretical blind alleys of modernism. The history of consumption and modernist design is beset with rhetoric that has become normalized; therefore, a thorough understanding of its use is necessary in order to avoid language that may be steeped in misogyny. Feminist critics have described how the consumer has historically been seen as feminine, if not wholly female, and the associations assigned to femininity, such as passivity, naiveté, triviality, gullibility, and weakness, pervade the discourse on production, design, and consumption. The process by which this occurred is not dissimilar from that which Ruskin and Morris observed regarding the alienation of the artist from the process of production as a result of industrialization and the resulting division of labor.

Similarly, as Penny Sparke described in *As Long As It's Pink: The Sexual Politics of Taste*, activities and ways of making traditionally associated with the home and with women's work became devalued and trivialized as less and less production occurred in the home (Sparke 1995: 1–12). Finally, the role of women became associated with consumption as their role shifted to acquiring ready-made goods. Ultimately, women bore much of the blame for consumerism, to the point that modernist design itself was seen as threatened by a process of adulteration brought about by consumption. Rhetoric regarding consumption is still saddled with much of this viewpoint, and a healthy dialogue on the subject devoid of this language is necessary as we reconsider both production and consumption in light of sustainability.

Establishing a new aesthetic not only describing sustainable graphic design but also truly initiating a movement for positive change will demand that we disassociate green from luxurious. Many of the products currently available and intended for green consumers exhibit a rarified aesthetic that is largely available in upscale retail environments. This isolates "Good Design" as it has often been in the past, as design under glass available for purchase at a price and set aside for contemplation apart from a world of problems and the problems of the world. This also contributes to the phenomena of green fatigue related to green associations with elitist forms and luxury lifestyles.

A related issue is that of good and bad consumption. Much of the dialogue on consumption in the popular media is a discussion of bad taste as bad consumption, as evidenced by the ills of Wal-Mart and less often of Pottery Barn, Design Within Reach, or Martha Stewart. The conflation of class and trash—and by extension race—began, as Susan Strasser pointed out in *Waste and Want* (1999: 75–77, 96–97, 138–140) at the end of the nineteenth century and early twentieth when the large-scale disposal of waste was engendered by an emerging consumer culture that devalued waste and assigned its collection to immigrants at the literal margins of society. In today's global economy, this dynamic needs to be carefully considered when we examine exactly what or where downstream is.

The issue of population growth also plays a part in this situation, because both the efforts to stem population growth and the dialogue on its merits have historically been riddled with what can at best be described as a Western bias and at worst racism, violence, and genocide. Buckminster Fuller addressed and disabused designers of the false notion of "scarcity" based on a control of resources and the inflation of their value by a few at the expense of the many as early as 1969 (34–35). As the number of societies that value a lifestyle based on consumer goods and devaluing waste increase, it is easy to see how critical mass is rapidly approaching in regards to environmental issues and design. An examination of the growth of consumption including where and by whom may be more appropriate than how growing populations are consuming or producing more waste.

The Consequences of Intention

Even the best-laid plans result in unintended consequences. As Victor Papanek related in *Design for the Real World*, no one anticipated that the automobile would become a bedroom on wheels (1972: 31). Facts like these might seem to negate the designer's creative vision, ambitions, and talents. All design is by definition, by intention, but not all is necessarily or equally inspired. By seeking inspiration, we will at once seek solutions that are sustainable. The problems design faces create the constraints that demand it. Sustainable design provides the opportunity for designers to once again define our practice, not only by intention but through inspiring others, drawing inspiration not from what designers make but from the natural world, from which we are made. Design has often been seen as that which springs either from the heart alone or from the mind alone. When it comes to our planet's future, let us have passion rule in the plans we make to secure it.

The visual essays in this introduction describe the divide between the relationship with consumption in North America and its effect on much of the rest of the world. They are about place and waste—where it is situated and the people who live among it and apart from it. The photos were culled from online stock photography sites. These sites, like many of the places you see in these images, are quite ordinary. They hold thousands of mundane images describing waste—who makes it, how it's processed, and where it goes. These images are among the ordinary, everyday tools used by the graphic designer. Because they are inexpensive and ephemeral, we underestimate their power and therefore their value.

A photo of a family shopping against the landscape of a superstore stands in contrast to the landfills that populate the horizon. A cursory search of images of "trash picking" yields both photos of happy, multicultural children collecting recyclables as a social activity and children living and working in landfills among the things that poison them. A search of "streams" pictures a lone hiker, at leisure, lost in quiet contemplation along a mountain stream as well as a group, working to sustain life in a polluted waterway.

Graphic designers have a unique relationship to consumption through the words and images that saturate our culture. Because this consumption occurs so rapidly, it often goes unnoticed even by graphic designers. The site at which images and words intersect is where the production of meaning occurs. It is the site where the dialogue on sustainability is happening, and it will decide how it will be visualized, framed, and remembered.

buy product

by-product

"It is our duty to criticize overconsumption/overpackaging.
We must express our opinion by coming up with design solutions
that are both creative and ecologically sustainable."
—Catherine Bourdon | student
University of Quebec at Montreal

refuse

reuse

"As graphic designers, we produce more than we should. Not many
of us know where it goes. Instead, if we made use of this waste, into
something else, with less environmental damage, then I think we can
consider ourselves much more effective and thoughtful designers."
—Gavin Mandrelle | student
Swinburne University of Technology

waste

want

"All the waste (beautiful trash) I was producing as a designer discouraged me
and left me feeling empty. I found the junk mail I created abominable and truly
felt I had no positive purpose in my professional life. I started asking myself
questions like: Why am I a designer? and What do I want to design?"
—Eric Benson | Professor
University of Illinois

upstream

downstream

"Designers have the advantage of being upstream of the production line. They can make a difference in influencing some of the decisions that have a significant effect downstream."
—Sylvain Allard | Professor
University of Quebec at Montreal

spread it around
12.5 tons of greenhouse gas each year.

Chapter One
Messages

On the surface, it seems simple enough to assume that the basic material choice of what paper to specify defines a sustainable approach to graphic design. Graphic design has been defined historically as design for print. Logically, the subject of paper choices has dominated much of the discussion surrounding sustainable graphic design for the last twenty or so years. But if we are to truly understand why this material choice is important, we must dig deeper and consider the very notion of materiality. We need to consider what set of circumstances led to the materials we now readily have on hand and how they came to dominate our material choices and define our limitations. As with many aspects of sustainable design, paper choices are predicated on what designers value and how we operate within larger economic systems.

Paper made from wood is the primary choice of material because the industrial process for producing it grew in parallel with the profession that came to be called graphic design. Before this development, cotton rags provided the primary source for paper production (Imhoff 1999: 18–19). It is worth noting that these were scraps compiled from millions of homes, creating a virtual patchwork paper industry. What today we would normally discard was reused and reused well. The process of collecting, sorting, and producing the cotton paper provided income for everyone involved in the cycle of production and consumption (Strasser 1999: 80–91), because the value of the material was not overlooked. Ordinary household waste was seen as a resource. It also was associated with nascent consumption in the nineteenth century, allowing individuals—especially women and immigrants—to trade their waste products for new industrially produced goods (Strasser 1999: 3–19).

Mary Bateson addressed the question of what materials we value as resources in the book *Design Outlaws on the Ecological Frontier* in describing her definition of a weed. She argues that a weed is something you do not value, something that does not represent wealth, until you come to recognize it as a resource (Zelov and Cousineau 1997: 92–93). Once we come to value a plant from which we can derive paper, sugar, or fuel, we see it for what it is—a source of wealth. The value of agricultural waste and textile scraps resulting from the production of cloth are currently being revaluated as a source for making paper and therefore producing wealth. It isn't yet clear whether sustainable paper production can either make or create enough demand to supplant systems of paper production that are currently unsustainable. The value of things is so often assigned in terms of dollars and cents that we have come to overvalue what can produce an immediate return.

With industrial systems of paper production so tied to private-sector and governmental economic incentives, it's difficult to imagine how a change might occur. Consumer demand is certainly a vital component, and it's driven by the graphic designer, who most often specifies that paper and thus the material upon which the content will exist, but not necessarily drawing attention to the materiality of the artifact. The byproducts and other waste produced in one process may—through the vision of designers and other innovators—be repurposed, shifting perceptions of their usefulness and therefore value. Utility can then be seen as not simply what is useful but that which can generate ideas beyond mere material uses. The idea that trees equal paper results from an assumption that only these hold value and can supply our need for printing substrates, though the very word *paper* originated not as a reference to wood but to papyrus. It is a belief in the idea that a single source, such as paper made from trees, is of such rich value that designers often overlook the many negative effects of its production, such as overconsumption of water and energy or emission of poisons like dioxin. Paper as a luxury item, bearing watermarks, was one of the first branded products, which speaks to its cultural significance and legacy. It is up to designers to mine it as a resource both culturally and in its ability to transfer knowledge and relay those values as a material resource.

Graphic design is not about paper consumption alone, the waste produced, or what the consumer in turn discards, nor is it defined entirely by its ephemerality. Ultimately, it is about what is valued, which is determined by how value is created. What designers should value most should first be their own work—not only the things

Green-Busters

Instructor: Peter Fine, University of Wyoming
Students: Michele Burgess, Jason Pawela, Casey Webb, Matt Ortiz, Amanda Democ

Objectives

1. Use your graphic design skills to interrogate green claims to turn an advertisement or entire campaign on its head.
2. Employ the methodology of culture jamming to analyze the ways media frames a subject.
3. Advocate, persuade, and inform using satire while also effectively balancing the verbal and the visual.
4. Appropriate and subvert the rhetoric of the original piece using the very words and images it employs.
5. Maintain high production values.

Process

1. Use the greenwashing site, http://greenwashingindex.com, to locate and choose greenwashing examples. Pick two to discuss with the class: one you feel is most authentic and one you feel is least authentic.
2. Research the green claims made in a campaign you feel is worthy of satirizing. Use the twenty-one key factors for analyzing green claims. Reference third parties that monitor the industry.
3. Focus on the specific claims made in the piece to avoid generalizations in your own work.
4. Work in pairs and small groups to help each other write and design.
5. Build maquettes, conduct photoshoots, create original illustrations, use stock

Figure 9

Fiji Water: Every Drop Is Wasted
Student: Michele Burgess

This piece demonstrates the use of the twenty-one key factors for analyzing green claims: The claim made in the headline that every drop is "green" ignores the larger problem by focusing on a single drop that works to represent the whole. The claim is certainly vague and misleading. The design hierarchy focuses attention on a single drop rather than on the much larger set of issues that actually result from the packaging. The consumer is directed to a website that cannot be accessed directly from a print ad. The copy in the original piece clearly misrepresents the facts and focuses on the small steps Fiji Water is taking to offset its larger misdeeds. See the following key factors: #1, #4, #6, #16, #21.

Figure 10

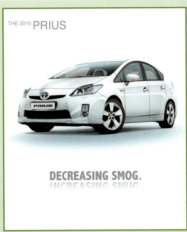

Figure 11

Student: Jason Pawela
Figures 10–11

US automobile advertising provides plenty of source material for this assignment. An advertisement for a Chevrolet resting quietly in a field of flowers is redesigned along with an advertisement for the Prius. In each case, the license plate is used to subvert notions of what is green and consumption of luxury lifestyles sometimes associated with some green products.

photos, and visit corporate websites for graphic standards.
6. Further research: AdBusters, John Heartfield, Barbara Kruger, James Victore, Hank Willis Thomas

Challenges

1. Avoiding simplistic counterarguments, generalizations, reductive practices of advertising, as well as simplistic spoofs and inversions
2. Effectively merging form and content
3. Creating a piece that achieves verisimilitude

Project Description

Design and write a subversive print ad in which the verbal and the visual and the form and content are effectively in balance. The student will employ the methodology of culture jamming, made popular by AdBusters. This methodology uses the tools that corporations employ through branding and advertising to question green claims. The piece should not simply counter a claim but should work to persuade an audience in a manner similar to advertising. One crucial component in this project is to use exacting production values, as seen in print and on screen. If the green-buster is to truly speak to green claims with authority, it must use the same verbal and visual rhetoric of large advertising and branding firms. Approach your culture jam piece as a dialogue, speaking *with* the audience rather than speaking *to* them. A hectoring tone or scolding insistence that overstates the issues is ineffective. The consumers should be able to laugh at the satire, and it should pique their interest in what truly lies beneath the surface of consumption while being made aware of their complicity in systems of waste. In many cases, highly successful products have created their own culture of consumption, in which the user identifies so thoroughly with the product that it appears to facilitate his or her lifestyle. This is the manner in which effective advertising and branding works to win over an entire demographic and can also be used to subvert the same.

Steps

Begin by questioning assumptions—your own as well as the advertiser's and its client. What is the piece proposing through the use of text and image? What formal choices were made

regarding font, color, scale, placement, and so on that influence the meaning? What does the piece assume the audience believes to be true, and how does it depend on the audience's ignorance of the subject to persuade them?

1. Look through the site and rate at least a dozen ads.
2. Pick two to discuss with the class: one you feel is most authentic and one you feel is least authentic (bogus).
3. Begin doing research on claims made in a piece you feel is worthy of satirizing. If the corporation you are investigating doesn't issue a corporate statement of responsibility (CSR), or other form of self-reporting, then find another that offers more transparency to learn what best practices look like. Locate third parties that provide oversight of industry practices such as the Forest Stewardship Council (FSC). Avoid oversight groups that are funded and maintained by the industries they police and learn the difference.
4. Use the twenty-one keys to distinguish among true, false, ambiguous, and misleading claims. Stay focused on specific claims the ad is making, both in images and words, to avoid making your own generalizations. Effective criticism means fair but pointed interrogation of specific words and images.
5. Overlay a copy of the original piece and diagram the visual and verbal arguments made. Make notes about questions you have about claims, fine print, or the veracity of images and text.
6. Copy down words and phrases from the piece onto three-by-five-inch index cards. Rewrite each word or phrase in the form of a question on the flip side of the card, leaving space below for the answer. Include

Outcomes

1. A highly refined piece that both employs the forms used in the original while effectively satirizing the content
2. A piece that looks as close to camera ready as possible and engages viewers through a mutual discourse, persuading them to subtly question their assumptions and those proposed by the original

4. Leveraging humor to turn the words and images against the original

Figure 12

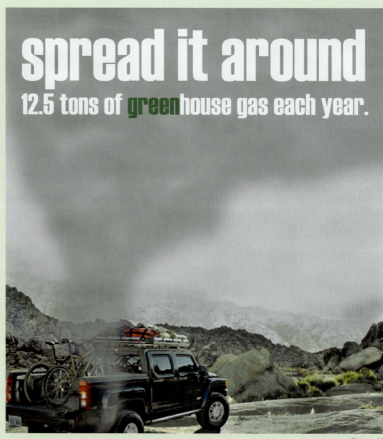

Figure 13

Figure 14

Figures 12–14
Students: Casey Webb, Matt Ortiz, Amanda Demock

The Hummer makes for an easy target when examining US attitudes toward automobiles and conspicuous consumption.

new information you have gathered on the product or service that may contradict the green claims.

7. In a similar method, translate imagery from the ad onto three-by-five-inch index cards in the form of simple graphics and basic symbols using a thick black marker. On the flip side, sketch rough images that contradict or invert the images on the front.

8. Write a minimum of twelve alternate words or phrases that subvert the original message. From this activity, develop three of your own ads using simple black marker drawings. Diagram these drawings to elaborate on how your piece interrogates the green claims.

9. Pair up with others in class to help each other refine your ideas by taking turns at copywriting or art directing for each other.

10. Once you have three solid concepts worked out, splice each one together as one PDF file with the original to produce three parings. Critique these concepts with the full class to make sure that your work addresses specific claims.

11. Small-group critiques should follow with full-color mock-ups leading to two equally compelling concepts exhibiting high production values. Choose one piece to finalize.

12. The final piece should be highly refined. Do whatever it takes to make it as ready for print as possible. Build maquettes, enlist models, do photoshoots, create original illustrations, use stock photos, and visit corporate websites for actual graphic standards for logos and marks.

they make but also their process and what they accumulate in knowledge and understanding as they develop a design practice, the ability to generate not only services or goods but also the ideas that create the value on which culture rests.

The Durability of Ideas

In graphic design, the life of the piece is often significantly shorter than durable objects of design and is often defined by that ephemerality. On the surface, graphic design artifacts appear to hold less potential to accumulate value or meaning over time, except perhaps in the form of collectibles. The multiplicity of so many reproductions and their innumerable exchanges powers and transports their meaning and therefore their value. The significance of graphic design to creative production is typically not a singular durable product but instead its collective power to move people, shape meaning, and to persuade through dual visual and verbal means.

Design for communication grounds how we understand and ultimately value all design experiences, no matter how intangible they may appear to be in the present digital age.

The graphic designer has moved from producing ephemera to creating, often, intangible experiences in which no material seems to be consumed and no product is produced. The decreased visibility of production and consumption and their environmental impacts require that graphic designers pay closer attention to the consequences of their work and the degree to which they cover their tracks or make visible their process. This highlights the importance of the graphic designer's need to embrace and advocate for new sustainable materials and processes. The need to understand and employ these is in fact no different from the need to understand what previous processes and technologies afforded the graphic designer.

In the 1980s, print design was digitized and democratized, as was eventually most cultural production, including film, music, and new interactive modes of communication. This democratization did not bring—as the word seems to imply—an equality of access and ability to utilize digital technology, nor did it limit the necessity of design professionals. Design professionals in fact became more visible and in demand as the digitization and dissemination of knowledge expanded exponentially.

These new developments decentralized creative production, but the larger systems in which that creative production occurs still hold sway and demand to be upheld through sheer inertia. With the digital reproduction of images and words in the hands of the individual, a renaissance in personal expression has occurred much in the same way the Kodak camera democratized image making via the snapshot. Like the snapshot, digital reproduction altered the scale at which the images are produced and disseminated.

Being made smaller and more widely available produced greater individual control of personal identity through direct access to the means of production. Larger systems simply increased to meet the demand for this control of individual ownership of image and identity formation. The means of production in the hands of the individual has actually increased consumption through more immediate and direct access to that means. This ubiquity has not led to an increase in an understanding of the larger systems in which creative production operates, but it has led to a greater appreciation of the value of graphic design as integral to those systems. The film *Helvetica* (Hustwit 2007) reveals the contribution of graphic design to the texture of the consumer's daily life as constructed by individuals and the ways they consume. It would be a mistake to consider the film as simply a product of a fussy design subculture, waxing nostalgic for a period represented by an appreciation for a now-ubiquitous font from 1959. Rather, the film serves as a bellwether for an increased sensitivity to graphic design as aesthetically valuable and enduring and therefore meaningful to sustainability.

Everything New

Sustainable design practices provide an extension of the designer's practice, and although these practices bring new constraints, they amend design practice rather than limit it. The materials and technologies used are incidental to this practice. They are incidental but not accidental, and they need to be valued but not fetishized. Designers need to continue to value their work while simultaneously keeping abreast of new materials. What designers do will define the visual rhetoric of sustainable design, but only if they take stock of materiality and consumption. An esoteric and fastidious devotion to typographic forms is not enough to move design beyond material limitations.

How do designers move to implement new methods and materials, and how can it be done efficiently and in keeping with what graphic designers do already? Print design has been around much longer than current systems of consumption and waste in which paper, made from trees, has come to be seen as the default substrate. The very rapid escalation in paper consumption, waste, and harmful byproducts leading to the unsustainable system in which graphic designers are entangled only emerged in the second half of the twentieth century.

Machined Aesthetics

The relationship between design for communication and mechanical reproduction has its origins in the fifteenth-century invention of movable type. For better or worse, this model has been perpetuated over the centuries. It does not necessarily

iConsume

Nicki Wragg
University of Swinburne
Students: Henry Fuller, Sarah Law

Objectives

1. Promote best practice in all areas of technology consumption, from raw material extraction through manufacture, from the sale of commodities through product after-life.
2. Inform and educate consumers about the life of technology, in the hope of molding them into responsible future consumers, and show consumers how to recycle their old technology.
3. Identify the responsibility of the advertiser in relation to consumption.
4. Successfully implement the use of advertising methods without connotations of mass consumption, rather using a balanced economic and sustainable future.
5. Monitor economic gain juxtaposed with social and environmental concerns.
6. Develop and promote concepts in "truth to materials" in social and production markets.
7. Offer new meaning to the word *progress* in relation to technological development and consumption.
8. Strive for a reduction in waste across all levels of manufacture, to increase reuse of obsolete

Figure 15

Figure 16

Figure 17

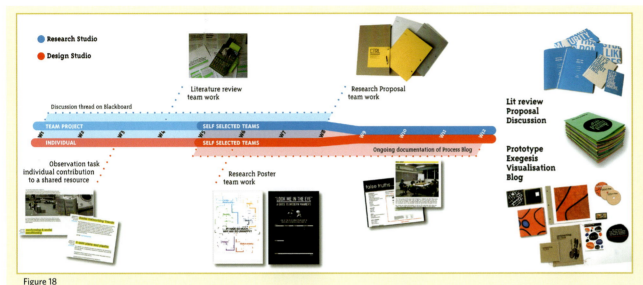

Figure 18

3. Other: iConsume Poster; Website, Blog, Proposed Exhibition
4. Always disseminated but not always a specific design artifact
5. Slowly sinks in over time that sustainability is key, as part of the self

Quote

"Fundamental skills are to enhance the students' ability to analyse and synthesise a variety of information and see patterns of behaviours. They begin to understand in much greater detail the importance of the audience and the new understanding of the user required in design today. It also encourages design entrepreneurism as students are finding gaps and developing work that can fill the gap and is useful and respectful. The students suddenly see design as a much deeper and complex set of issues that is

technology, to be more transparent in recycling, and to honor simplicity.

Process

1. Conduct twelve weeks of comprehensive research using books, articles, journals, internet sources, and the triangulation of questionnaires, case studies, and observation methods.
2. Design an application that is informed by research: research poster, archival blog, prototype development and exegesis.
3. Combine traditional research methods into the formative phase and throughout the design process.
4. Analyze and synthesize a variety of information and see patterns of behaviors.

Challenges

1. Shifting the ways in which design students brainstorm ideas and innovation
2. Introduction to research methods and the rigors of ethics
3. Realizing that anything is possible
4. Constraints of a twelve-week timeframe
5. Not relying on design empathy but actual interest

Outcomes

1. iConsume brand
2. iConsume Publication includes mini publications "101 Things to Do with Old Technology," outline of concept event: eight artists and eight computers and a profile of the project

Figure 19

not just about the design industry per se but about people and the need to connect with and communicate to people."

—Nicki Wragg

Description

Students: Henry Fuller, Sarah Law

The waste created from obsolete technology, in particular computers and mobile phones, is a major economic and environmental issue. Technology is too often replaced by updated models after an all-too-short life cycle, without consumers understanding or justifying a need for it. As consumers, we need to be informed and educated as to how we can be more responsible in our choices, from buying to disposal. It has become apparent that we cannot simply purchase new technology without a sustainable plan for the old. With this in mind, we began our research by asking ourselves, could technological waste be the greatest environmental concern of the twenty-first century? To reach a better understanding of the research topic, we used the triangulation practice of comparing and combining different sources of evidence. First, we conducted a questionnaire asking people about their consumption habits, expressly relating to the purchase, usage, and disposal of technology products. Case studies of a select range of volunteers' homes were undertaken to gain more qualitative results, looking at what technology they own and how they dispose of those products when they are upgraded, replaced, or broken. Finally, we documented a range of photographic and cultural references of overconsumption. The results of the research show that Australian consumers are willing to dispose of, or recycle, their old technology thoughtfully if:

- There is an easily accessible way to dispose and recycle.
- They do not have to pay fees to dispose and recycle.

Research showed us that most consumers either hold onto their old technology—unable to dispose of it anywhere they deem thoughtful—or throw it into their trashcans because they don't know about or have easy access to a technology recycling program. So, who is held responsible for the millions of tons of e-waste? Is it the unsuspecting who buys all the technology? Is it the producer who manufactures it? Or is it the advertiser who tells us we need it?

require the depletion of the natural environment, nor is it inherently wasteful. This system has been sustained not by inertia alone but because one of the first processes to be mechanized and standardized was the reproduction of the written word, which occurred centuries before the advent of industrialization. Second to that was the struggle to marry words and images in a single impression, which was finally achieved during the industrial revolution. The basic skill set now associated with graphic design originated to reproduce words and images. Graphic design is a system based in the book arts, which evolved into the craft and trade of printing, embracing a system that was later hitched to mechanical and academic arts education during the industrial revolution.

The written word distinguishes graphic design from the other design disciplines that arose from and in response to new ways of mechanical production. Graphic design was there first. It was systematized by Johannes Gutenberg and spread the ideas and technologies that would ultimately result in the industrial revolution. Therefore, the very essence of mechanical reproduction resides in the reproduction of words and images. It is no small matter to untangle the ways that the reproduction of ideas both written and visual informs all other systems based in mechanical reproduction. In its present form, graphic design could not exist save for these complex and enmeshed systems. In understanding the machine age, graphic designers can distinguish the effects of machine production on the reproduction of words and images—and therefore ideas and ideologies both produced by and encoded in graphic design. Gutenberg's genius was not simply that he produced a machine out of seemingly disparate parts but that the machine became permanently tied to a mechanical aesthetic that itself defines how knowledge is reproduced.

It is vital that graphic designers recognize the significance not of the printing press but of the book as the defining representation of the original machine aesthetic and that this form transcends its own materiality. It does so through the transmission of ideas in multiples that created a new mobility of ideas and that for another two to three centuries outpaced all other systems of production. During this period, ideas continued to move further and faster than systems could absorb them. This is more than likely where designers now find themselves in terms of design history and in their efforts to define sustainability. It's also just as likely that designers have been struggling to come to terms with sustainability even as they have celebrated the machine for its own sake, so that graphic designers may still be engaged with the subject for some time to come.

The modernist's devotion to the machine and to a variety of progressive ideals may not be in contradiction but may well represent the inherent tension in designing for the past, present, and future all in one breath. Their chief failing may be in not recognizing what William Morris had rediscovered in the book—the definitive machine aesthetic. This was easy to miss among the plethora of materiality in which they found themselves, wherein machines seemed to be themselves reproducing and wrecking havoc and destruction all at once.

Inventing the Natural

Written language, which separates graphic design from other design disciplines, is a closed system. It is incredibly simple and profound, requiring in English the mastery of only twenty-six letterforms, with which any and all ideas can be formulated and communicated. It is a sign system with each form existing in relation to the other twenty-five letterforms. Graphic design students tasked with creating a twenty-seventh letter of the English alphabet soon realize the sheer magnitude of what it takes to invent something new—something that appears to be so obvious, operate so naturally, and so simply to make sense of a highly complex world with such facility. This closed system remains static not just because of the weight of time and mechanical systems bearing down and controlling the way we all see and speak and learn and talk but because it works, and does so beautifully and potentially with great originality.

What graphic designers do apart from designing for print using words and images is to create designs intended to communicate meaning. Design disciplines that do not engage directly with written language, which seems to preclude any further need for invention, often stress invention as the primary means of creativity. Creativity is not always synonymous with invention. The digital revolution, which continues to unfold, was born through the invention of new technological systems and forms. These were first utilized in design for visual communication or—as it's practiced and usually called—graphic design. These systems of visual communication, apart from photography and cinema, remained largely unchanged from the 1450s to the 1980s, except for a very brief period in the 1960s and 1970s when analog systems were tied to new emerging digital technologies. Graphic design is perhaps in some way a series of alternatives to the limits of written language through the artful combination of words and imagery. It is no wonder designers often feel limited by it in fully expressing themselves. It's often remarked that not everything can be expressed

Greening the Grocery Store

Katie Meaney
University of Cincinnati
Students: Nida Abdullah, Britt Cobb, Susan Wilso

Objectives

1. Educate the US public about materials and recycling
2. Undermine assumptions about recycling
3. Emphasize investigation of materials before designing
4. Reduce passive consumption

Process

1. Research the current system.
2. Tour a local Material Reclamation Facility (MRF).
3. Study and diagram Germany's Green Dot system (Grüne Punkt): http://www.gruener-punkt.de/en/.
4. Visit and photograph two supermarkets.
5. Conceive public information campaigns.
6. Students pitch ideas: one is selected; brief is created.
7. Focus on the consumers and their interaction with products in the supermarket and at home.
8. Class collaborates to design a supermarket system that takes advantage of multiple spaces.
9. Publication of work on *Design Observer* to stress the importance of dissemination and dialogue.
10. One student—Darwin Campa—produces an educational website as a living document of the work product.

Figure 20

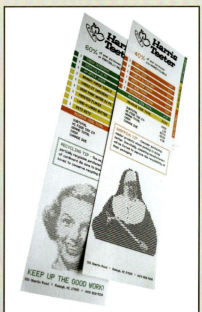

Figure 21

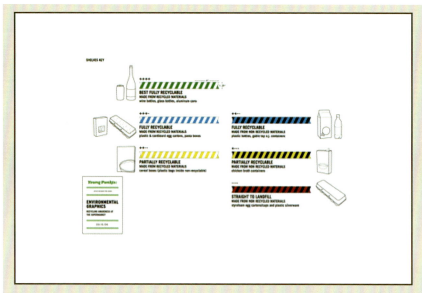

Figure 22

Figure 23

Challenges

1. Lack of consumer awareness
2. Vast differences in systems and standards between the United States and Germany
3. Learning to ask the right questions and to develop one's own assignment

Outcomes

1. Creation of rating system that makes you "proceed with caution" as you purchase
2. Redesigned receipt organizes your purchases into three categories: recyclable, partially recyclable, and nonrecyclable
3. Postcard campaign puts pressure on the manufacturer without boycotting the product

4. Redesigned supermarket flyer
5. Design brief
6. Dissemination of results through online journal, website, and blog

Quotes

"For the case study diagram, I first focused on how different materials are treated in Germany versus America. At first I wanted to depict their different routes or life cycles. I moved off the computer and worked on the glass bottles. This dealt with the materiality of glass and how many times it is or isn't used. I wanted people to really pay attention to the bottle and what happens, so I used the materials themselves to create the message."

—Nida Abdullah

"We took our research and applied it to the supermarket. Each student had his or her own approach to educating the public about recycling, but I felt that consumers just don't know what is and is not recyclable. I chose to educate through applications that were already preexisting in the supermarket. Like rethinking how to better use a receipt and slightly altering sales ads."

—Britt Cobb

"Conscientious Design was a topical junior studio in the spring of 2008 at the NCSU College of Design. The warm-up assignment was

Figure 24

Figure 25

Figure 26

a research project probing into Germany's Green Dot program (Der Grüne Punkt). The students were required to make a diagram comparing Germany's practices with the United States."

—Katie Meaney

"Too often, we work under assumptions. Or, too often, we work without investigation. This class was structured to recognize the former and reverse the latter. The class was not about recycling *per se*. It was about understanding the systems we live in, finding the flaws, and evaluating them. The three Rs were research, rethink, redesign."

—Katie Meaney

The class operated under the following assumptions:

- There is a huge waste problem.
- People don't know what materials they are buying in the supermarket, and this adds to the problem.
- Throwing something away doesn't mean it goes away.
- The supermarket can be a place where people start to think about the life cycle of materials.
- The supermarket is a place where most people must shop for food.
- The supermarket can be made a place of awareness, to learn about recycling.
- Manufacturers simply cannot make materials that can't be recycled any longer.
- Purchasing power is influential.
- Information about recycling is lacking.
- People need help in knowing what can and cannot be recycled.
- Through awareness, change happens.

The class investigated these research questions:

- What can I do about such a big problem?
- Why is it important to recycle and reduce waste?
- Why should I think about this—what consequences do I personally face?
- What are the effects of my purchasing patterns (what impacts do my decisions carry)?
- Do I add to the problem of waste?
- If I'm concerned about sustainability, what should I consider in my purchases?
- What are some easy ways to be green in my purchases?
- How can I get insight into my buying practices?
- Can I influence manufacturing through purchasing power?
- Can I learn more about materials from this information?
- Can I shop more strategically?
- Will this change my habits?
- How do you convince people to change?

Fundamental design skills the project teaches while also enlarging the student's application of these skills to sustainability include the following:

- To work backwards
- To learn basic research practices
- To ask the right questions
- To learn how to recognize a flawed system
- To develop one's own assignment, under an umbrella topic, not driven by the teacher's limitations or preconceptions
- To understand how to design for systems
- To create a proposal or design brief
- To persuade a target client
- To make a presentation
- To advocate

Terms & Conditions pedagogy site: http://www.termsconditions.com/pedagogy/?p=195
Design Observer article: http://observatory.designobserver.com/entry.html?entry=6937

Project Description

We started with Germany where 65 percent of municipal waste is recycled compared to 32.5 percent in the United States. With Green Dot, the onus to recycle is placed on the manufacturer, under a "polluter pays" principle. They are responsible for the life cycle of their product—a strategy changing the way things are made. Recycling starts before manufacturing, *at the point of design*, not as an afterthought. And this made a lot of sense.

When shopping, you'll notice that each shelf is coded with colorful construction tape. Green/white stripes indicates a fully recyclable product, made from recycled content. Red/black stripes indicates a landfill product, and is made from nonrecycled sources. Other colors refer to partial recycling. This rating system makes you "proceed with caution" as you purchase.

Upon checkout (and to help the consumer later at home), our redesigned receipt organizes your purchases into three categories: recyclable, partially recyclable, and non-recyclable. An ASCII image of a ruler-wielding nun appears on a receipt with too many straight-to-landfill items.

In America, recycling is a problem that exists on the systems level. In other countries, manufacturers are responsible for the life cycle of their products—but not in the United States. In the United States the onus to recycle is placed on the consumer. Education about materials and the recycling of materials is often invisible or cryptic. In every state and every district, recycling practices differ. Yet the products are the same. Manufacturers make products that pollute the environment, and they are allowed to do so. Citizens are arguably not aware.

The students were asked to design for the supermarket—to educate and instigate. We focused on the grocery store, because that's where people need to go; it's where they buy the things that will eventually find their ways into recycling systems, compost, or landfills.

in words, whereas no one says not everything can be expressed in color, shape, and line. Graphic design limited by a discrete set of signs overcomes these limitations in what Barthes described as the semiology method, wherein "the semiologist is entitled to treat in the same way writing and pictures" (1957).

The initial thrust of the digital revolution for print design is essentially over, but it continues to stubbornly resist larger systems, which over time will diminish in their transformative ability and will be eclipsed by new technologies driven by new ideas and given form to by graphic designers. As long as graphic designers remain grounded in negotiating new ideas and materials through language, both written

and visual, they will continue to affect how others see and hear. Because we deal in signs, graphic designers should hold to understanding all visual and material culture as sign systems. They will then understand how to communicate the essence of what is being produced, not in the concrete but in cultural meaning. Graphic designers deal in cultural production, in crafting a context that can make sense of the material world. This of course now includes the meaning of sustainability. To the graphic designer, a thing, a designed object, is not the content but that which holds meaning and signifies the many cultural associations latent in the artifact.

Finding Meaning in Destruction

The Modernists, especially the Dadaists, Constructivists, and Futurists, sought new meaning from and through the machine and believed that it would produce a new aesthetic complement to the things it produced. They also saw very clearly that it produced chaos and destruction. They made efforts to comprehend whether any meaning resided in that destruction, but they ultimately opted to further rationalize design, as epitomized by Swiss design, and largely ignored its potential for destruction. Ignoring this key dynamic of the machine age, they whitewashed the short- and long-term ecological damage caused by industrial processes that were abstracted in service to the machine and commerce. Current assumptions about the resourcefulness of new technologies to constantly improve our lives have been challenged by design as the engine of consumption. This process appears to be creative in that something new or "brand new" emerges, but it relies on the destruction of resources as the means to achieve growth, which is defined exclusively by economics. Designers cannot assume that one technology replaces another in succession as in the production of new artifacts for consumption. These concepts are not in fact necessarily related. This is what Buckminster Fuller described as "negatives moved out of sight from their familiar location" where we are willing to pretend "that problems have been solved" (1969: 12). The language now associated with growth, creativity, and innovation has been co-opted, perhaps corrupted, and therefore lacking in meaning and ability to redefine contemporary problems. As designers of messages both verbal and visual, graphic designers need to not only redefine the present language related to creativity but also instigate the visual rhetoric it will require to challenge ingrained ways of thinking.

It was assumed by many and perhaps rightly that digital design would or should replace by as much as half all design for print. Most people have now resigned themselves to the fact that more paper is being consumed in its wake. This is an example of just one system that graphic design remains tied to but seems unable to challenge. As Heather Rogers rightly exposed in *Gone Tomorrow: The Hidden Life of Garbage* (2005), desktop computers and printers aestheticized the rapid increase in the consumption of printed materials produced and the increase in digital delivery of designed experiences via the luxurious surfaces and screens. Aesthetic experiences have increased as a product of popular culture since the dramatic increase in broader, faster access to the web. Many nondesigners now count themselves as type and design aficionados through the ready-made designs they can now access and produce. This creates the question of whether graphic designers can retool their own practice and invent new ways of working or if others might eclipse them.

Print remains as important, but in new and varied ways, and it is likely to increase as a result of the availability of all types of information both new and old. As Buckminster Fuller asserted, the book was the first information-storing and information-retrieving device. This is what Fuller described as a principle or original notion. As he stated, it was in the "graphic writing of words and ideas" that "we have the beginning of the computer" (1969: 105–106). The computer is therefore not simply a tool, as many graphic designers claimed when it was first employed in the profession. That would make it only a prosthetic, a means to extend and apply what we already do. It was the beginning of what Fuller called, in his now much-abused term "synergy," the comprehension and use of whole systems but now within the digital domain (1969: 65, 68–90).

The Revolution Will Be Digitized

The term *information age* is deceptive, because what it actually refers to are systems of storage and delivery such as the personal computer, the internet, databases, servers, and software. It assumes in its definition that knowledge, understanding, equality, and perhaps even wisdom reside in technology. It anticipates a critical mass in which everyone, everywhere, will have access to not only all the information they need but also the technology to use it. This is typical of what Roszak saw as the invisible ideology of the technocracy (1969: 8). This technocracy represents in large part the unsustainable systems within which graphic design operates. The term *digital revolution* speaks more accurately to what has occurred over the past thirty years in making not only seemingly unlimited information available but also the means to reproduce it accessible to so many more people.

What users need are ways to make sense of the information they already have, which is legion. What they need is someone to design information in ways that are accessible, interesting, and beautiful. Whether information holds meaning for readers is more important than whether they can access it or disseminate it. The conflation of the delivery system with what it delivers originates the conceit that technology represents knowledge and the means to employ it. What would be the use of transporting durable goods somewhere faster and in larger quantities if they were not wanted or needed? The same is true of information. Marketing already exists as a way to offload too many things to people who don't actually require anything more. The world wide web is not, as some supposed, entirely a communication technology like the telegraph or telephone; it is more akin to a mash-up of railroad and telecommunication technologies of the nineteenth century. It has, like the railroads, increased at tremendous scale and speed, but it is unlike them in that it resists total control by virtue of its fluidity.

The progenitors and scions of the digital revolution are not the robber barons. For graphic designers, this is crucial to understanding what they are working within. The notion that information is all that is needed overlooks the need to contextualize that information through and within the very ways in which it is being delivered. Designers often lose sight of how this plethora of information is aggregated and digested, when they should be much more aware of this than their contemporaries, causing hardware and software to shape what they believe their role to be. This role persists in many young designers' imaginations as a phantom, a residual memory of man and machine. Today, most people no longer work at a machine creating durable goods, or if they do, they have no connection to how these goods are finally realized. The Mac is not a machine. Its outcomes are not tangible products of consumption but the molding of meaning.

Shrouds and Skins

Because industrialization separated design and production, the concept was freed from material limitations and was put in service to create new meaning in the rapidly transforming industrial era. Through this dynamic, new ideas also increased, and the need to ground them to human experience increased in parallel. As ideas became unmoored and objects unloosed themselves from experience, the power of visual phenomena was propelled and fixed through photography, a process of discovery initiated during the Enlightenment but finally coalescing in the industrial age as a mechanical art. This combination drastically changed the way that designers and others saw the world as fundamentally visual. Oliver Wendell Holmes predicted that photography would allow men to hunt and skin any object off of its original surface (1859).

Once skinned, any material thing could be reattached to any new idea, creating the true engine of modernity. Time and place then became redefined by the object's dislocation and its portability through and upon contemporary ideas. Film and eventually television only increased this dynamic and enforced the hegemony of the visual over the concrete. The implications of Holmes's statement are clearly informed by a colonialist mindset, which expressed the unlimited resources of the industrial age as "ours" for the taking. Today's graphic designer, still operating through these phenomena, must come to terms with the history of how meaning was defined by the supposedly unlimited resources of the industrial age, an age that demanded that others provide the abundant labor and materials needed to feed the machine. Historically, mechanical reproduction of printed matter differs not at all from the mechanical reproduction of any and all designed objects except in its power to define and describe all other forms of mechanical reproduction.

Today, the question of meaning is crucial to the young designer who must cope with increasingly larger systems of consumption and waste, which compound the excesses of the industrial revolution and consumer capitalism. When designers experience a sense of futility over their relationship to waste and consumption, they are simply coming to terms with their own limitations. This is not necessarily a bad thing, although they may experience with it a sense of resignation and perhaps failure. In fact, knowing one's limits is essential to leverage one's strengths. When designers feel overwhelmed by their complicity in overconsumption, they may be ignoring what they can do in favor of what they cannot. Designers need to break down or move through the barriers between design disciplines and other ways of knowing and making. They also need to hold true to what they do and in it find what's needed to change themselves and the ways they work.

What Remains

Graphic design provides us with extensions of our thoughts. What is a book but a means to hold memories, to contain ideas and consciousness, and to move them about from place to place and over time? The graphic designer thinks in images and words, not with a set of tools as extensions of their physical abilities. Designers need not envy other design disciplines, nor should they mistake one set of skills for another. Consider the impact of the International style of architecture; its legacy remains in part as an expression of state control, corporate domination, soul-killing conformity, and egotism. But among these, like most creative activities, there also remain soaring examples of pure form in the very best sense. Consider also the tiniest expression of the International style—Helvetica set in nine over ten point. Designers and users may grow tired of it, perhaps resent its omnipresence, but there are no calls to tear it down because it breeds social ills. It remains because it fills in the cracks of our material existence with words. Words remain in the form of typography, and this form provides the fulcrum on which graphic designers work. A building retains memories as a book does, each is different, neither form is superior; what matters is the transport over time of collective values. What designers must do is try to anticipate what will come, not only to avoid professional failure and ecological destruction but also to hold in reserve what they value. Design is currently experiencing the rapid escalation of obsolescence. It is literally overwhelming designers' ability to absorb not only the waste they make but their understanding of what they are doing and what they will do.

All Things Being Equal

All things being equal, all design is equal in value. Confusion as to the value of graphic design results from what is assumed to be graphic design but is actually marketing. This is the result of many decades of confusion about the role of design and even what design is. Design is not marketing, because it does not assume to sell something to someone before ascertaining whether it is needed. Marketing has come to seem a natural extension of graphic design, which is itself assumed to exist as an extension of advertising. In fact, design is the reverse of marketing. Marketing is a short-term solution to a sales problem, whereas design in all its forms should serve the user beyond the point of purchase. Marketing suggests the inevitable and relentless consumption of products and packages regardless of their necessity. Marketing does not depend on an idea but on novelty. It propounds the very visual clutter in all its manifestations that sustainable design would diminish. This clutter is what occupies so much space in landfills and in the public psyche. It is what frankly gives graphic design a bad name and creates the assumption that it is made to be thrown away. This is no more true than the assumption that all film, television, or fine art paintings are disposable because so much of it—and in fact the majority of it—is poorly conceived and produced.

Marketing is not a medium of art or design; it is a distribution system for goods. This system developed in the nineteenth century to produce and sell more goods and was based on a rapid increase in affluence that depended on cultural and material hegemony. This dynamic remains through an economic system of obsolescence and a tidal force of goods that has dominated entire cultures and demanded systematic dependence. Garbage, much of it designed for disposal, is the visual manifestation of an ideology in which multinationals have more economic muscle than many nations and states. This ideology has led many to speak of "a market" as encompassing all the values of a culture in relationship to what can be sold to it, often at its own expense using materials derived from it. A market is a small, localized venue for selling and trading, not an ethnographic substrate of consumers. The domination of markets is the very basis for what is unsustainable.

If designers are to help revolutionize markets in order to make them sustainable, then they will need to dispense with the marketability of cultures as simply niches or avenues for brand extension but as culturally rich and sustaining beyond their own borders. It is a specious argument to make the case for more of what is unneeded, which will only continue the deluge and undermine the reason for our efforts. The dominance of gigantic brands in the last thirty years cannot be overlooked, especially when considering the degree to which they have influenced notions of identity. Persons formerly identified with nations, cultures, and ethnicities find themselves identified with brand tribes (Klein 2000: 3–26, 27–61).

Green products and green brands have proliferated in recent years as a means to define a green market or particular tribe of green consumers. The search for this elusive, largely undocumented group continues in the hinterlands of consumer psychology. Ultimately, the green consumer is the same in this scenario as any other, except for a desire for expression through a conscious decision to improve themselves and others. Most importantly, consumers make greener choices because of the benefits these choices accrue to them. The green consumer is not a niche market, an exotic breed in need of preservation, but is a series of delicate strata across all of culture.

Preservation

Because the environmental movement emerged in part as a wilderness movement, this has led to ingrained thinking regarding environmental issues and most discussions of sustainability. The focus and therefore the limitations have been based in preservation. The effort to preserve or maintain a certain space or to set aside a small patch of wilderness undermines a holistic pattern of positive action. Designers cannot hope to preserve and maintain a particular number of specialized green consumers. They need to spread their efforts across a wide spectrum of citizens, who will in one way or another identify themselves as green. The fact that culture wars continue to belabor and nurture competing interests that are constantly at

loggerheads and with the hope that one interest group might win out is itself a defunct idea. It only serves to isolate one idea or value from another and create a situation where no progress can be made. Ultimately, one group gains an advantage as a newer generation begins to generate a different set of ideals. In this scenario, environmentalists find themselves besieged and defending even what were once thought of as secure strongholds, not only in physical space but more importantly in the public mind. The graphic designer can help a great deal to change the way the public thinks about the environment and sustainability in trying to save not just a small slice of green but a wider spectrum.

Denaturalized: The Case for a Critical Methodology for Sustainability

It is clear that a suite of critical approaches is necessary to deal with the variety of forms and historical contexts that have produced or engendered graphic ephemera over the last 200 or so years. Because of graphic imagery's direct influence on the founding of stereotypes in the public mind and their wide availability through print, made even more accessible through the internet, there remains a need to apply critical methodologies of race and feminist discourse to the study of graphic design before undertaking a consideration of how to establish any new critical model for sustainability. In these, as well as other cases, a critical approach sets the historical context for imagery and sets it apart by denaturalizing it. The very technologies and media that made for the plethora of output via lithography, photography, and typography cemented in the public mind the tropes we associate with reproducibility and multiplicity, which once established and widely distributed, repeatedly act out prescribed narratives. The internet now serves as never before to create and widely distribute images and words as well as unearth and decontextualize historical images.

The twentieth century provided critical methodologies that are easily adapted to the study of visual imagery of graphic design, allowing the student a way to discern the relative meaning of an individual image and the signs it contains in a historical and critical context. This first serves to denaturalize the artifacts of graphic design and together can supply a methodology for the examination of the ways we consider words and images related to discussions of sustainability. Many of these questions originate with the dichotomous relationship of nature and culture exhibited in many designed images and artifacts since industrialization. In essence, what has come to be regarded as natural is very likely influenced by what has come to expect to be seen through the design of human artifacts and systems. For the graphic design student, the ability to see beyond the expected is necessary for the production of imagery that transcends those expectations. Therefore, the student of graphic design must learn to look beyond what has been regarded as natural. The history of consumption realized through visual culture parallels the development of consumer culture as visualized by graphic designers. A critical methodology for sustainability would invite the design student to participate in a critical debate about and through design. This is in stark contrast to a formalist approach to design, which when combined with an education emphasizing professional practice, doesn't leave much room to consider what precisely the role of design is. Is it in service to industry, business, or perhaps humanity? Changing the way graphic designers think about what they actually do as designers will tell them what, why, and how they should be reacting to environmental issues and unsustainable practices. A critical approach grounded only in a historical appreciation of good or even great design barely begins to describe how to meet the future of design that is already unfolding.

A critical approach to sustainable design must avoid simply criticizing some work as less sustainable or lauding work that improves incrementally upon existing forms. The term *greenwashing*, coined in 1986 by Jay Westervelt, reveals the limitations of this type of approach and indicates the absence of a serious critique of consumption in contemporary culture. The term has lost some of its punch, being perceived as too sweeping a declaration or too broadly painting a product or product category as to be misleading. There is no strict definition of what might constitute efforts by a corporation or any institution to deceive the public about either their ecological damages or their efforts to mitigate that damage. It is more important that graphic designers who are concerned with sustainability must understand where the hidden biases lay in the words and images they use and reproduce. To do this, graphic designers must appreciate the inherent constructedness of design and the ways it can keep us from taking a holistic view of sustainability.

It is increasingly difficult to move outside the problem given the role of design within systems tied to nearly all human activity. The designer's complicity in the production and consumption of material resources and capital of all kinds resists the questioning of such complicity and of finding ways to work for positive change. To ask new questions—to ask the right questions—designers must at times work outside of their comfort zone. It is widely assumed that graphic design was established to support consumption and engender materialism, but historically graphic design has been equally powerful at critical junctures as an agent of change. Its seemingly passive role in supporting the status quo requires a more critically oriented approach to graphic design—a critical approach based in sustainability that can develop young designers whose default method is critically engaged.

To establish a flexible enough methodology for examining graphic design's myriad relationships to production and consumption, designers will need to allow for the assessment not of printed ephemera alone but will need to include many, if not most, of what is termed popular culture, especially that which is fundamentally visual. This assessment will also need to include what is broadly termed the decorative arts, because much of this work relates to the design of artifacts that operate in systems of commerce. The built environment also figures, as does material culture studies, which can provide a means for analyzing a wide variety of artifacts. Contemporary art also can further describe the reach of designed images and systems, beginning with pop art to the digitized and mediated experiences of contemporary life. A sustainable methodology would consider pop culture fundamentally to be visual culture. It would also assume graphic design to be defined by a complex intertexuality between type and image. Based on these twin assumptions, it would go further in treating graphic design as a critical discourse unto itself and require that training in the practice should employ a critical sensibility that may appear to undermine its position.

There exists, in fact, a duality within graphic design seen in the work of AdBusters and other intertextual critiques by guerrilla and street artists who subvert dominant corporate narratives while employing them for effect. Artists working in these forms have seen their work as an undermining of media as the monolithic enforcer of conformism and carving a line between art and commerce in a quixotic pursuit of authenticity. In reality, they are reading between the lines. Although they seek to undermine large corporations as all-powerful, they tend not to bring attention to their own positionality as actors debating who holds sway over human agency. In most cases, the work is situated within an urbanized context and rarely questions that position as oppositional to nature and reinforces "the corporation's" purpose as foil to the natural systems. This necessary critique emerged in the mid-1990s against corporate domination in the form of a few increasingly monolithic multinational players, but it is at times hyperbolic, reductive, and occasionally juvenile. Big Brother is in this case visualized as a father figure in a paternalistic foil to youthful rebellion in a revival of the hackneyed pastiche of left-leaning politics and detached urbanity. A critical methodology for sustainability therefore must acknowledge the duality of graphic design to avoid blind spots that occur in the activity of producing designed images that may serve more than one master.

Work that makes its mark directly upon the mediated, urban landscape does serve to authenticate spaces as human and therefore more true to the role of design in the everyday lives of people. By inscribing words and images upon mediated spaces, this work leads the viewer to question from where creativity originates and who has authorship over not only texts but the very images and objects with which we speak collectively within the public sphere. A critical methodology for sustainability should then be humanistic and be naturally suspicious of work that seems to deny this role. Victor Papanek made the case for this when he claimed that "design is basic to all human activity" (1972: 23). By attaching vernacular forms to and within mediated images and spaces, guerrilla artists are questioning the heroic within art while also dethroning the corporate mouthpiece. These small gestures by virtue of their diminutive quality provide a kind of "mouse that roared" effect. However, like claims of greenwashing, these gestures also fall short of the goal of sustainability.

A critical examination of graphic design must always question what appears to be natural and assume, as Drucker and McVarish assert in *Graphic Design History:*

A Critical Guide, that the more natural something appears, the more apt it is to be constructed (2009: xxix). This goes to the heart of the subject of denaturalizing the designer's relationship to design. The very words designers use to describe design's relationship to nature imply a dynamic wherein they cannot without the aid of a sustained critical approach appreciate the very ways in which designers contribute to their own blindspots. Contructedness is by definition cultural and therefore designed and not of nature. Design's position in culture positions it, and rather precariously, as the façade on which society reflects on nature. It is then not only an affront to what joins together human society but also a seam between that society and a truer, more "natural" self. The nature/culture dichotomy is therefore not simply a false divide but an inherently complex device for simplifying society's relationship to complexity as individuals.

The duality of text and image in graphic design presents the point on which a critical methodology for sustainability rests in the production of images for mass reproduction. It would be a mistake to assume duplicity on the part of the designer in this interaction. Typography is the fulcrum on which graphic design rests, because written texts separate graphic design from other design disciplines and most contemporary art. It is not strictly speaking words but typography defined as movable type that produced the original divergence of graphic design from handwriting and other letterforms. Because the innovation of movable type was a harbinger of the systemization, standardization, and mass production of the industrial revolution, it placed graphic design in a separate category. Typography brought modularity and with it the dislocation of the individual letterforms and their members. Once these were in play, the line between verbal and visual communication expanded to provide the means for a specialist to be employed to both negotiate the differences and employ the power of intertexuality. The graphic designer then worked in the ambiguous space between visual and verbal imagery in the exchange between implicit and explicit content. In this space the form and content are in flux, and one can serve the other or both. In a critical examination of the conjoining of the two forms is where designers can investigate the potential of the work to enforce or subvert the notion of a nature/culture divide.

Summary of Case Studies

Green-Busters

Green-Busters is an introductory assignment in sustainable design employing the methodology of culture jamming made popular by AdBusters and put to good use by guerrilla artists and activists worldwide. The students turn an ad campaign on its head, using their design skills to interrogate claims of green practices in advertising and in service of large brands. They learn to co-opt the tools and language that corporations employ through advertising design to question not only corporate claims but also the ways that the advertising frames a subject. The assignment begins with questioning assumptions, especially students' own, but also those being broadcast. The students question what the ad campaign is saying through the text as well as the image.

They ask what advertisers assume their audiences believe to be true and what they will accept as true with little evidence. Are they depending on the audience's ignorance of the subject to persuade them? The research process originates through content available on https://greenwashingindex.com, a website devised by Kim Sheehan and Deb Morrison at the University of Oregon School of Journalism and Communication to help consumers become more savvy about evaluating the environmental marketing claims of advertisers. They worked in tandem with EnviroMedia, an Austin, Texas–based media company. The user is provided with ad campaigns espousing environmental claims, which they rate on a scale from one to five, five being "bogus" and one being "authentic," with three being "suspect." Users may also post ads for others to rate. Valerie Davis of EnviroMedia describes the site as helping consumers to see "what a corporation is doing with the left hand while obscuring the right."

The impetus for the site originated with events in 2007 when the Advertising Federation, an industry group in the United States, fell short of actually recommending that the Federal Trade Commission institute new federal guidelines limiting green claims in advertising, branding, and packaging. Despite the voluntary nature of the proposed guidelines, large advertising firms resisted the possibility of their environmental claims being even tacitly examined by the federal government. Recently, smaller advertising and media firms such as EnviroMedia, seeking to change the ways that advertisers use green claims, have come into competition with boutique firms set up by larger agencies to deal exclusively with green branding. Smaller agencies such as EnviroMedia have far more incentive to challenge conventions because of closer links to the local communities in which they work. Through the Greenwashing site, students are immediately exposed to the immense amount of advertising and branding that either co-opts the language of environmentalism in the name of consumption or possibly employs sustainable practices as part of their product or service. Many of these ads exist as either broadcast or print campaigns within complex integrated campaigns. Often the purpose of the work is to encourage lifestyle choices among consumers that appear to be "natural." In other cases, they seek to offset poor practices that adversely affect natural systems and the health of consumers.

These campaigns are not strictly speaking public relations because they don't exist as part of journalistic practice. Many are most certainly intended to create a buzz of the sort that viral media now occupies in the zeitgeist. The students follow up on what they find on the Greenwashing index with additional research into the larger context of the green claims. The site engages students with the notion of greenwashing as a means to insinuate research into the process before students realize they are researching. As an added benefit, students are also exposed to the shortcomings of such cursory internet research. Often they are unaware that the products or services they consume are proprietary or protected and also lack any kind of transparency. The Greenwashing site develops an awareness of the practice of greenwashing, something many students are not aware is occurring. Davis asserts that most designers working in advertising are equally unaware of the implications of the work they do. Greenwashing often occurs inadvertently as designers begin to explore the visual language of greenwashing tropes in the form of trees, flowers, globes, and the ubiquitous leaf, as well as empty descriptors, such as "gentle," "natural," and "friendly."

The scale at which greenwashing is occurring is made clear through student presentations of two campaigns, one they feel is most authentic and one they feel is bogus. The presentations demand that students explain the command corporations maintain over the rhetoric on green consumption and even that of the environmental movement, and the lengths to which corporations will go to establish the dialogue on what constitutes green while they often operate outside of ethical practices and through a system of regulation that winks at environmental impacts. The costs to the environment of doing green business are exposed through this simple exercise by both the extravagant purchasing power of these corporations and the highly polished aesthetic of advertising and the skilled work of designers, photographers, illustrators, animators, and copywriters who are put to work in arguing the case for green consumption.

Following these presentations, the students join together in groups to discuss which campaign they feel is worthy of spoofing. This is the point at which collaboration is first used as a process tool and in the interest of developing a skill set that is fundamentally interdisciplinary. Group dynamics play out as a means of evaluating the individual contributions each student might bring to a group project. They then begin the work of dissecting the green claims that will provide the best opportunity for satire. They are encouraged to stay focused on the specific claims made both in images and words to avoid generalizations or simplistic verbal puns or inversions. They both rewrite and redesign the campaign in most cases by subverting the images and words present in the work. In certain cases, there are themes so common to green claims that they may posit a single image as typical for a more generalized satire. Students are encouraged to pair up with someone in their group to help each other refine ideas. Taking turns at copywriting or art directing for each other are useful tasks in instigating collaborations similar to the methodology devised in the 1950s at Doyle, Dane, Bernbach, which ushered in the golden age of advertising.

The student is tasked with being both the copywriter and the designer. The ways words and texts entwine with graphic design messaging existing as advertising, signage, motion graphics, logotypes, and the myriad of interactive graphics we encounter daily is denaturalized. This dynamic can be seen in fig 9, where the student inscribes directly onto the copy attesting to the green value of the product and then formally in the use of the package, first as the water is poured out and wasted to demonstrate how Fiji actually wastes water, in addition to many other resources.

The package is enlisted against the brand's wasteful packaging and shipping, seen crushed and rejected in the corner.

The final piece should be highly refined, with the student doing whatever it takes to make it look as ready for print as possible and create a sense of verisimilitude. Fig 10 operates through this truth effect, engendered by advertising's smooth and polished integration of text and image. The use of vernacular forms may be used to bring into relief the highly polished quality of large campaigns, as seen in fig 12, a sendup of advertising for Hummer. The tactics and formulas used by the advertisers are subverted in order to not simply make the student aware of greenwashing as a phenomena but also to produce a piece that educates, advocates, and persuades. Balancing the verbal and the visual is vital to both enlarging the students' appreciation of the power the two forms have when carefully considered in tandem and teaches them how ideas emerge as graphic designs. Both figs 13 and 14 employ the advertiser's use of Hummer, situated against the backdrop of nature as a visual trope, and the way the copy often contradicts the scene, while simultaneously encouraging the viewer to lust for the brute power to overcome natural obstacles.

What is fundamentally important about this assignment is how it demonstrates the ways that graphic design affects all of our perceptions of sustainability. This is most evident in fig 11, wherein even an environmentally sound product such as Prius commands an inordinate amount of attention and therefore rhetorical power over the dialogue on what constitutes sustainability due to the scale at which it is produced and advertised. At the heart of this issue is the act of crafting messages using words and images. This activity sets graphic design apart from the singular act of writing or of producing images. It is not simply a method for explaining text or illustrating that text; it is an intimate process wherein the designer marries word and image and in this creates new meaning. By reversing this process through a subversion of a design that results in a satirical reinterpretation of an ad, a new narrative emerges that harnesses the persuasive power of multiple forms and the means to carry that across various media. When media critics tackle these same issues, they deal in the discrete, albeit powerful methods of the critic, whereas graphic design as a process brings a host of methods to bear on the way language and visual communication work. A more critically oriented approach to graphic design in general and specifically as it relates to sustainability can develop young designers whose default method is critically engaged. This assignment serves this purpose and educates students about the potential rhetorical misdeeds of those that produce messages, as well as producers of more exceedingly wasteful objects tied to systems that pollute minds and bodies—either could be considered greenwashing.

iConsume

The iConsume project deals directly in design thinking as integral to sustainable design and is typical of research projects the students pursue in their Honors year. iConsume is focused on the user of technology, especially portable and desktop technologies, but it holds specific relevance for the graphic designer who designs with and for these devices. The consumption of technology through use and eventual disuse provides the basis for this twelve-week, semester-length group project. These projects are intended to enable students to analyze and synthesize a variety of information in order to locate patterns of social behavior. The students begin to understand in much greater detail the importance of the audience and the new understanding of the user required in design today. It also encourages design entrepreneurship as students find gaps and develop work that can fill those gaps with design that is useful and respectful. The students suddenly see design as a much deeper and more complex set of issues that is not just about the design industry but also about people and the need to connect with and communicate with groups.

The main premise of this project is to look at social patterns and how these overlap with new technologies and then, in the studio, to create applications or tools with the user at the center. In the end, iConsume became a book, but the intention was to produce solid design thinking surrounding technology usage that first considers the user. Multiple outcomes could have been achieved, because multiple structures and systems were analyzed. Although iConsume represents and explores social patterning facilitated through technology, it is about how in a complex mediated world users act to mediate their lives. Messages therefore must originate from people. Users must define how they want to be communicated to, and the designer must serve that need first and develop a message that speaks with and for the audience. Solutions as defined by users must inform the designer's response, even where complex problems stymie the users' appreciation of their own complicity in harmful and unsustainable practices.

Greening the Grocery Store

Katie Meaney teaches what she calls "conscientious design"—design for the good. The outlet for her ideas and her own education in environmental issues is a thematic studio course she taught at North Carolina State University. She starts with nothing and everything, a no-limits brainstorming session designed to uncover what lurks beneath all the many things we consume. By treating the classroom as a place where she should be learning along with the students, she reduces her bias regarding the content and allows the students more freedom to explore. The work produced by the students and the fact that the process has changed her own design practice validates her approach. The result for the students is that they want to share the information they find in a very public way. Once the research is done and the readings are finished, both Meaney and the students find their motivation. The students better appreciate the value of the research in their process, because they know it must be translated into a form that can compete in the retail environment. Like many of the educators featured in this book, Meaney likes to take the classroom outside and bring the outside in. As she states: "design education would include a hike." This is (and should be taught as) the beginning of a design process. The point is that students should be connected to the world directly, not abstractly. This is important because it reduces the abstraction that has created much of the ignorance about waste in modern life. The class visits the local MRF (municipal reclamation facility), and waste experts visit the classroom.

Meaney began with the students looking at a waste reduction system that works—the Green Dot system of German fame. The class then compared this system with their own local and sadly broken system of waste reduction. In the United States, the onus is entirely on consumers to dispose of their waste, but in Germany under the Green Dot program, it is the opposite: The manufacturer must plan for the disposal of any packaging. Meaney situated her project in the grocery store, so the students could begin to understand what they were buying when they shop and the systems they are participating in at the site where consumers buy most of their consumables, a place everyone comes to and can relate to. Meaney's goal was not to create a class on recycling; the course remains fundamentally about the design process and the systems of design that surround us, both good and bad.

Initially, the class found it depressing to consider how far their local systems lagged behind Germany's, but once they understood more fully the size of the problem, the possible solutions, and the fact that most of the information was simply unknown to the local public, they became emboldened. By prioritizing the clear dissemination of the facts, the class was made more aware of their own strengths as designers—namely, their ability to convey the information visually and with impact. Whenever possible, they decided to stress wit and charm as ways to engage the viewer. Ultimately, the class was concerned with the way the facts regarding waste have been obscured by the systems of waste management. Typically, the average consumer has no relationship to the tons of consumables produced even in their local area. They seem to just "go away." The more designers understand the systems by which their own work is produced and where it finally comes to rest, the more they can appreciate the need to change this system, as well as all systems, from a linear to a cyclical model. As Meaney asserts: "understanding the printing of design dictates how you design printing. Know the process, then work backwards. Likewise, researching landfills may change the way you think about using Styrofoam."

Green, Greener, Greenest: Twenty-One Key Factors for Analyzing Green Claims

Here are some graphic designers' strategies for deconstructing green claims:

1. Does the claim isolate a particular feature or service that might distract the audience from examining how it impacts holistically?
2. Is the claim paired with images that picture the product or service in a natural setting that it has no specific connection with?

3. Is the claim paired with images that connote growth or wholeness, such as leaves, trees, or globes, in a way that does not signify anything specific?

4. Does the claim include rebranding through the use of a new logotype or other text that include the word *green* or the color green?

5. Is the claim paired with a mark or symbol for an industry-sponsored oversight group rather than an independent third party representing ethical consumption? Can the claim be substantiated through any third party?

6. Is the claim paired with a design hierarchy that implies greater relative sustainability through scale and the proximity of words and images? Does this include disclosures in small print or reference an unseen document?

7. Is the claim paired with small print, jargon, or fine details that obscure important facts about the actual percentage of post-consumer waste used or the proportions that are recyclable?

8. Does the claim use vague qualifying terms to disclose or obscure the product's actual percentage or average contribution to sustainability?

9. Does the claim make clear whether it is referring to the product, the package, or its manufacture?

10. Does the claim make reference to what is commonly assumed to be recyclable, as in the material properties of the product, such as a claim of recyclability applied to aluminum foil?

11. Does the claim properly communicate what portion of the product or packaging can be easily separated for recycling?

12. Does the claim infer that the product or package is widely recyclable within the geographic range in which it is sold, when it is not?

13. Is the claim technically true but conveys a broader application or false impression (such as a product like a garbage bag, labeled recyclable or biodegradable, which is normally destined for a landfill or incinerator)?

14. Does the claim conflate the terms *recycled* or *recyclable* with *post-consumer* or *repurposed*?

15. Does the claim ambiguously state a comparison but not reference whether the comparison is to a competitor or an earlier iteration of the same product or package?

16. Does the claim make a broad, vague, or misleading comparison, such as a claim that the product has the highest recycled content in a product category wherein very little of the category is typically recycled, or a claim of "less waste" or "less toxic" wherein a significant amount of toxic waste is common of manufacturing in that industry?

17. Is the claim really a shell game, stating that a paper product is non-chlorine bleached but its manufacture still releases other harmful substances of equal or greater toxicity?

18. Does the claim include unregulated or vague terms such as *friendly*, *gentle*, *safe*, *practically nontoxic*, *superior*, or *natural*?

19. Does the claim make assertions of *biodegradable*, *photodegradable*, or *compostable* when the item is likely to remain inert under typical conditions?

20. Does the claim encourage individual consumers to recycle or reuse in the absence of any collective government or industry waste systems to do so?

21. Does the claim represent an insignificant portion of the company's business and seem to overstate an environmental attribute or benefit?

Chapter Two
Process

GREEN GUIDE
LANDSCAPING
HEATING + COOLING
ENERGY + LIGHT
INTERIOR FINISHES
FLOORING
FRAMING
ROOFING
INSULATION
EXTERIOR FINISHES
GREEN CARDS®

This chapter emphasizes the value of the design process, ideation, and analysis. Graphic designers should place a high value on their own work—not only the things they make but also their process and what they accumulate in knowledge and understanding as they develop a design practice. Therefore, it is essential that designers communicate the value of what they do to audiences, users, and partners. The significance of graphic design in creative production is not always a durable product but rather its power to visualize, contextualize, and shape meaning through visual and verbal means. In the digital age, the graphic designer has moved to creating intangible experiences in which no material appears to be consumed and no product seems to be produced. In this context, the designer's process grounds how he or she understands and ultimately values all design experiences, no matter how intangible they appear. Designers must develop new ways of knowing and making and explore systems of waste and consumption and design's role in them.

This book defines research as any process of discovery in which the designer seeks new questions and outcomes, as well as interrogating accepted forms. Nonprescriptive approaches that allow for interdisciplinary work are highly valued under this definition. This chapter also investigates information design as a broad process for design research. The power of information design to uncover and visualize complex issues and how they exist within global systems of design that are normally outside the control of the graphic designer is crucial to mapping future design practice. Many of the wicked problems of sustainability are only now being recognized and defined, making information design a crucial process and product of design. It also serves to clarify complexity in the face of the current vitriolic atmosphere in politics and culture. This chapter also examines the creation of new, often highly original tools made by and for designers that change the ways they design, consume, or interact with the world at large. Many new tools are being developed as web resources, and digital apps are arising to address current issues, providing venues for graphic designers to influence user interaction and understanding by embedding narrative structures within technologies.

Understanding systems of waste and consumption and design's role in them is important to appreciating the value of design and realizing the true costs incurred in the process of design. This includes a consideration of not only the designers' personal impacts but also their processes and the impact of their designs. Designers need to learn to measure their own impacts and the value of their genuine contributions. For graphic design to continue to measure itself against itself will only limit it to a very narrow and eventually redundant role.

Collective Utility and Meaning

Design for reproduction lacks the advantage of other forms of creative production—often defined as art with a capital A—where the value of a work is assumed to reside in its singularity. An original or authentic work or experience may be enjoyed by many thousands of people but still retain its uniqueness. A work of art may be disregarded as useless by some people, but if it is assessed and found to have exchange value it generally only increases in value, despite the often subjective and seemingly arbitrary nature of the process. This also holds true if the work is entirely conceptual, producing no tangible product or utility. Though both design and art are commodities that may be bought and sold and may contain designed images and texts, design tends to be regarded as a product for consumption and therefore as discardable. Designers need to begin to better appreciate the more intangible aspects of design that are so often taken for granted in the same manner as perhaps fine art. This needs to include forms of process and discovery that are normally considered ancillary to design.

Designed artifacts acquire meaning largely through their use, which is defined collectively by the users, rather than through the viewer's singular and subjective response to a work of art. Each individual lends meaning to the design through use, contributing to its significance and ultimately its value. The ways in which multiple users encounter the many reproductions of the piece or experience determine its

Energy and the Environment

Instructor: Karen Cheng
University of Washington
Students: Nivi Ramesh, Andrew Chiu

Project Description

Karen Cheng loves type. The detail and sensitivity that comes from close attention to the little things informs her particular understanding of what design can achieve. Typography might appear to some to be an esoteric—possibly quaint—pursuit. But training in typography can bring to sustainability the very necessary attention to the tiny spaces that most people never see. The movie *Helvetica* brought home the ubiquitous presence of type in our everyday lives. Understanding that the little things do matter is especially important when we are thinking about what materials to specify. Remember that plastic never really breaks down; it just becomes smaller and smaller. It is ubiquitous.

Cheng teaches information design at the University of Washington, where she's been working with students on a project that looks at energy and the environment in the United States. Cheng focuses more on design thinking than simply on design practice. She wants her students to consider how design can affect every aspect of life, not just design as a commercial activity. The choices they make can affect them personally, and she wants them to figure out how. This is clearly demonstrated as they explore various energy sources and their potential to affect everyone's quality of life. Each student develops information graphics that delve deeply into a specific form of energy, its source, and its outcomes. The students have to worm through the data to realize the costs. The goal of design is to

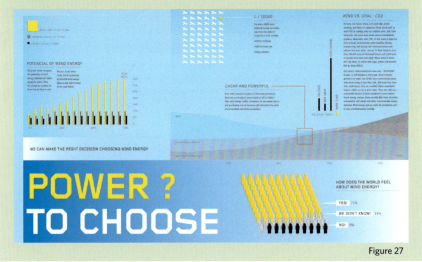

Figure 27

Figure 28

make people more aware and at the same time make the student/designer aware not only of the problem but also how large an impact he or she can have. As Cheng says:

> I tend to think that we (the faculty) may have more impact in the long run by developing students' overall thinking/problem solving approach. That is, making sure that students understand that preserving the environment is a continuing responsibility (not just one aspect of a single project). And, making sure that students understand (and have the tools needed) to research, understand and evaluate new information/ potential solutions that could be adopted in their personal and professional practices.

First, Cheng makes sure she's done about half of the research herself so she knows how far to take the students before she frees them to figure out how to best frame the information. The students stretch the research by making presentations. This forces them to consider how the information will be received and how important editing is to how one gestates complex problems. The process entails building a story and editing it to create a narrative. Reportage and investigation are key steps; as one uncovers new information, more details emerge. Finally, the student finds that being aware is as important as the ability to visualize. The end result is something that is not simply beautiful, nor does it function only to provide the facts. The information graphics are persuasive both in form and content. They beg to be seen and read; they engage the viewer.

Figure 29

value. The power of design therefore resides in its ubiquity and its ability to naturalize a common experience through repetition made possible through multiplicity. Each user must bring his or her own singularity to each design in order to use its collective utility.

One example is Barbie and her companions. Many children share some experience with the doll, even if she was denied to them and resides with them only as an ideal object or image of desire. Each child may play with the doll or other similar dolls, altering the doll to fit a unique narrative. Though designed for young girls, Barbie holds special meaning for all users and embodies their own unique stories. Even if the doll is discarded, the individual can still recall her experience through multiple duplicates, even if years have passed. If the doll is not discarded when it grows old, signs of wear may hold even more meaning for the original owner as traces of identity formation. The power of a designed artifact to exist not only in the moment but also to hold value and extend the experience over time has been largely ignored in assessing value, especially in graphic design. This experiential dimension of design that exists beyond the artifact through memory and aspiration reveals how meaning is created through user interaction. It also reveals the potential for creating extended narratives based on these experiences, which designers can utilize to bring more meaning to their work.

Sustainable Use-Value

The value of design therefore lies in its ability to accumulate equity through use. The more sustainable the work, the more equity is created and the more value that must be communicated through use. Therefore, all true value is sustainable use-value. Sustainable use-value is chiefly cultural and can be referred to as capital but is often not because the work is shared by so many and the value is so widely dispersed through use and reuse by multiple people through multiple units. In order to understand the value of design and build its equity, designers must understand its larger ability to accumulate meaning through use by groups both large and small. This phenomenon has been seen most clearly with the recent emergence of social media and its ability to move tens of thousands of people to act on every issue of

Figure 30

Figure 31

Objectives

To use information design to analyze energy issues in the United States and worldwide.

Process

1. Two weeks: Topic research
2. Three weeks: Design exploration/ideation
3. Five weeks: Design development and refinement of final publication series

Challenges

Difficulty researching, collecting, and understanding energy and related data

Outcomes

1. Realization that US energy policies are flawed
2. Realization that there are no simple solutions to global energy issues
3. Realization that information design can play a significant role in helping others to understand complex issues around energy consumption

Quotes

"Designers don't just make things look good, we also have the power to 'alter' how people view the information, and further change how people perceive the information."
—Andrew (Chao-Ying) Chiu

"Good design has the ability to make ideas powerful, interesting, bold, trendy, cool, catchy, and most importantly, accessible. Because of this ability, we can use design as a way to make the environment a priority."
—Nivi Ramesh

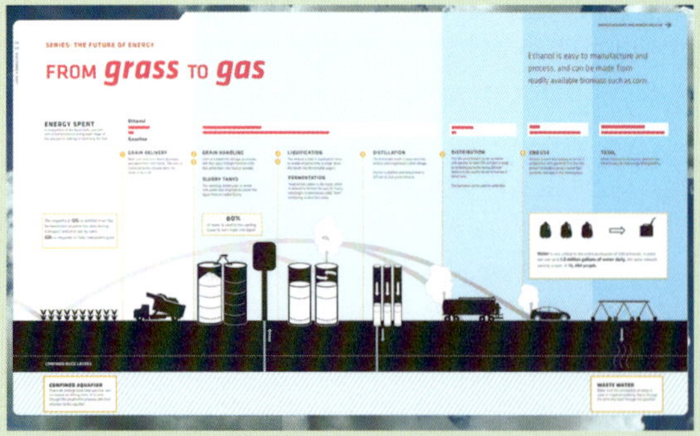

Figure 32

society, from the extraordinarily mundane to the truly revolutionary. The very nature of this phenomena is its self-revolutionizing and democratizing effect on how people interact through real and virtual sites. Although defined as media, it overlaps significantly with design through the access it offers to the means of production for ordinary people across the developed world. In contrast to this access, the digital divide offers a very real opportunity for designers and technologists to bridge the gaps that remain through direct interaction with communities. Through designers working with communities that operate beyond the digital firewall but are affected by e-waste, the very meaning of community takes on increased relevance for designers.

Framing the Problem

Although it may seem obvious that all design should begin with research, this crucial step is often forgotten. Young designers often begin at a computer, struggling to fashion a result from nothing but the basic toolkit supplied. This work is almost always superficial and bears the stamp of a particular set of software, which can yield reasonably good results almost instantaneously. Young designers hope that through continual and repeated use, their work may bear some imprint of themselves. However, this prefabricated set of solutions, although fairly easily mastered and seemingly unlimited, actually narrows the scope of their designs. So admitting that designers often do not begin with research is the first step in researching and designing with intention and with specific attention to issues of sustainability.

When faced with issues of sustainability, designers frequently find themselves unequipped to handle or even frame the problem. It often appears that such thoroughly complex issues lie beyond the expertise of graphic designers and belong to others who are trained to specialize in science or technology. In fact, the graphic designer's skill set overlaps with a variety of other disciplines and is especially well equipped for synthesis and therefore framing a problem that utilizes the efforts of many people.

Designers must first overcome their own resistance to reimagining what they do. It is a matter of reinventing themselves for a new era, something they were trained as designers to do for others in their role as creative professionals, but often at a remove from vital issues surrounding production and consumption. Designers cannot wait for the right client to come along and offer the opportunity to improve our world. It is in both cases a matter of self-preservation. In order to remain relevant, designers will need to invent new ways of working that include original models and tools to help them make the transition that will redefine what they do as research in application.

Beyond the Vanishing Point

Research in application takes place through a process that must be defined, often with each new project. Both intuitive and systematic, it is geared to deal with very large and complex systems that the graphic designer has typically ignored. This speaks to Buckminster Fuller's warning about the pernicious nature of specialization, leading, as he surmised, to extinction. As he described in *Operating Manual for Spaceship Earth*, specialization has been the key to graphic design's success and marketability, but it limits its ability to be truly visionary. Fuller clearly saw the role of design in uncovering hidden truths that were not yet visible to the human eye (1969: 12–13). The designer is equally equipped to see beyond the plethora of information inscribed in and through design to make sense of complexity. In order for designers to access their abilities as visionaries, they must look beyond the vanishing point. They cannot stand alone at the center of their own universe and expect to transcend their own place and time. To do this, they must literally reject many of the formal design lessons of the past that limit their perspective.

Curiosity Made Visible

Graphic designers have at their command a well-developed understanding of how to work with language systems and the tools of creative production. This includes not only how to use systems but also how tools speak as designed artifacts and what they tell us as designers. One such powerful tool that deals with how to comprehend complex ideas is information design. It is a process of coming to grips in high detail through that which is visually persuasive and compelling. In this case, the form and the content meld so that both macro and microelements can be discerned at once.

Green Cards

Sara Alway-Rosenstock
Project: MFA Thesis

Objectives

1. Create a thorough resource of sustainable building materials for residential home-owners and remodelers.
2. Broaden consumer awareness of affordable and available sustainable materials and building methods.
3. Encourage consumers to choose sustainable materials because they're more energy efficient, better for the environment, as well as cost efficient.

Process

Fifteen weeks: Comprehensive research, design, and production

Challenges

1. An enormous amount of materials to research and deciding what materials are appropriate to include
2. Creating an interesting and engaging way to design symbols and booklets for immediate information absorption

Figure 33

Figure 34

Outcomes

1. Extensive resource of available sustainable material benefits and drawbacks
2. A project that is easily updateable with advancements and additions to the field

Question and Answer

What was the original intent of your project?

As a baker, I am constantly finding healthier ingredients to be alternatives in my favorite recipes. When I started working in the architecture field I discovered that architects, engineers, and inventors were trying to do the same thing with building materials. In today's climate where "green" is a buzzword, more and more environmentally friendly building materials are becoming available. Unfortunately, these materials are mostly marketed toward the commercial industry, leaving the typical homeowner largely unaware of green alternatives. The intent of Green Cards was to educate the homeowner through an easy-to-digest

information design piece about alternative building materials for their specific residential projects.

What motivated you to tackle this question?

When I started this project, I had several family members building new homes or remodeling their existing ones. I realized that even my green-minded family was unaware of several alternative methods and materials that could have been utilized in their homes with the same budget, as well as decreasing their footprint on the environment. When I tried to find information to send them, I found the existing research materials to be convoluted. Though there is existing information on alternative materials, it was hard to find out how much they cost and where to find them.

How did the project evolve/change?

I originally planned on designing all the information about each product as individual recipe cards. As my research developed, I decided to group the product cards into project-based booklets. For example, all the countertop, paint, and wall products were grouped as interior finishes, while all the stone, stucco, and siding was in exterior finishes. Grouping these products allows the user to only look at the booklet that addresses their current project without spending time reading through extraneous information.

What was your process?

I began by researching products on the internet, to see what existed as the most up-to-date information. Then I researched what books were currently available on the subject, and I

reviewed them based on their content and how easy it was to get essential information out of them. That essential information was average cost, ease of installation, health benefits, energy efficiency, and environmental impact. Finally, I contacted a local store (Greenable in Philadelphia) that specializes in green building materials. There I was able to see and feel the actual products and get more recent information on pricing and how many ways the materials could be used.

How did you balance research into the subject matter with the practice of making?

For most of the products featured, there was a lot of information that was hard to absorb. My goal was to create a product/layout that made it easy to digest the information in a short period of time. I achieved this by developing a consistent grid that highlighted easy-to-understand symbols, a brief description of

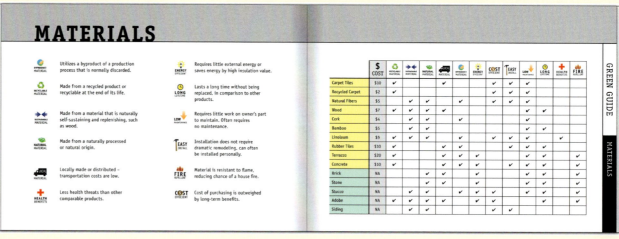

Figure 35

the product, and the benefits and drawbacks of using it in your project.

What problems did you encounter?

With some products I was inundated with information, much of it contradictory, while researching other products was nearly impossible. Toward the end I utilized my relationship with Greenable to suggest certain products that I should feature and which ones I could omit from the booklets. At the end of the research I had a lot more products than I originally planned on, so it took a great deal of time to design all of the booklets.

How did your professors inspire/motivate you?

During the time that I was working on my project, many of my professors showed their excitement for the green building subject, and in fact many of them asked for my advice concerning their own building projects. Their excitement made me feel that the end product, Green Cards, was a practical product that could actually be utilized in the real world. As

a designer (and a student), that aspect was very exciting.

How did you change?

I have become very aware of how I use things. As a financially challenged student, I began purchasing products that were built to last longer, rather than get the cheapest. I also consume a little bit less. I try to reuse things a lot more or find other purposes for them. I dazzled my fellow students when I made notebooks out of all the paper scraps from the semester for gifts.

What is the future of this project and where will it take you?

Because of this project I redesigned the Greenable website (www.greenable.org), to highlight my easy-to-understand symbols and benefits/drawbacks system. It was almost an interactive version of the booklets. I have also gotten interest in commercially producing my books, but if that opportunity pans out, I'm sure another handful of new products will need to be included.

The process by which information design is best implemented is synthesis, where designers learn and develop the subject matter as they design to inform. In the process, both form and content emerge to find a common voice. How this process unfolds is often idiosyncratic, but it follows basic patterns. It is an act of patterning through the visual assemblage of complex information, rendered in simple terms. Because the act of finding and then creating larger patterns is repeatable, the principles can be taught and applied both intuitively and intentionally. As designers work with raw data to uncover how to communicate information, their own curiosity is made visible and acts to inspire users. Through the process of information design, designers can develop generalized methods for devising other systematic processes or tools that are in and of themselves proofs. These tools for learning can be used repeatedly and

adapted for other uses and contexts. Graphic designers are well equipped to communicate to others—not only information in raw form but also as compelling ideas simultaneously from multiple points of view. The further value of this process lies in its ability to be continually mined as it is being formulated.

The Power of Multiple Ideas

One advantage of graphic design's adaptive process, as in the case of information design, is that designers can rapidly utilize modeling and the creation of new tools through multiple iterations. This is essentially what technologists associated with design disciplines such as architecture and engineering do in concrete terms. Designers create models for design thinking, systems of thought that depend on their iterative ability to create and reliably duplicate the creative process. In this case, the ephemeral or transitory nature of graphic design serves as its strength. This iterative ability is a process of multiple ideas that, while producing many more failures than successes, relies on multiplicity to conjure up enough solutions to eventually hit on one that works. This approach parallels the power of mechanical reproduction, but in a model that constantly recycles its own waste to reenergize the creative process. The constant flow of new ideas and the discarding of nonworking ideas on the fly is what the graphic designer brings to any process where design must be flexible and where the power of multiple ideas is essential to success.

Synthesizing Meaning

The tools that graphic designers make are not hammers and anvils that depend on durable materials and intense heat to adapt them but are themselves idea generators. They are of the sort that make sense of a constantly changing world. They are not technical but are about the ways in which designers understand technology and use it to make meaning. The reproducibility of meaning since Gutenberg's invention has meant that in the modern era ideas could be infinitely disseminated not only through words and images, but they can also be attached to all material culture of both the highest and the lowest forms. This implies that all of what graphic designers make is itself language, as all of it exists in systems of meaning. All that designers build or make has symbolic meaning, because it has both a fixed purpose and the ability to change as it is recontexualized. Graphic designers' ability to make meaning lies in their facility to understand the history of a complex modern world as it is constantly refashioned. As they synthesize meaning from diverse historical and contemporary sources, new meaning is created; this ability is what designers bring to organizing the world we all create. Because design is a universal, everyone designs, but the graphic designer sorts and distills the variety of meanings attached to all that is made to decipher its meaning in the present. This process is not predictive, but it does equip designers to formulate ways of dealing with the future and to model and create ways of thinking about sustainability. The solution resides in understanding materials and reproduction and their ideological constraints.

The things now being made that will define sustainable design are transitional tools, but not in the concrete sense. What will follow cannot be entirely predicted. Designers cannot assume that simplistic notions will suffice. For the graphic designer, sustainable design cannot function through a limited definition. Victor Papanek's assertion that "Design is concerned with the development of products, tools, machines, artifacts and other devices" (1995: 29) is not a sufficient definition for the graphic designer who deals in the more ephemeral strata of text and images. This definition seems to assume that only things and not ideas "have a direct influence on ecology." If we assume that concrete things alone—and not ideas about them—are having impacts, then designers operate with a blind spot. Papanek's definition supposes the preeminence of tools as the original catalyst in the creation of human culture rather than the acquisition of language. To assume that one preceded the other is the type of folly that will only deter progress toward sustainable design. The graphic designer's ability to synthesize all manner of form making and meaning making will coalesce sustainable design practice. It was likely not Papanek's intention to limit the influence of graphic design on sustainable design practice, but simply his bias in favor of tool making and invention over ephemeral, especially two-dimensional, processes that he saw reductively as skins or shrouds.

Although Papanek may have had an instinctual suspicion of two-dimensional design as that which covers the workings of systems and therefore masking what we

Re-nourish: Project Calculator

Project Description

The Re-nourish Project Calculator helps you minimize waste on any print project, reducing your environmental impact and saving your client money by using less paper. As you input your selections you can watch as the Calculator automatically provides recommendations on the right. You can save your projects for future tracking and client reporting.

The book you hold is itself a case study meant not to simply serve up facts on sustainable design but as much as possible to

Figure 36

Figure 37

integrate the arguments made within the design. Control of both the production and consumption of the book is largely in the hands of the designer. I have already in Chapter one made the case for the book as a form that is inherently sustainable in its ability to hold and transport ideas over time. Because print remains a principal medium in which designers specialize, it is important that this book advocate for sustainable book design. As I've pointed out, there are very few reliable open-source tools available to the graphic designer for understanding even the most basic constraints and imperatives of sustainable design. *Re-nourish* serves not only the needs of designers as a tool but also offers us a positive proof of workable solutions to common design problems. More importantly, it demonstrates the need for designers to create original tools, new methods, and processes for designing sustainably.

The creation of tools that utilize new technologies for designers are the very artifacts of design that are most important in the transition to the widespread adoption of sustainable design principles. The creation of tools associated with new processes and methods demonstrates the emergence of design thinking as a broader and far more critical engagement with design problems that were previously seen as beyond the graphic designer's purview.

Figure 38

need to understand to work sustainably, he clearly saw the power of the visual, as evidenced by the cover of his book *Design for the Real World*. On its cover, a photograph predominates of a man likely living in the Asian subcontinent and struggling beneath the weight of a very large console television. It is literally strapped to him and he stoops, bent perpendicular at the waist by the weight of it. Wearing traditional clothing along with sneakers, he is clearly struggling to adapt a modern technology produced by a monocultural and hegemonic entertainment and information industry. The photograph states the inappropriateness of what the Western world assumes is both meaningful and useful design for all times and places. This photograph should not lead us to assume that visual technologies are at fault for many of the world's problems, because they are in fact a powerful means of communication and way of seeing that marries art and science. Graphic designers have an inherent advantage in this approach, because the visual is their default, seeing most of what surrounds them as visual source material. This constant flow of material is now more readily available than ever in the form of a gaggle or google of images. This wealth of material should not be wasted but rather put to good use by graphic designers who are schooled in its use.

Beautiful and Meaningful

Even before the most recent crisis of concern over ecological destruction and the desire to find truly sustainable solutions, Richard Saul Wurman recognized a lack of expertise in dealing with what he described in *Information Architects* as a "tsunami"—a total lack of preparedness for calamity (1997: 15). He saw the designer's lack of readiness to deal with too much information as being insurmountable without training to deal expertly with complex information. At that time, designers and technologists lacked the ability to communicate in print the complex knowledge structures that would come to define the world wide web, a sphere now dominated by information technology corporations of global proportions. Wurman wasn't calling simply for better facts or matrices of facts but for beautiful and meaningful new forms that faced uncertainty without fear of failure. Wurman's particular love of learning, coupled with a curiosity and unique insight about how design is shaped by learning, encouraged designers to face their ignorance rather than flee in fear. His description and example of how to encounter and welcome complexity is exactly the model designers need to deal with actual calamities, both natural and technological. His insights dealt specifically with the ways designers learn holistically; learning new material in relation to what they already know could be described mechanically as creating context but is truly about the very creation of meaning. To work sustainably, designers will need to continue to create new meaning based on what they already know about design, cultivating new meaning as they collaborate with other disciplines and knowledge systems. The meanings designers now hold will need to evolve to meet new problems and, in order to do that, take on new structures both mentally and in the ways they design information that are truly meaningful rather than simply factual.

Presently, the phrase *design thinking* is becoming a commonplace description of how design actually works to shape not only design and the systems it operates in but also how it shapes thinking. Nondesigners are now recognizing the value of design as a discrete system of thinking with broad application to complex and diverse problems. The term also speaks to the intentionality of design being more explicitly utilized to highlight its application to both concrete problems and more intangible realities of contemporary life. Ultimately, the term describes how designers think through problems by reshaping both their own thinking and a potential audience or user. It further implies the use of that thinking as an actual model for developing other new ways of thinking that can take virtually any form. This also implies a media and material neutrality emerging in contemporary design. This promises greater possibilities for design, as formalist design education is abandoned and the ideological implications of industrial production and materials become a legacy of twentieth-century design imperatives.

Summary of Case Studies

The case studies featured in this chapter highlighting process include designed research, information and systems, as well as proofs and tools. Often these topics all thread through the designer's unique process as a complex methodology focused on creating new ways of developing knowledge and innovative outcomes. For the sake of clarity, each case study featured in this chapter highlights a particular thread.

Textile Recycling

Elsa Kurniawati
Raffles Design Institute (Singapore)
Project: BA Thesis

Project Description

The designer began with a mind map exploring ways in which to combine shopping and recycling. As the concept unfolded and was refined, one mind map was followed by another. This was crucial to ferreting out what is essential to the idea of a "second life." This ideation provides the underpinning of a successful graphic visualization. Without this process, any weaknesses in the concept will manifest themselves later in the execution of the concept.

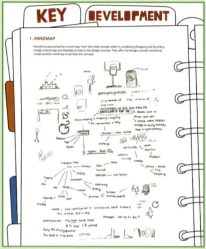

Figure 39

The designer searched out inspiration from various design books in the National Library, and with those images in mind, she began to sketch out some of the key concepts from the mind maps. The loose methodology of the sketches informs the graphic character of the design and allows for a diversity of ideas. The mind maps, sketches, and collaging led to a visual diary, which inspired her to emphasize the story of the clothes and provided a hook for the concept.

The designer used a series of marks as a means to define the brand. These marks first emerged as logotypes, linking the verbal and the visual in a phonetically pleasing manner. The first was "upgrade," emphasizing the many positive associations sought through the campaign and the exchange of old for new. The second is "shiok!" a Singlish word meaning fantastic or marvelous that is commonly used to describe good food, places, or experiences. Its Singaporean derivation bolsters

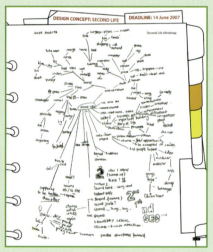

Figure 40

the campaign's resonance with locals, who are needed to embrace the campaign to make it successful. The final marks were produced to be more in keeping with Giordano's image and as instructional pieces telling the consumer what and how to exchange. This was done as a means to emphasize Giordano's role as a mediator between the buyer and the Salvation Army.

The designer created several posters to support and bring public awareness to the campaign. These were developed further and extended to T-shirts that served as walking, breathing billboards. The T-shirt carries the message beyond the shopping district to reach those who are not typically first adopters. The visual diary was the seedbed for all these images and graphics. The result was a campaign that used its own process and methodology to emphasize the life story of production, consumption, and reuse of clothes and other material items. The final poster series was a design made of multiple articles of clothing. This design informed the consumer not only about the campaign but also about what types of clothes could be exchanged. It also emphasized the multitude of clothes awaiting a new life, the material abundance of the consumer, and how diverse individuals can come together for a better purpose that is unattainable to one individual when acting alone. Quotes and facts about reuse and value also help convey the message.

The designer created an original font to further execute the campaign. The font made the overall design more cohesive by marrying text and image with the whimsical character of the visual diary.

Objectives

1. Create inspiring and emotional designs that connect with an audience.

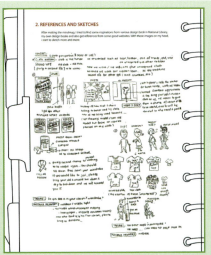

Figure 41

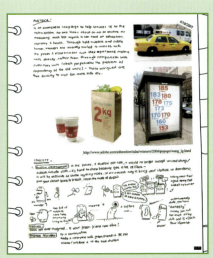

Figure 42

2. Create greater awareness of textile (apparel/cloth) recycling.
3. Engage consumers to recycle in a more convenient, easy, and fun way.
4. Influence consumer preferences while promoting sustainable products.

Process

1. Three months—Comprehensive research: books, articles, journals, and internet sources
2. Three months—Mini thesis and a project plan, experiments, conceptualization, and visualization

Challenges

1. Lengthy experimental and conceptualization phase
2. Locating source materials and avoiding copyright infringement
3. Discovering a fresh and engaging concept versus a stale, top-down approach

Outcomes

1. Changed thought process and perspective on environmental issues
2. Learned designers can contribute to the society and the environment using their talent and creativity

Question and Answer

What was the original intent of your project?

My original intention was to give people a new and fresh perspective on how to deal with used

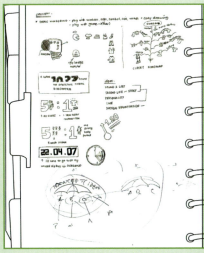

Figure 43

Figure 44

clothing. The project aimed to create greater awareness of textile (apparel/cloth) recycling and engage people, especially Singaporeans, to actively recycle in a more convenient, easy, and fun way. The project was also meant to influence consumer preferences and promote sustainable products that are gentle on the earth.

What motivated you to tackle this question?

The reason was actually quite personal; my father works in the textile industry, and thus I wished to have more knowledge about textile recycling. Textile recycling is quite rare, and most people do not have much knowledge of it. This project was a medium for me to help educate the broader public about the benefits of textile recycling.

How did the project evolve?

The project changed as I obtained new inspiration from a lot of books and resources. There were additional problems that haven't been addressed before and other people's innovative ideas/designs, which can contribute to the problem-solving process. The school environment also inspired me on how to approach this project. Nevertheless, the purpose of the project remained the same, which was to educate the broader public about textile recycling.

What was your process?

My first step was to conduct comprehensive research mainly through books, articles, journals, and internet sources. This was followed by a mini thesis and a project plan, which were used for the design process. The last phase of the project involved experiments, conceptualization, and the visualization processes.

Figure 45

Figure 46

How did you balance research into the subject matter with the practice of making?

I didn't create the designs at the same time that I was researching. According to the school's procedure, students are given three months' time to do the necessary primary and secondary research and prepare a comprehensive proposal and mini thesis. Knowledge of the issues is the first step. At the conclusion of the research, the school gave us another three months to design and produce a fully documented portfolio. Personally, I think it's easier to do research first and get important information and ideas about particular issues before designing. Having the necessary information helps me to define a clear purpose and direction in my work.

What problems did you encounter?

The major challenge came during the experimental and conceptualization phase, which took more time than anticipated. Another challenge was to make sure that I did not violate any copyrights from the sourced materials. I also ran into some problems finding a fresh/engaging and original design concept, as sometimes people perceive recycling as a government program that is simply informative and boring.

How did your professors inspire/ motivate you?

My professors always gave me encouraging input, valuable advice, and feedback throughout the project. In the initial phase, the discussion with my lecturer (class tutorial time) helped me a lot to make sure that I was on the right track. My professors also helped me to further develop the design concept and gave

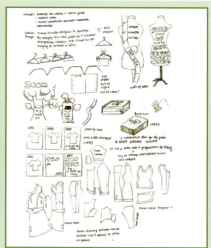

Figure 47

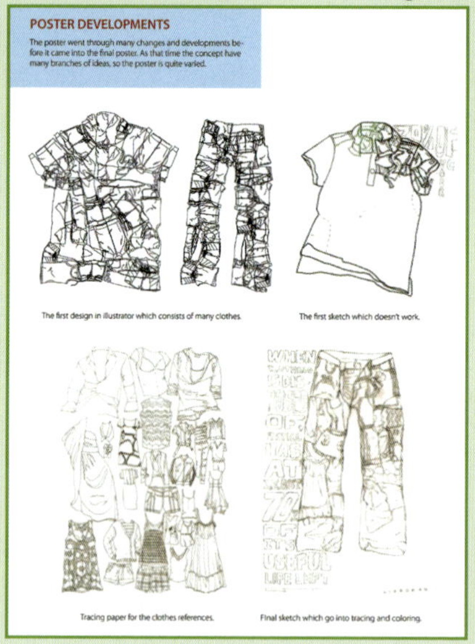

Figure 48

encouraging feedback on how to improve the visual design.

How did you change?

This project changed my thought process and perspective on environmental issues. I learned that designers can contribute to society and the environment by using their talent and creativity. This project also taught me about the capabilities of designers to help the world.

What is the future of this project and where will it take you?

My original plan was to introduce the concept of textile recycling to clothing manufacturers.

I tried to approach a few well-known manufacturers, such as Giordano, where I hope to take the project to a new level. However, I did not have the chance to pursue this project further, as I needed to go back to Indonesia due to family reasons. Still, I hope that my project helped to inspire other bright minds to consider textile recycling and help push the concept forward.

Figure 49

Figure 51

Figure 50

Figure 52

Information Design

The work of Karen Cheng's students in her information design course details the visually persuasive power of information design, a process of investigation unto itself that makes visible the workings of systems we often take for granted. Information design is not simply an end in itself. It is a process of research wherein form-giving is determined by which details can be sifted and refined to create the most visually compelling revelation of the facts, leading to the simplest and most persuasive argument. Information design employs some very basic elements that we often take for granted but that, when used by trained designers, produce new ways of seeing information that is also typically taken for granted. As described by Richard Saul Wurman in *Information Anxiety* (1989: 55), we have at our disposal three elemental forms for graphic design expression: (1) words, (2) numbers, and (3) pictures. Typically for the graphic designer, the first form predominates except in the case of information design. These elements, along with hierarchical structuring of information, are largely overlooked in basic two-dimensional design courses. These courses tend to celebrate the formal qualities of line, shape, and color, leaving most design students to discover the value of design hierarchy through courses on typography—or not at all. The preponderance of words, imagery, and numbers in our designed experience demands that information design be among the basics of a sustainable design education. This is especially true when many questions remain unanswered as to the complex details of sustainability and in projects like these where the designer is defining not only the question but also his own methodology. In many ways, the crucial question of sustainability is "How?" How do we work to make sense of an uncertain future while surrounded by an avalanche of information?

Proofs

In the case of Green Cards, Sara Alway-Rosenstock used her MFA research process as a graduate student to develop a new green product. Research into materials was the principal goal of the project, as this was the problem posed by the dearth of knowledge regarding ecologically friendly building materials and sources. Although a particular product arising was an unforeseen outcome, this highlights the very power of design to discover and anticipate simultaneously. The importance of universities and colleges offering students the opportunity to work through a thesis project experience is made visible through the work of Rosenstock and other students. If not for research conducted through the work of students and professors, sustainable design will likely remain in its so-called green phase, never reaching maturity. If graphic design is to have a voice in the rapidly growing discourse on sustainable design, then educators learning along with students will make it possible, along with young designers entering the field and implementing sustainable models and ethics.

Rosenstock's project contains great breadth and depth, exhibiting important dimensions of research, information design, entrepreneurship, and tool making coalescing into an original product. The mix of these dimensions developed organically as she began defining her thesis question and then grew until it became clear through the process that what was needed was a guide for consumers who are seeking green building products. By keeping the end user in mind and joining that with advanced design process and conscientious design decisions, she ensured the success of the project. This success extends beyond the three-legged approach to sustainability that recognizes human culture, economics, and ecological concerns. It achieves this through the craft of the designer and extends sustainable value through its direct engagement with production and consumption. This is complemented by graphic design's ability to define a question through multiple modes and iterations and to create tools that transcend the tangible through new ways of thinking critically through making. In Rosenstock's case, the majority of the work was spent in research and then was realized through a modular template. This inverse of what we commonly suppose graphic design to be makes clear the need for intense and ongoing research for sustainable design where the designer's process drives and defines a question that may result in any number of outcomes beyond what we define as graphic design.

Although much progress has been made in a short time regarding how to source sustainably, the importance of materials, materiality, and materialism remain paramount. If we as designers mistake the materiality of our own work with the materialism we often associate with overconsumption, we will miss the chance to impact production and consumption, the very places where we can leverage some influence. Objects of beauty and desire are still important aspects of any culture and are not themselves a form of degradation or corruption. What is important about design is its ability to shape values and impact the things that remain with us after a designed experience or object is consumed. By influencing what, how, and why we consume, designers can greatly influence the definition of *sustainable*. Rosenstock's project guides consumers to make lasting choices that resonate with meaning beyond the typical experience of delight with novelty, thereby reducing trivial consumption. The fact that people are consuming is not the principal issue for the designer. The designer's role is to define new limits and possibilities for conscientious design and consumption.

Research: The Book and Its Cover

This book is itself a case study, not simply a treatise serving up facts and notions on sustainable design or acting as an illustration of these. As much as possible, it integrates the arguments made in the book through its design and use. Because print remains a principal medium in which graphic designers specialize, it is important that this book advocate for sustainable book design.

The design of this book relies upon the *re-nourish* website as a tool of production. There are very few open-source tools available to the graphic designer in understanding even the most basic constraints and imperatives of sustainable design. *Re-nourish* serves the practical and daily needs of designers as a tool and a positive proof of workable and sustainable solutions to common design problems. More importantly, it demonstrates the need for designers to create original tools, new methods and processes for designing sustainably. Sites like *re-nourish* that utilize new technologies in the design of tools for designers are the chief artifacts in the transition to the widespread adoption of sustainable design principles. The creation of tools associated with new processes and methods demonstrate the emergence of design thinking as a broader and far more critical engagement with design problems that have previously been seen as beyond the designer's purview.

The Project Calculator and Paper Finder located within *re-nourish* were used in specifying the production of the book. Ultimately, the users of this book provide the impetus for a more sustainable book; those who buy, handle, read, and consume the book will hopefully over the long term retain or pass the book on. A book should have many lives and persist in many ways, but most especially in how it shapes how we think about design.

Tools

In 2002, Eric Benson was working as a graphic designer for Texas Instruments in Dallas when one evening he attended a lecture by Michael Braungart. Braungart, the coauthor of *Cradle to Cradle*, was giving a talk on sustainability to a group of graphic designers. Near the end of his talk, Braungart—a chemist and now a leader in sustainable design and business—began to cry. He cried over all the damage he had done to the environment as a chemist. It just so happened that Eric's father was a chemist, so what might to some have appeared to be theater hit a nerve with Eric. Eric was moved to act and returned to school to get his MFA in Graphic Design. While studying at the University of Texas, Eric began work on a project to be named *re-nourish*, a website he designed on sustainable practices for graphic designers. What he intended to be simply a tool and a jumping-off point for designers looking to get started designing greener work became a conversation about sustainable design. Before long, Eric became a recognized expert on the subject and the content of his site became something of a commodity. He designed the site as his thesis project, and that seemed to him to be the end of the subject. What followed surprised him; *re-nourish* entered the mainstream design community, creating a honest dialogue, and revealed the hunger designers have for real information on sustainable design practices.

Today, Eric teaches these practices at the University of Illinois as an Associate Professor of Design, and his retired father now works on issues related to clean water. Eric's process started with designing an architecture that would simplify questions into easy-to-digest components. He decided on this route as a way to imagine what type of questions someone who was initially only somewhat interested in the topic would ask upon finding the site. Eric felt that if the site was architected with the same framework that the user was thinking, it would be more intuitive. From the beginning, he decided the site should act as a narrative whose story would grow into further discussions. He began with the metaphor of a seed as a conversation starter online or at a casual night out at a pub. The key ideas communicated on the site were designed to be provocative enough that the user would want to share them with colleagues and seed future conversations with sustainable topics that would later germinate.

In 2008, Eric joined with Yvette Perullo to integrate her online tools from their original location on her site *rethinkdesign*, which she developed as her MA thesis project. Perullo realized that change needs to start at the beginning, because designers cannot make a substantial difference through attempts to clean up waste. The greatest impact a designer can have on minimizing waste is during the concept phase. Given the negative environmental effects of graphic design, her goal was to compare these traditional processes against new possibilities for sustainable processes. This investigation would lead to developing a solution to minimize the impact of graphic design. She was especially motivated by a particular piece she designed that included 400 extra printed pieces left sitting on a shelf. This direct-to-trash postcard left her somewhat embittered by all the waste produced through the design of just a single piece. She then developed her project calculator as an interactive, real-time tool for designers to have the most up-to-date information immediately. Yvette turned to a simple and clean design with an uncluttered layout focused on the toolset—the most important content on the website. And because designers respond better to visual cues, her goal was to provide the maximum amount of information with a minimal amount of text.

Systems

The work of Indonesian designer Elsa Kurniawati, who studied design at Raffles in Singapore, uses her design process and methodology to produce a total system to reduce consumption and through which the consumer is able to recycle unwanted or underused clothing for new, more sustainable items. In addition to designing the system, the documentation of her thinking-through-making represents the other designed outcome. The system visualizes an infrastructure employed by consumers, acting through retailers, to realize their own values and enlarge their understanding of the systems through which they find self-expression. The principal process she employed was ideation through repeated refinements, a basic process that all design students learn in their undergraduate training. What makes her process important is its focus on how sustainability is linked to all people, both collectively and individually.

Kurniawati chose to explore textiles for her project because of their ubiquitous presence as a basic necessity surpassed in significance only by their cultural meanings. They are woven and knit into the daily lives of each person in the form of clothing, adornment, covering, and ritual, and as indicators of status among the constant flow of the fashion industry, which defines contemporary ephemerality and unfortunately obsolescence. Not only do buyers end up with too many clothes that are dated, but producers also end up with extra stock that they must dispose of. In Singapore, where land area is very limited, especially landfill, and with a high rate of waste generation typical of an urban society, waste is a critical issue in any type of design.

Kurniawati's project seeks to integrate recycling with fashion as a lifestyle choice, operating through a designed system that is rooted in a visually provocative brand and convenient leisure activity. Perhaps more important is the possibility that the project might help recenter youth consumer identity around a more sustainable lifestyle. How a consumer identifies through the choice of what to buy, although considered by many critics to be an expression of trivial and irrational impulses, can be a fundamental tool in changing how and what we buy. Kurniawati's project engages consumers in a literal give-and-take, where they exchange old clothes for new. This reciprocation is what drives the concept of recycling as fashion. Used clothes are donated through the now-fashionable process of recycling using the already exchange-based retail site as the conduit to carry old clothes to those who can use them. The designer has employed the twin motivations of status seeking and altruism to not only waste fewer goods and increase the reuse of clothing but also to elevate the status of recycling. Twice the benefit is derived from the single act and yields to the buyer greater value and therefore satisfaction.

With more Singaporeans participating in recycling, the cost to the government for the disposal of used goods and waste is abated. In addition, consumer demand is in part shaped by the desire to give back in locally responsible ways at no additional cost to the individual and society. Currently, several fashion retailers in Singapore are attempting to sell virtually the same merchandise to the same shoppers. This demographic when defined by shopping is characterized by deriving self-expression via fashion choices. What many may view as impulse buying is more likely a consumerist-oriented image of oneself as young and current. This self-consciousness could also be harnessed to include environmental and community consciousness through this system.

Chapter Three
Packages

A package is a container of ideas, a vessel that holds meaning for individuals and groups. Victor Papanek responded to Marshall McLuhan's claim that "the medium is the message" with "the package is the product." This statement is true not only of iconic products that transcend both the package and the product through a personality beloved by the masses, but also of the ordinary packages thrown away every day because their value is overlooked. Understanding the value packages hold is extremely important given the plethora of packaging that fills, by some estimates, 30 percent of contemporary landfills.

The materials used in packaging and their material qualities also add value and meaning. Designers now need to be made aware of how the material is also the message. In designing for sustainability, what the designer chooses can make a dramatic statement and can advocate for better design. The simple act of choosing a ready-made pack or pioneering a new material choice has increased significance in the present. Sustainable package design is by definition distinct from graphic design only in the way the marketplace demands specialization. The material is the message, and the package is the medium with which the graphic designer can impact users and lessen the impact of packaging design on the environment while advocating for change.

Sustainable design should consider the package in two distinct ways. The first is as a container of ideas rather than things. If designers make this small leap, it will be apparent that all of the things graphic designers produce operate in much the same way. The second is as a material choice that, once made, cascades through a series of choices that, once taken, have a vast downstream effect. The best choice marries form and content sustainably, where each works to reinforce sustainability rather than working against the other. The things that packages contain may not in most cases be of primary interest to graphic designers, unless they are the product designers. Perhaps they should be the product designers, and at the very least could have some effect on the production end in order to reduce the amount of packaging. In that case, the marriage of form and content expands to include the product as content. In the end, the package may lend meaning to the product in ways that are unforeseen by the product designer in the context of consumption. Consumption is the site where what designers do matters most. How much will be discarded through use and what will remain? Is it important to simply reduce what gets discarded or to create meaning (i.e., value) for what remains? What, if anything, can be reused, recycled, or can reside in memory through remaking? Is post-consumer really ever the end of a thing?

Designing Over Time

A Coca-Cola bottle from 1907 provides an example of designing over time. Stamped on its bottom is West Palm Beach, Florida, which is close to where it was found nearly 100 years later, having just been dug up by street workers. The bottle lay just a foot or two below the surface in soft white sand that left it with a pearlescent patina over its green surface. It has considerable heft to it, is iridescent in the tropical light, was made locally, and reused repeatedly by the local bottler. It is, in short, not disposable. It continues to hold value (brand equity) for the product nearly a century later in ways that brands today seek to accomplish in the matter of a few short years. It speaks to the importance of designing over time so that a package will resonate with the user beyond the original experience, perhaps across generations.

So what happened? How did the reusable become the disposable? The bottle remains, but why end reusable, locally bottled soda? Why dispose of the brand equity contained in the glass bottle? Even given the ubiquitous presence of plastic and aluminium, it isn't entirely clear, especially if we consider packages of Wrigley's gum, Campbell's soup, or the Hershey chocolate bar, which remain virtually unchanged (Hine 1995: 8). The case study Re-Label, Re-Size, and Re-Design (see fig 82) offers a whimsical examination of this question by comparing the limits of one-way cans to the ways in which their impacts cannot be contained but are forever expanding.

Eco-Packaging

Instructor: Sylvain Allard
University of Quebec at Montreal, Canada
Students: Louis-David Noël, Camille Blais, Audrey Blouin, David Théroux, Jessika Brunner-Gnass, Jolin Masson-St-Onge, Mélissa Pilon, Pier-Philippe Rioux, Pierre-Luc Desharnais, Stephanie Malak
http://packaginguqam.blogspot.com/
http://labdi.uqam.ca/packaging/

Objectives

1. Create a sustainable package based on the 3R principles (reduction, recycling, and reuse).
2. Create greater awareness of environmental issues in package design.
3. Learn to integrate life-cycle analysis as a key paradigm in package design.

Process

- Five-week project (one of three in a 15-week term)—research, exploration, and design development of a packaging proposal
- 15-week term = three 5-week projects + two exercises
- Exercise 1 : Single sheet exercise—week 1
- Project 1 : Branding project (traditional packaging as communication design)—weeks 1–5

Figure 53

Figure 54

- Project 2 : Breaking the codes (nontraditional packaging methods)—weeks 5-10
- Exercise 2 : Variable exercise—week 7
- Project 3 : Eco-Packaging project—weeks 10-15

Challenges

1. Create a functional package to gather, transport, or protect one or more objects of similar or different nature.
2. Minimize the use of material in maximizing the functionality.
3. Offer a service that accompanies the experience of the product.
4. Reduce the ecological footprint by the use of biodegradable, reusable, or edible materials.

Outcomes

Recognize the immense environmental problems generated by packaging; the young designer is challenged to think about the role of design and to aim to be part of the solution.

Project Description

Further along in the course I have the students solve a functional packaging problem with minimal impact on the environment. Many aspects have to be considered in evaluating the sustainability of a package. The choice of material, the energy needed to produce and to transport such a package, and the weight and size effectiveness are only a few of the many aspects one should consider in a realistic approach to eco-packaging. Without a full and complete understanding of all these aspects, one can easily fall into greenwashing. One thing is certain though: less materials with more functionality is always a good approach. The students have to redesign a common object that could potentially be repackaged in a more creative and effective way. Their solution should be designed from a single piece of material with a minimal amount of transformation, no gluing if possible, and a maximum degree of recyclability.

I generally design my projects along my own research with specific objectives but that allow for a variety of explorations. I'm expecting to be surprised by the students and have my own perceptions of package design challenged. Therefore, I always give projects that have a large spectrum of potential solutions. I see design as a problem-solving discipline, and I help my students to develop an analytic approach. These projects are designed to reject preconceived ideas on sustainability and address specific solutions to specific problems. Exploring new

Figure 55

Figure 56

Figure 57

Figure 58

Figure 59

Figure 60

possibilities and stimulating students to think outside of what they know generally brings surprising results. They come to understand that real change in package design requires freedom to be creative. They also realize how much of a strategic position they are in being upstream from industrial production. I often tell my students to start by questioning everything. Since nearly all packaging on the market isn't sustainable, I encourage them to rethink packaging from scratch.

Once they are familiar with materials and how they are produced, they can explore new ways of approaching each problem. The most environmentally friendly package is the one that is not produced. That being said, should we have to design one, it should be along the lines of optimization. I tend to promote extreme reduction and optimization of material. I believe it is the only certainty we have to avoid greenwashing among all the other virtuous principles. The other aspects, such as recyclable products, nontoxic materials, and second-life are often difficult to measure without a serious life-cycle analysis of all aspects of a package's production. A green package transcends its basic function and takes a position by carrying a message that talks about the values of the brand. The customer endorses that value by its purchase. It becomes a communication that goes way beyond the simple commercial exchange.

Figure 61

Figure 62

Figure 63

Buying is voting in that sense. It is to a certain extent an act of adherence.

I am not a specialist in LCA, and I'm not expecting my students to be either, but each year, I have a specialist come to our design school to talk about it. My goal is that my students understand that all of the aspects of a product—from production to distribution and finally to disposal—should be considered in designing a package. Many significant aspects of the ecological footprint of a product have to do with transportation and energy and are not really related to the primary package, so I try to explain basic principles like reducing weight and size of packages. I put a lot of emphasis on avoiding multi-matter packages and avoiding using material that comes from the other side of the world even if it is green. It is important for students to understand that no material is evil, and it all has to do with case-by-case problem solving. It's the only way to avoid or at least reduce greenwashing. Students first feel a little lost in the complexity of it all. In the time frame we have, we stick with basic principles, and it seems to work well in terms of results.

Paper Exercise

I always start a term by giving my students a basic paper exercise involving a single sheet of paper. The exercise consists of designing a wine label out of a single sheet of

Figure 64

Figure 65

Figure 66

In the case of Campbell's, the history of the seemingly insignificant tin can was born in the midst of global change. War and conquest motivated the tin can's creator to invent a reliable way to provide a consistent, portable diet to armies and navies that could be transported everywhere. It was developed in an age of conquest couched in terms of exploration, discovery, and the spread of liberal democracy. It is on the surface a package, a container, but inside it held all the promise and the heartbreak of imperialism, colonization, and domination of many of the world's resources, which were also then packaged and distributed the world over. Wherever expansion of markets occurred, the packages that carried the goods also carried industrial processes that maximized efficiency and linked systems of production to systems of government and economics.

All around the world, crates, boxes, bottles, cans, barrels, and tins have been left behind in the wake of national economic progress for some and the detritus of that progress as a legacy to others. From the insignia of the Dutch East India Company literally branded on crates to the 50-gallon drum that became the basis for vernacular music of the islands of the Caribbean, these objects carried with them ideologies and lifestyles. The packages were reused because they were still useful to people who were reliant on the largesse of wealthier peoples. What of the other things consumed from these packages and then strewn across the developing world? What else did they contain? Incubating inside them were the toxins that litter the food chain, especially in places where people are undervalued and resources are overvalued as a means to someone else's gain.

Ideas in Motion

In today's economy, companies speak of bundling or piggybacking one product onto another. What are they truly transporting along with what they believe is their primary product? Are they overlooking the meanings and the materials that, though latent, will express themselves through some other form once the process of consumption has ended? Often the actual contents are left for someone else, who lives on the periphery along with a legacy of poor health and an even more rapidly diminishing future. This ecological and cultural blowback occurs unintentionally

paper excluding any image, print, or typography. The exercise helps students gain a respect for the material they use. They understand that it is exciting to search for great optimization concepts. When they get back to a more applied project, they tend to be more conscientious about each material they choose to use.

I believe that in order to teach packaging design to graphic designers, you need to start with what they know: that is bi-dimensional imagery, with a single flat sheet of paper. We tend to forget about it because it is so accessible, common, and yet sublime. The exercise is a pretext for paper exploration; I don't give them any constraints regarding partiality, functionality, or cost effectiveness. I let them explore the possibility in cutting, embossing, and creating shapes using light and shadow.

There is no intelligence involved in overdesigning packages with tons of layers, coats, material, and ribbons. The real challenge lies more in reducing and removing unnecessary items instead of just adding layers. What could look like a loss of creative freedom is in fact a challenge. The era of carefree design is on the decline. The environmental approach inevitably leads to a new aesthetic based in efficiency and restraint rather than excess.

Quotes

"I think we are at a tipping point in environmental matters now, because being green is no longer perceived as a hippie thing. . . . Being green is now mainstream, and the emerging technologies make the possibilities almost endless. Young designers can now run with those tools and propose even more creative solutions."
—Camille Blais | student
University of Quebec at Montreal

"I realized that most of the people I know had never paid attention to the toxic warnings on the product. At that point, I noticed that most of the packages we buy have lost their information vocation. As a consumer, we must understand the environmental impact of the things we buy, and that is why my packaging is almost strictly informative."
—Audrey Blouin | student
University of Quebec at Montreal

"I often end up having long conversations with students, and I am now realizing how important it is that the next generation be more aware of the issues. I find it to be very rewarding. The students feel they can make a little difference instead of being cynical about the ecology."
—Sylvain Allard

"Integration of environmental ethics starts by endorsing the values as a teacher and avoiding any cynical and destructive thinking about what has to be done."
—Sylvain Allard

"I think designers are often ignored in the chain of production. Design is generally perceived to be superficial or even useless, whereas good designers can really make a difference if they want to. My main goal is to fulfill their needs in a way that I also feel comfortable with, and that involves respectful and intelligent design."
—Camille Blais | student
University of Quebec at Montreal

"I wanted to use a minimum of matter to create this package: the Paillasson is still produced in a way very close to its origin and to its environment. Hence, I created a folding pattern that allowed the cheese to be wrapped in a single sheet of paper, without any glue. I also limited the amount of printing to make production simpler and to showcase the beauty of natural paper. Moreover, I thought of a possible second life for the wrapping: the closing tab could be detached and used as a label to identify the cheese."

—Camille Blais | student
University of Quebec at Montreal

"I first thought of a familiar object that we use everyday. I not only wanted to make something eco-friendly by using less ink, less glue, and recyclable materials, but also something useful and practical for all users, by combining two inseparable things, a facial tissues box and a garbage can."

—Louis-David Noël | student
University of Quebec at Montreal

yet systematically. If we became aware of what we are actually packaging and leaving behind, what could we do with that knowledge? These packages are not simply containers but vehicles and, as such, ideas in motion—ideology embodied and mobilized. They possess a kind of agency because, although they are made within strict parameters for a specific end, their impact exceeds any expectation or original intent. As vehicles, they travel, and the notions they carry still remain but in the form of unintended consequences. Strictly speaking, they were not designed for the future but only for the present and to last only until the point of purchase.

Local and Unique

The development of packages and containers such as tin cans, paper bags, and paperboard boxes coincided with the development of lithography, chromolithography, and offset printing, which when applied to packages increased their visual appeal and their power to communicate. These didn't just contain or move things; they motivated consumers. Their power to contain and move ideas remains, and the systems by which they continue to assert themselves are grounded in the larger systems that they support. They are tied to a way of thinking, which molds ways of living. At their inception, they were transported by rail and steamship. Today's ideas move over little more than currents and are not made concrete until someone acts, such as a designer to give them form. This means the graphic designer crafts the message and the means that will decide how we think not only about today but, more importantly, tomorrow.

Historically, package design has always been a visual expression of the substance within, as well as a distinct carrier that spoke to the origins of the product. The unique local qualities of the contents were perfectly in sync with the package. The package originated with the product, and the form and content were assumed to originate together. This history suggests that responsible sourcing, just as recycling, remaking, and reusing, is not a new phenomena or unique to what we currently seek to do and communicate through sustainable design. The materials from which both the package and the product were produced were both locally sourced and perfectly suited to their roles. Durable packages that could travel over time and distance are rooted in ancient trade routes, which are also not unique to the present. The value of the product resided in its individual relationship to a local area and increased in value as the distinct qualities of the product were sold or traded farther afield.

Communicating Value

Our current notion of locally produced items as boutique and rarified luxury goods misdirects our attention from their role as the basis of sustainability. Today these goods compete against monocultures as an antidote to mediocrity, homogeneity, and poor quality, but often, unfortunately, at a high price and as class signifiers. The association of sustainable goods, especially food-stuffs, with elite culture is currently undermining their potential.

The role of sustainable package design is not only to buffet the product and to reduce the costs and impacts of transporting goods, but also to maintain the health of the user all along the life cycle of the package and beyond its consumption and reuse. Communicating the value of the product as a sustainably produced good that increases in value as it is transported in sustainable packaging is imperative. Sustainable packaging can make visible systems of production, distribution, consumption, and recovery. This contradicts the role of packaging in the recent past, which further abstracted processes and divorced production from consumption, blinding the consumer to its ingredients and impacts on the environment and people.

Memory

Designers should now seek to invert this previous paradigm so that the consumer identifies with products as components of ethical systems rather than with an ideology associated with systematic control and hegemony. Designers should speak through the package to the consumer's better selves—grounded in informed citizenry, acting in their own best interests and the interests of others. Consumer capitalism has been based largely on aspiration. This is not in itself a bad thing, but it should be harnessed to other, better values associated with creating a better culture rather than status seeking. Because packages carry an object over time and distance, part of their role as sustainably designed objects should be to maintain a memory of their life cycle. This was the case with the earliest packaging and early forms of writing that emerged with it in Mesopotamia. This hasn't changed, it has only been abstracted through modern systems of production and consumption. Products that are pioneering efforts at returning to this essential aspect of design are positioned to entirely reorient consumption. This will not be achieved through dominance but through influence—the kind that shifts cultural paradigms.

Remediating Relationships

It is no longer necessary to convince the consumer of the need for packaged goods or their benefit as standardized and widely available. The challenge in sustainable package design is to introduce that consumer or user to the value of his or her own agency. This agency allows consumers to act to make change not through mediated relationships to food and life's other necessities but in what they owe to themselves. Users' true personality and character should be allowed to act through their purchases to initiate systematic changes. This is fundamentally different from the notion of the consumer who was manufactured in the nineteenth century and served by proxies, such as the Quaker Oats man, who was introduced to wean consumers away from first-person relationships to life's basic necessities. Rather than supplanting ordinary human relationships with objects and environments, we should seek to enforce and rebuild them. The effort to revive the relationship between who the

ReBrand and ReNew— The Total Package

Instructor: Peter Fine
University of Wyoming, USA
Students: Michelle Rivera, Jack Barnett-Queen, Sean Hudson, Adam Isleib, Nick Zemek

Objectives

1. Renew the brand to reflect the consumers' desire to actively change their lives to reflect their genuine and ethical aspirations.
2. Perform well at every level to be sustainable, persuasive, beautiful, smart, and accurately describe its contents.

Figure 67

Figure 68

Figure 69

Figure 70

Figure 71

Figure 72

Figure 73

Figure 74

Figure 75

Figure 76

Figure 77

Figure 78

Figure 79

Figure 80

consumer is and what he or she consumes is not a search for novelty or niche markets for new goods, nor is it a return to a bygone era populated by kindly and paternal store clerks, patent medicine hucksters, or the friendly figures that first sold the promise of packaged goods.

Peeling Away the Label

Packaging has not only moved things but also transmitted important ideologies. As the book literally carried all of the progressive notions of the Reformation, Renaissance, and democratic movements and many other less benign aspects of Western culture, the package has held all of society's beliefs regarding the products of the culture of the industrial age. These contradictory, often competing, values are so inextricably linked that they have in large part been invisible to those who have profited and those dominated by them. If designers examine package design, they can glimpse what is at work through the design of images and objects of desire and consumption. They visualize not only the things everyone consumes but also the systems of design that carry goods and ideas. Many of the key products associated with world trade in the modern era, such as tobacco, coffee, and sugar, arrived in unique packages that set the stage for modern graphic design in the industrial era. Many of these packages defined the consumer's relationship to goods, which they literally consumed along with notions of race, gender, luxury, hygiene, and a host of other complex modern notions. If designers will peel away many of their labels, they will find that they, along with the larger culture, have absorbed an entire set of ideas. The lesson in this is that *how* things are made and consumed is as important as *why*.

Ethical Representation

Graphic designers trade in a language of visual representation. At the heart of that language rests many fundamental assumptions about the profession. We need to take responsibility as designers to create honest and ethical representations and new avenues for doing so. To do that, designers must know how representation operates rather than simply respond to visual communication problems with a formalist or

Process

1. Visual audits
2. Ideation—name and tagline generation
3. Design of logotype
4. Feedback—multiple presentations, critiques, focus groups, and small-group interactions
5. Life-cycle analysis—intensive analysis and research followed by the creation of a rough model for conducting the LCA
6. Design of new package—including sketches, maquettes, comping, and rapid prototyping
7. Information design—unique, integrated narrative about the package and product

Challenges

1. Negotiating the morass of complex systems tied to package and product design not typically addressed by the graphic designer
2. Developing the right questions that challenge assumptions about waste and produce a persuasive package

3. Constructing a method for developing an LCA from scratch
4. Project management over the course of a semester while navigating small-group dynamics

Outcomes

1. Student-derived model for both analyzing and designing for complex sustainable problems and solutions
2. A portfolio-ready comprehensive mock-up that is persuasive and engaging, as well as one that advocates for the consumer

Steps

ReBrand and ReNew rebrands the package as the vehicle for sustainable design education and practice. The product must be something ingested or used upon the body, and the package must have a contemporary retail presence.

1. The students take a trip to a Target store, where each picks one package and then returns to class, where each group then

Figure 81

chooses one package that demands to be redesigned.

2. Each group performs exhaustive research into every aspect of the package and the product, including visual audits, complete LCA, and multiple ideations.

3. The students perform a comprehensive visual audit of the product line as well as for two competitors. This begins the process of revealing and detailing the visual language of the product.

4. The students conduct research into the primary consumer for their product, reimagined with a greener persona.

5. The students create a minimum of three interventions in the production and/or consumption of the package, one of which must include some material component of the packaging.

6. The students are tasked with defining and implementing a methodology for conducting the life-cycle analysis, without any previous knowledge or specialized tools to conduct it, ferreting their own way through a tangled web of information, half-truths, and misdirection.

7. As the students discover bits and pieces of the LCA, they record them on three-by-five-inch index cards. On the flip side, they draw simple icons or symbols of these components, building a visual lexicon to be translated into a complex information design.

8. The students consider unusual forms for information design that resist the urge to simply inform through illustration. These may include books, videos, games, or other narrative forms. These should inform implicitly without attempting to convince an audience to embrace a particular point of view but win them over through the merging of form and content in a manner that seems to transcend the issues and assumptions about consumption.

9. The first step in the redesign is to name the product in a manner that speaks to its newly emerging green value. Each student in the group contributes thirty-six to forty-eight ideas for product names, which they narrow down to the twelve they feel worthy of presenting to the entire group. In addition, each student contributes another thirty-six to forty-eight ideas for taglines that they also narrow down to twelve for presentation. Once the name is chosen, each student designs an original logotype with the tagline set with it.

10. The package takes form through a series of sketches, diagrams, elevations, and simple maquettes. The material considerations given to the life cycle are presented along with or upon the package. The final mock-up for the design is realized through rapid prototyping and other comping techniques.

11. The students work with Industrial Engineering students to develop a prototype of the package, where they are developing plastic made from canola oil.

utilitarian approach. Central to the ways in which visual representation operates is in defining who dominates in any society, but especially those who are equipped to mass produce themselves through mechanical reproduction. Historically, this was accomplished by comparison. Westerners have historically defined themselves not only by what they consume but also through the labor of others who they saw as different.

Sugar as an industrialized product is related to establishing the consumption of packaged goods and, along with tobacco, cotton, and other goods, was fuel for the transatlantic slave trade. This is historically important to understanding sustainable design because (1) it is linked to basic modes of representation that operate by defining "the other"; (2) the concept of race has historically defined the very limit of the success of Western liberal democracy, and still today represents a barrier to people trying to share in it; (3) products and packages were sourced from regions that were dominated through colonization, imperialism, or conquest; and (4) race has been central to defining the value of people, which continues to affect where the waste we produce is currently redistributed.

Embodying Consumption—The Labor of Others Provides for Your Comfort

If designers will consider products distributed worldwide and packaged along with racialized images of Africans and other misrepresented peoples, they will see how these images have embodied the ways we all consume. These characters were originally designed in the United States to serve as proxies for the kindly storekeeper. Their role was to guarantee comfort and the reliability of the product divorced from the day-to-day trade in goods in a new age of industrially derived foodstuffs. Most importantly, the products represented by these packages and their characters would have been impossible without new forms of packaging. These packages allowed manufacturers to market and distribute ordinary foodstuffs in unique combinations. The revolutionary power of ordinary paper bags, paperboard boxes, and tin cans and how they radically changed how people eat cannot be overlooked or overstated. In fact, color lithography emerged as a means to label tin cans. The message of these products and the characters' faces upon them in the nineteenth century was clear—the labor of others provides for your comfort.

There is a deeper meaning, especially in the form of images such as Aunt Jemima. Aunt characters were common in the post–Civil War period in the United States and other areas of the New World as wet nurses. The message of nurturing and sustenance cannot be denied. The story of Aunt Jemima as a fictional character who shilled for a pancake mix is as complicated as all race relations are, but her representation of race, labor, and comfort are clear. She is also related to a common theme in these packages and popular literature regarding the passing of secrets in the form of recipes from enslaved people to their owners, which describes a very intimate and ongoing relationship. That she was displayed on the surface of the package declares the power of the package as an ideological object that wholly contains desire.

An example of this concept can be seen in three packets or wrappers from different countries, single-serving sugar packs, the kind readily available in cafés for use with coffee and tea, and one candy wrapper. Each one contains a representation of blackness in the form of a small character. One is from Italy, called Caffè Moca Roma, and holds the image of a smiling African character in a straw hat. Another is from the United States but was originally created in Austria in the 1920s for Julius Meinl, a Vienesse coffee company and café. The well-known Viennese graphic designer Josef Binder, who later emigrated to the United States, was the designer. It has on its cover an African boy who, in a larger poster image, is making coffee upon the desert sand, presumably for someone else. The third is a candy wrapper for Kismi from India. It has on its wrap the black figure of a man, against which the profile of a white woman is overlapped in a clever figure-ground relationship. Each of these examples is a package, a single serving, and a sweet substance. Sugar is sweet not only in taste but as a symbol of status and a luxury item that once indicated middle-class status and taste. High-quality serving utensils and containers made from precious materials were used to serve it. These were well designed and crafted, representing status, luxury, and refinement.

Packaging first emerged in the modern era to hold luxury items such as cosmetics, perfumes, and soaps along with tobacco and tea. The link between luxury and leisure time is directly connected to the cheap and often entirely free labor of

Relabel, Resize, and Redesign: Repackaging the Single-Use Beverage Container

Students: Darold Ross, Fangshu Zhu, Candace Barnett, Joel Zamora, Carmela Martinez, Danielle Garcia, Matt Ortiz

For this project, the students relabel and redesign one of three of the most common beverage containers, the plastic two-liter soda or pop bottle, the twelve-ounce aluminum soda or pop can, and the now ubiquitous twelve-ounce bottled water container. This project ideally takes two forms: (1) an actual model of the height each container would have to reach to accept all of the new labeling required and (2) a new redesigned beverage container. The redesigns reflect new labeling requirements according to the group's recommendations as to what consumers most need to know about the impact of one-way beverage containers.

Here the students use research methods they developed in earlier courses to ferret out the LCA information, working in groups to streamline their efforts and individual skill sets. This group chose the twelve-ounce Coke can as their subject. Instead of creating a taller-than-life Coke can based on the can's footprint, they chose to expand the can in all directions to accommodate the plethora of information necessary in describing the can's entire life cycle and health concerns. This piece includes cheeky references to the risk of diabetes associated with drinking soda and the actual fluid ounces contained in the gargantuan can. This group created a single can at the height of five feet and used forty-five cans to describe some of the can's larger impacts. Included on the can's label are several aspects of the life cycle of the can and its contents, including high-fructose corn syrup, transportation impacts, and aluminum while white clouds puff with industrial off-gasses.

Figure 82

Figure 83

Figure 84

subjugated peoples. These tiny packages are at once connected to these notions in a variety of ways that are so inculcated that their relationship to brutal and, yes, unsustainable practices of the past go largely unseen. Their representations remain as nostalgic or kitschy characters, but we also cannot and should not support their practices. Is it any wonder that designers have been complicit in practices that sideline countries and cultures and that allow many people not to see how negatively they are affected through consumption? The consumption of sugar, whether in the form of molasses, rum, or its now more familiar processed state, serves as a window into how our culture literally consumes products, packages, and the things that bind them together, often without considering what is smuggled in every package.

Between Consumption and Waste

Today's consumers must question whether they should continue to consume people and resources as products as long as they are nicely packaged and branded to abstract the systems that keep them at a remove. This issue has now been foregrounded by the downstream effects of what designers make, as globalization rapidly shrinks the distances between consumption and waste sites. Consumers may feel they cannot do without the consumables that crowd their daily lives, which they perceive as necessities, but they would not pay the difference if asked to absorb all the actual costs. They would soon realize that what they lack cannot be made up at someone else's cost. They would not pay the cost either to their health, the health of their families, or the environment. They accept many of these throwaway packages because they are cheap and convenient, and so are the products and ideas they contain. In doing so, they underestimate these packages. Their power is not in their low cost, consistency, and wide availability but in their ability to contain a world of interlocking bits and pieces. We have literally overlooked their power to inform because they entrance us as a display through the ways in which they perform. The package's primary display panel doesn't reveal on the retail shelf the host of lost labor, materials, and health that the total package holds. Designers need to search out what is currently not visible but still just below the surface. Most consumers rarely consider the life of their purchases once it leaves their hands, much less where it began. What in

one case might mean the world to someone is just as likely to be considered trash by someone else.

The Iconography of Representation

The first brand manager was instituted at Procter and Gamble in 1930 to manage a line of packaged products (Hine 1995: 117). This was in part a false conceit, because the distinction in the products was only created so that Procter and Gamble could place highly similar products in the same category in competition against each other. Once again, as in the case with race and representation, we have a thing that exists only as it is differentiated from another and is manipulated by a larger entity for the exclusive profit of a small group of people at the expense of others. What is being consumed? Why? How have consumers formed themselves in response to products designed and packaged for disposal and in contrast to others?

In considering packaging, designers need to look at iconic packages, those that define and embody the ways consumption occurs. This is defined first by production and what is valued. Designers should consider how these packages began as mundane throwaways that created whole categories of consumption. These packages, and in some cases the products, pose a different problem than obsolescence, which is rightly associated with durable goods. Their iconic quality is defined in large part by their package and its ability to define a product to the point where both merge. The problem they present is doubled in that disposability gains greater value through convenience than sustainability, leading to hegemonic domination of an entire product category.

This branding of a wholly disposable product/package category truly defines not only that category but also what the consumer believes a brand is and how it should operate. In some cases, these products not only dominate a market but also represent the cultural dominance of US-based consumer culture. This dominance occurred at a rapid and titanic scale both during and after the Second World War. In some cases, these products represented the distribution of an American-style democracy, especially in the case of products like Coca-Cola. Its popularity, though certainly boosted by a worldwide youth culture that rode the coattails of the baby boom, was grounded in associative power. This throwaway culture was defined by Victor Papanek as our "Kleenex culture" (1972: 96–106). It is no accident that he chose this product as a metaphor for large-scale systematic consumption. Kleenex literally defined disposability and hygiene as a product category beyond the kitchen and bathroom. In the public psyche, there is no substitute for the Kleenex; it is not simply shorthand for "facial tissue" but *is* facial tissue. Few products designed as packages occupy this position, therefore they reveal much about what packaging means culturally; they include Coca-Cola, Scotch tape, and Kleenex as words in the form of logotypes, with a host of others that very nearly eclipse other brands, such as Clorox or Hershey.

Alongside these brands emerged certain technologies and industries that defined systematic obsolescence as a lifestyle, such as the auto industry. The power of these iconic products and services is contrasted with their need to remain current or, as the case may be, replaced by newer versions in order to drive production and control consumption. The novelty of the Kleenex box seems to have served it long enough to lodge permanently in the public imagination so that even a more sustainable alternative could not displace it. In most cases, the public has come to expect that packages will at times change, often offering novel ways of dispensing the product or disposing of it but most often through meaningless attributes.

If a product like Kleenex can be defined by its package and meanwhile also define the very category it occupies, what else might it signify? What space might it occupy in the public mind? In *The Total Package*, Thomas Hine describes packages as embodying and resolving conflicts by positing the product as a panacea to a new or longstanding problem (1995: 164, 214). It matters not that these products may be solving problems that don't exist.

On-the-Go Packaging

In addition to products packaged for retail sales, convenience foods, especially single-serving products, are another system of design focused on packaging. With nearly 60 percent of all packaging designed and produced for foods and beverages, the waste associated with these products ranks high on the list of ecological issues.

The anti-litter campaigns of the late twentieth century focused only on the removal of trash to the boundaries of our built environment. These campaigns, like the television spots created by Keep America Beautiful, were produced largely for the packaging industry. The Keep America Beautiful spot featuring a weeping actor in red-face on horseback conflated the mythology of the American West with modern notions of hygiene and waste in which we separated ourselves from the ugly truth. Sustainable design should make visible the ways in which all systems overlap and the way a more holistic understanding of our environment can serve us better.

Throwaway fast-food packaging as litter is only a single symptom of an unsustainable food production model. Food, for a variety of large-scale, systemic reasons, is the number-one category through which the individual negatively impacts the natural environment. The food consumed often travels long distances, as much as 2,000 miles within the United States. This distancing of source and consumption obscures the fact that ecological or bodily contamination cannot be avoided. The package designed to contain and protect the product over time and distance obscures the fact that it cannot protect anyone from the downstream effects of industrialized food production and consumption. The tolerances are simply too narrow and the skin of the package too thin. Although the majority of the costs of packaging result through energy consumption, extraction of resources, and emissions, graphic designers typically only engage with the package design, and yet this is where their leverage resides in how they specify materials and therefore production. They can also leverage the package to create more sustainable forms of consumption within a closed loop.

The process by which we so quickly eat prepared and fast foods and then dispose of their packaging diminishes not only food and our health but also the very ritual of eating. The goal is only the quick and easy aspect of meeting a basic need—and even that fails to occur. The entire ritual associated over eons with eating is reduced to a solitary and anonymous moment interchangeable with any other. There are, of course, many satisfying examples worldwide of the cultural richness of sharing food with others. Many of these activities involve the ritual discard of ephemeral elements that, though temporal, describe eternal verities. Many of our present packages associated with food emphasize only the hygienic function of food containers; this emanates from the dangerous quality of food in the industrial beginnings of packaged foods and in the modern and contemporary eras as well. Though consumers are protected from the immediate, harmful effects of unsustainable food production, they lose contact with the food as a sustainer of life both bodily and culturally. What they are left with and what is bequeathed is the baggage they are unwilling to cling to.

To Signify or to Obscure

Graphic design can mediate our relationship to food and invest it with meaning, value, health, and a legacy of quality. The labels that cover the packages purchased also hide the complex and damaging systems associated with food production. This is accomplished via the branding of these food products through the use of highly reductive images and logos. The logo itself or, more often and more accurately, a logotype is a visual device that combines and reduces very complex, technical systems down to a single identifier. It serves less to signify than to obscure. What are signified are not the complex and destructive systems that produced the product, the package, and all their wastes, byproducts, and side effects but a notion of an abundant supply that is constantly and literally close at hand. For the graphic designer who is employed to design packages, the real work is to define the links between what is consumed and the consumer. Foods and beverages provide the clearest and most necessary example of the process of mediation that occurs through design. To literally consume food and drink is also to eat and drink of the cultural fount of industrialization. Because the things typically ingested as foods were industrialized incrementally, consumers have been late to sound the alarm about their ill effects that serve as metaphors for a life based in industrial processes and technocracy.

Designers cannot simply employ a passing interest in what cultures produce and why. Despite their disposability, packages are still linked to ritual, preciousness, and a host of essential human values that cannot be discarded. To truly engage with this system implies a much more interdisciplinary approach to design in concert with other forms of discovery. It would also mean a dramatic shift in foundational teaching in art and design. Ethics would feature prominently in this teaching as the hub of how to understand cultures apart from and within the designer's sphere of influence, not as simply abstractions of difference. If this is not the case, designers can easily fall into the trap of making more of what they don't want and don't need that will continue to negatively affect many more people in the future.

Plastic Is a Noun

Aside from paperboard, plastic continues to retain and expand its centrality as a primary material solution for packaging and in its influence on how we define consumption, waste, and material abundance. It retains its influence through phenomena similar in significance to the mechanical reproduction of words and images. Just as design for visual and verbal reproduction has created a sense of unlimited supply of ideas, synthetics have manufactured the sense that plastic is an unlimited source of cheap material abundance. This is coupled with the literal and metaphoric plasticity of chemically derived synthetics. Plastic synthesizes these notions at the foundation of modern materiality. The material is boundless in its capacity to be molded to accommodate any dimension and therefore any modern notion. Plastic's material qualities have informed our current notions and practices of consumption to the degree that we no longer recognize them as constructed. We have eaten and drunk from plastic to the point that we cannot conceive of a time when disposability was not essential to sustaining our basic physical needs. What we could not have imagined is how such an apparently unlimited abundance could tie us so closely to industrial systems beyond the control of the individual.

Plastic's association with artifice—through its original purpose as a substitute for rare and precious materials used in the production of cheap and common consumables—had by the 1950s been eclipsed by its association with all things artificial. In the postwar period, its cheap and easy availability further enforced this notion and through its systematic adoption by beverage companies, food packagers, and fast-food outlets led to its rapid devaluation in the public mind. The ubiquitous visibility of litter in the form of plastic and paper both escalated their devaluation and also reinforced the seeming inevitability of wasted material abundance. This occurred despite the increasing degree to which plastic was finding its way into nearly every object of design and material culture. As described by Susan Freinkel in *Plastic: A Toxic Love Story*, "plastic had become the skeleton, the connective tissue, and the slippery skin of modern life" (2011: 6).

The synthetic and the artificial were then also linked, materially and metaphorically, in the age of plastic. This age was defined by unlimited resources and therefore optimism, but in reality was constrained by synthetic polymer's origin as a chemical byproduct of oil refinement. Like much of what has come to be regarded as natural in an era awash with synthetic materials, plastic is tied to the systematic obsolescence of automobile culture and its hegemony over systems of design. This dynamic, along with plastic's democratization of consumption at the broadest and highest levels in human history, caused a further conflation of consumer capitalism with democracy. In the marketplace of ideas, the most marketable material is the most valuable and the least esteemed.

Today's designer is faced with this legacy in the form of plastic's enduring materiality and in its dominance through ubiquity, despite its low status. Its durability is furthered in the way it remains even as it degrades and continues to poison, ecologically and bodily. The bits and pieces scattered throughout natural systems and human tissue fail to return anything to the earth that can sustain it. The brute force of industrial systems that are dependent on oil production simply lack the nuance to deal with the smaller matters that affect intricate systems. The result is a dearth of rhetorical, aesthetic, and critical assessment of design, which is so closely associated with consumption. In allowing plastic to mold, shape, and contain so much of our material culture, design has failed to define how and why we should give so much agency to something that is commonly regarded as disposable and unworthy of our esteem. In the end, we waste too much of what is needed and ignore what value remains. Plastic promised the designer unlimited flexibility and control over the natural world but produced unmanageable waste as a result of the true material constraints of synthetics. In the end, plastic is not a thing but a temporary placeholder for whatever it contains. Once it has served this purpose, it finds its true meaning in its disposal and lingers in its ability to resist natural forces, as Barthes described, "the first magical substance which consents to be prosaic" (1957).

Summary of Case Studies

Eco-Packaging and Paper Exercise

Sylvain Allard inherited a course at the University of Quebec, Montreal, entitled The Object, which he admits had grown fallow and was in need of a fresh approach. Allard decided that packaging was the best place to start in a graphic design department where the emphasis had been on design for communication. Because "the package" implies that everything comes included, is neatly boxed, and ready to go, this seemed to him to be the best avenue to pursue new ideas. Given the ubiquity of packaging and how intimate the average consumer was with the form, a sustainable course in packaging seemed to encapsulate what he wanted to achieve.

Allard was in pursuit of better practices concerning design and the environment, as well as ways to engage directly and practically with the design profession. But where to start? There were no precedents for what he was considering. He realized that education had waited too long on industry to make a change and that neither a passive approach nor simple agitation for change would work. He began by starting a blog where he initiated a way to communicate what his students were doing with the goal of getting their work into production.

He also determined that he would need to question how all kinds of things get conceived, made, and used and that this demanded a more holistic approach to teaching design. The ways in which both he and his students perceived design would need to change. It would require them to question the very definition of design, because all the actors would have to be educated, not only the students. The results were sure to be uneven, as the integration of environmental concerns would happen in small steps, at different locations, and at different times—in small revolutions. Instead of teaching what already exists in the profession, he pushed the students to generate their own innovations, to search for better solutions that could then be adapted to the market. This emphasis on original ideas helped clear the air, freed the students creatively, and avoided replicating existing ideas. It wasn't long before he realized that design education was shifting:

Design has to start with the complete integration of the green concept in every designer's mind. If one doesn't realize the importance of environmental issues and the consequences of our design decisions on ecology it won't be possible to go very far. On the other hand, if the students are exposed to information about the situation, they will discover for themselves the importance of making a difference. It is an educational issue more than anything else.

Much of that education happens through discovery and occurs while seeking out new materials and processes. For Allard, that begins by reducing the amount of materials used and maximizing what remains:

With this economical and ecological approach to design, you can't help but respect the materials and try to optimize as much as you can their characteristics. Sometimes, the quest for an optimal solution leads to new forms and new materials.

Through new processes and materials, the package becomes a mechanism for better practices. The box—often overlooked and tossed aside—becomes the site at which design connects consumers to their own desire for a safer, cleaner planet. The pleasure of discovery is important to the design students' long-term goals as designers, citizens, entrepreneurs, and parents, because they are the pioneers of a new movement in design. Because of the joy of discovery, the designers will come back for more; in solving big, complex, abstract problems, we need more than a task-oriented approach.

ReBrand and ReNew

ReBrand and ReNew rebrands an existing product not to look green, greener, or green-ish, but to be sustainable. The vehicle for this is the package. The contents, the product contained within the package chosen for the redesign, must be ingested or used upon the body: topicals, foodstuffs, liquids, clothing—anything that might come in contact with the body. It must be an existing product whose package has a presence in the retail environment.

The students take a trip to a Target store where they can find a wide array of toiletries, medicines, foods, beverages, cosmetics, and clothing, all in one location where "design for everyone" is declared to be a core company value. Each student picks one package and then returns to class with it, where they form small groups to discuss which package demands to be redesigned. The chosen design may be performing well in terms of aesthetic value or utility or already in need of a redesign. The redesign should include a new logotype as the core identity of the package's primary display panel. The identity of the parent brand, if any, should remain the same in order to retain brand equity. For instance, the redesign of the Twinkie package would not include the redesign of Hostess, although its presence would persist on the package. The final redesign includes all of the elements present on the existing package, from bar codes to volume of contents, and so on.

The basis for this collaborative design project is exhaustive research into every aspect of the package and the product, including visual audits, complete life-cycle analysis (LCA), and multiple ideations. The students perform a comprehensive audit of the product line beyond the package and including branding, advertising, point-of-purchase, and web presence. The students also collect the same information for two competitors. If two direct competitors do not exist, they choose something akin to the product in the same category. This begins the process of revealing and detailing the visual language of the product, its product category, and its consumer.

The students also conduct research to determine the primary consumer for their product if reimagined with a greener persona. This is the entry point that allows the students to name and define the principal user. They discover what the package and product hold for this particular consumer in terms of his or her desire to act and consume as a form of conscientious self-expression. At this point in the project, the student has the opportunity to connect production and consumption through design to the very identity of the user. This stimulates empathy in the student and produces a more heartfelt response to the users' needs as people rather than simply consumers left, at the end of the product's life cycle, "holding the bag." The designer then acts as facilitator of the consumer's desire to freely identify with the product as a further manifestation of that product and as an ethical consumer.

Through the redesign, the totality of the product is expressed through the package. The total experience of a package and its product are not constrained by the limitations of the final design but possesses a life beyond itself—through reuse, recycling, remaking, and reclamation of valuable waste material, all as a tangible reminder of consumers' relationships to their essential needs. In reality, the line between a package and product is thinly drawn. A tension exists in the ephemeral quality of the materials and the properties of the product as they relate to addressing fundamental needs as users experience the design from sourcing of the product to reuse of the package. Users then understand how their lives and health are tied to the products' origins and life cycle. Transparency is key in this dynamic, with the product wearing its heart on its sleeve in the form of the package. By including key components of the product and package LCA on or in the package, users are able to view what they are actually ingesting. This occurs in terms of product, messages, and acculturation.

The visual audits culminate in the digital presentation of all the research produced. What results is nothing less than the visual language of everyday items, such as razors, toothbrushes, soap, mouthwash, and the like. The ubiquity and mundane quality of these objects of design and their companion packages tends to hide them in plain sight. Through the design process, the students come to see the ways that designers construct our visual environment. Prior to the digital presentation, the group presents all their work on boards to the class in order to gather feedback from the other groups.

The students create a minimum of three interventions in the production and/or consumption of the package, one of which must include some material component of the packaging. As part of this, the student is tasked with defining and implementing a methodology for conducting the LCA. The purpose is to learn how the product and package is made (in total), where it's sourced and by whom and for whom, why it's made, who designed the product, the package and brand, how it's distributed, who buys it, how it's used, and finally how it's ultimately consumed and what waste is produced.

This process highlights the student's primary role as designer, acting as mediator between production and consumption. To fully appreciate this, the student must understand how both ends unfold. In the space between, the designers leverage their skills to enlarge the dialogue on how things are made and especially how they are consumed. The goal is to eliminate waste by altering the linear process of production and consumption through interventions that create a cycle. The students begin work on the LCA without any expert knowledge or additional tools to conduct it and must find their own way through a tangled web of information, half-truths, misdirection, and obfuscations of a product and package life cycle. The typical cradle-to-grave life cycle is not on the surface a linear one but rather a maze that ultimately ends in one spot: the waste heap. Ultimately, it is more profitable for the students to ferret out the details and learn the basic concept of the LCA, along with the difficulty in deciphering the facts.

This difficult hurdle helps the students realize the overwhelming body of knowledge required for any complex design project and the variety of skills and participants involved. It also reveals the limitations of ad-hoc research using readily available online information. This duality provides the students with just enough information to begin to define the problem while exposing them to their own limited access to factual information about the product, the producers, and their sources. The students often find it necessary to cobble together several sources to create even a cursory visualization of the LCA.

The lack of transparency exhibited by many corporations reveals to the students their necessary role in visualizing information. It highlights the need for designers to advocate for consumers at the point of purchase. As the students discover bits and pieces of the process, they record what they find on three-by-five-inch index cards in the form of simple phrases or words. On the card's flip side, they draw simple icons or symbols of these components, building as they go a visual lexicon that can later be translated into complex information designs. The plethora of information on the seemingly ordinary designed artifacts we interact with daily is revealed, along with the stunningly obtuse nature of large institutions and corporations. The design students who have not yet been exposed to research as a distinct aspect of the larger process of designing learn a great deal more from encountering the frustration of teasing out an LCA than simply by using an LCA calculator.

The verbiage and images collected in gathering the LCA are used to produce simple diagrams and schematics that make up a rudimentary information design piece detailing the LCA. At this point, the students can more readily consider the steps they might take in redesigning the package and potentially the product to create a cycle in which waste is reduced or eliminated. The students must implement at least three interventions in the LCA in addition to replacing petroleum-based plastics with renewable or biodegradable plastics.

Once the students understand the mechanics of how a product and its packaging are produced and consumed and the possibilities for altering how these occur, the goal is to translate the facts into easily understood visual narratives. In some cases, the student will choose to work within what is commonly called information design. The students are encouraged to consider unusual forms for creating information design pieces that resist the urge to simply inform and harness the form's potential for describing the great beauty of complex systems. These may include books, videos, games, and so on. These pieces should inform implicitly without seeming to be an attempt to convince an audience to embrace a particular point of view. Rather, the piece should win them over through the merging of form and content in a manner that seems to transcend the issues. The piece may employ whimsy, irony, satire, or other strategies in order to engage the audience in a dialogue rather than speaking at them or to them. The result should draw the outlines of the argument for sustainability beyond the margins it typically occupies to capture a broader audience. By avoiding simply illustrating the argument, it should be folded into the form seamlessly, creating a new way of visualizing how each of us is empowered by our role in systems of production and consumption.

Once the students have spent time with the ways the package's design is caught up in the complex systems of contemporary design, they are ready to peel away the labels that surround and obscure the packages and that hold all these complex relationships. In this step, the student considers the consumer's relationship to the product through the design of the package as a brand that co-opts the identity of the consumer and seeks to make them the object of their own desire. The first step is to name the product in a manner that speaks to its newly emerging sustainable value and to package it so it holds and maintains that value by extending its useful life while

operating to inform and educate. Each student in the group contributes thirty-six to forty-eight ideas for product names, which they narrow down to the twelve they feel are worthy of presenting to the entire group. Throughout this ideation, they are encouraged to feel free to generate as many ideas as they can, even if they seem ridiculous or inappropriate.

The reasoning for this approach is that if these ideas are not exorcised early on, they tend to reveal themselves later. Essentially, the notion is that all of these ideas already reside in the public mind, and if they are not explored early on, they may undermine the message later. This may happen when the client inadvertently and perhaps subconsciously makes an off-the-cuff remark about the design. It may also occur through the consumer's interaction with the package, creating dissonance and possible rejection of the product. In the end, unless each iteration is not thoroughly expressed, it may be difficult or impossible later to persuade the client or consumer of its green value. The green value of the package must be maintained, and this by definition cannot afford to be undermined.

In addition, each student contributes another thirty-six to forty-eight ideas for taglines that they narrow down to twelve for presentation. The tagline is intended to support and enhance the product name as a key component of its primary identity and may serve several functions in advertising, web, and other collateral design. The modularity of the written language designed, along with the name and logotype, demonstrates to the students the ways in which identities are served best by a simple but fluid modularity. The student groups then cull their several ideas down to three names and taglines, presented in black on plain white paper. During the presentation, the individuals rotate between the groups, giving feedback on their impressions of the names and tags. This feedback employs a larger number of voices in reaching a final decision on the name that will then serve as the basis for an original logotype. This group interplay helps alleviate any myopia that may occur, further refines the message, and contradicts the sycophantic relationship of marketing to design, which asks focus groups to respond to prepackaged solutions.

Once the name is chosen, the individual student then moves on to designing an original logotype with the tagline set with it. If the research and ideation have been thoroughly conducted up to this point, the logotype should easily express the identity of the product and transcend the normally flatfooted approach given to package design. Rather than simply apply a label to a surface, the logotype is designed in concert with both extensive research and the design of a new package that reduces waste and increases efficiency.

At this juncture, the package should begin to take form through a series of sketches, diagrams, elevations, and simple maquettes, the identity of the product being formed through the package along with the logotype. The material considerations given to any aspect of the life cycle can now be presented along with or upon the package. This utilizes the package not only as a container of the product but also the aspirations of the user as a conscientious and ethical consumer. The package becomes an expression of all the students' efforts to remake and rebrand a product or product category as sustainable and a knowing awareness of the impact and import of package design.

The final mock-up for the design is realized through rapid prototyping and other comping techniques. The process of creating a well-realized mock-up not only serves ideation and the acquiring of craft skills but also demonstrates to the students the potential of design as a tool for visualization.

Relabel, Resize, and Redesign: Repackaging the Single-Use Beverage Container

The purpose of this project is to make visible the many hidden costs of a one-way beverage, bottle, or can in the form of an accurate accounting written upon the product's label. Although there is a whimsical aspect to this project, it seriously considers the history of packaging and labeling of consumer goods, especially foods and beverages. In 1991, all food packagers in the United States were required to begin providing nutritional labeling on their containers. This initiated a massive redesign of many of the ordinary food packages we encounter daily. This sometimes led to humorous results, with nutritional labeling of soda, junk food, and other food products that are clearly unhealthy if not wholly unsustainable. What if an even more massive redesign was required to reflect not only individual health concerns but all of the impacts associated with the product—and especially its package?

What size or shape might the present US two-liter bottle of soda take if all of its actual inputs and outputs were recorded on the label? Would it rise to the height of a small building? Can the average US consumer be expected to appreciate the significance of the liter when the metric system is largely ignored in the United States by government and industry? If Coca-Cola or Pepsi were required to record on their labels all of the energy required to make, transport, and distribute the package and its contents, that alone would require a complete rethinking of all their labels and containers. If we add to this how the product and package is sourced and made, along with its impacts on the health of the average US consumer, the subsidies given to farmers to continue growing corn to make high-fructose corn syrup and that monoculture's effect on the environment, the four liters of oil needed to make a single two-liter plastic bottle, the label would certainly exceed the present package to a staggering degree.

Following the Second World War, beverage companies in the United States began expanding and consolidating rapidly, gobbling up most of the small, independent beverage companies that were common to most local areas. At that time, virtually all bottling was local, and most bottles were refillable. This practice continues in Europe, where it has been expanded greatly and to positive effect. In the United States, however, bottlers began aggressively implementing one-way beverage containers as a way to cut costs, expand operations, and make use of cheap and abundant new plastics. They were also very aggressive in fighting and defeating any bottle laws, from the smallest municipalities to the state level. In the end, they virtually eliminated any regulation of their industry, which became essentially a packaging industry, rather than a beverage industry, with very little difference in the contents of the few competing brands. By the end of the century, this led to a cynicism regarding the limited choice of beverages, as in the false comparison of Coke versus Pepsi, and also metaphorically to a general malaise regarding US visual culture as representing the limits of popular democratic institutions.

This left the consumer and local governments literally holding the bag. There was a great deal of garbage to contend with and no infrastructure to deal with it.

Although there was some pushback from consumers, the beverage companies had proven they could defeat any regulation of their industry. The can and bottle lobby's response was to launch the anti-littering campaigns of the 1960s and 1970s; this approach shifted the problem onto the individual consumers to regulate their own trash. The public focus was now only on the visible signs of the ill effects of over-consumption, in the form of litter. The cultural significance of the individual as a representation in US culture cannot be underestimated and was widely co-opted by the beverage industry to avoid any collective action by activists or government. The image of the rugged American individual was greatly expanded in the postwar era through a broader consumer culture and associated with modernity in the form of convenience and new materials, especially plastic. In this community-wide context, citizen-based initiatives were curbed in favor of consumers' individual responsibility for controlling not their consumption but the visible signs of their waste.

Chapter Four
Space

This chapter on space connects the specific ways graphic design is tied to consumption and the ways our larger built environment—which we have created—affects the health of everyone and everything. The chapter challenges assumptions about the physical limits of the graphic design profession. It also makes clear the autonomous function of graphic design through the designer's direct response to the needs of communities in public spaces. It further analyzes how graphic design offers ways to interact in public spaces at the intersection of the built and natural environments, especially in underutilized or discarded spaces. Environmental design, way-finding, exhibition design, and installations are the sites where this occurs. Site-specific designs such as these serve not to mark the boundary between spheres but to highlight the ways they overlap. In the process, they denaturalize the supposed human-made environment and foreground the way ideology frames the contexts in which we live through artifacts and systems of design. It also offers an historical overview of the ideological legacy of human domination of the natural environment through design and describes how we have abstracted human impacts on this sphere and reinforced the dichotomy of humans versus nature.

The Collective Self

A sustainable view of the design and space requires a nuanced understanding of all local qualities and limits. A consideration of space begins with a single person, the individual self, as part of the immediate and larger environment. Design deals with the body's subjective response to its environment as a total experience that includes all of the senses. Where each person is centered in a space is crucial to knowing his or her part in the larger body, the collective or public self. The emphasis since the

Enlightenment on the individual requires each person to locate him- or herself as an individual in order to create connections through larger interactions with groups and environments. The subject-versus-object relationship of human versus nature has not only limited perceptions of these connections but also led to their possible destruction. Modern and contemporary systems of design, including the built environment, typically isolate the individual and tend to leave most of the consequences of collective impacts out of sight and out of mind. Design should work to upend that relationship so that people connect their personal health to ecological health and the health of all human systems as well, repairing the disconnect wherein the individual is separated from both society's larger collective self as well as from nature. Ultimately, this leads to the isolation of the individual from the self, where identity is built through a series of layered abstractions surrounding consumption of lifestyles and materials (Buell 1995: 1–27, 31–52).

Within this system, the individual is no more connected to him- or herself than he or she is to nature. Nature becomes something to experience through leisure and tourism or in the amorphous boundaries of suburban and exurban settings. These "edge cities," defined by the automobile, as described by Joel Garreau and idealized as a third space, exist and operate not as borders of town and country but as the site of the greatest amount of the production and consumption of labor, goods, and capital—both natural and human (1992).

Constant Crisis

The disconnect between the self and nature is situated in a very real place but one that is built on a mythology that hides the actual existence of the human relationship to the natural capital (Schumacher 1973), which we depend on to support a lifestyle of consumption. In this scenario, labor and capital are blanketed over by the promise of a life of leisure apart from the workings of industry, cities, politics, race, and especially the labor and resources drawn from others. Nature, placed aside as a force to be contained and subdued, is actually in a state of constant crisis. There is no real relationship in this state between the self and the natural environment, so that nature must be sought out by the individual, who lives apart from it and who seeks self in quiet repose alone with nature.

Make Change: Plastic-a-holics

Kristine Matthews
Professor, University of Washington
Students: Tom Futrell, Cassie Klinger, Erin Williams, Katherine Wimble
http://www.studiomatthews.com/sustainability.php?image=1
http://envirodesign.tumblr.com/

10 Personal Principles of Sustainability

1. **Rethinking:** We step back and think before we dive in, to find a different way to communicate our clients' needs.

2. **Reusing:** We aim to achieve more with less. We reuse things to create new. (Then when all is said and done, we recycle.)

3. **Using friendly materials:** Whenever we can, we use recycled and innovative products and ask suppliers to stock eco-friendly materials. We avoid specifying (and wasting) environmentally harmful materials.

4. **Saving energy:** We reduce our clients' carbon footprint by using sustainable energy sources. People power is best, or failing that, renewable energy is becoming more efficient. We design to minimize energy demand.

5. **Sharing new ideas:** We seek out and use new technologies and materials and

Figure 85

"The first step was to document our own daily interactions with plastic. Some were more obvious than others—packaging surrounding the food we ate, water bottles, household objects—and as we dove further into our research, the broad scale of plastic in manufacturing, building, and consumption. Because of the target audience, we chose to use materials that were more apparent in everyday interactions. As we started the design process, we challenged ourselves to reuse existing materials rather than creating new waste. Because we didn't want this to look like a recycling yard, we experimented with how we could use materials in a new way. How stacks of plastic could be used as structures, melting plastic to create a surface for printing, how multiples could create an impact, etc. We also wanted to incorporate plastic objects into our data—creating info-graphics out of color-filled water bottles, using plastic lids as plot points, and stacks of waste plastic to show scale."

—Kristine Matthews

PLASTIC-A-HOLICS

SITE VIEW FROM APPROACHING FROM THE EAST   VEIW OF WALL SECTION   PATTERN DETAIL

Figure 86

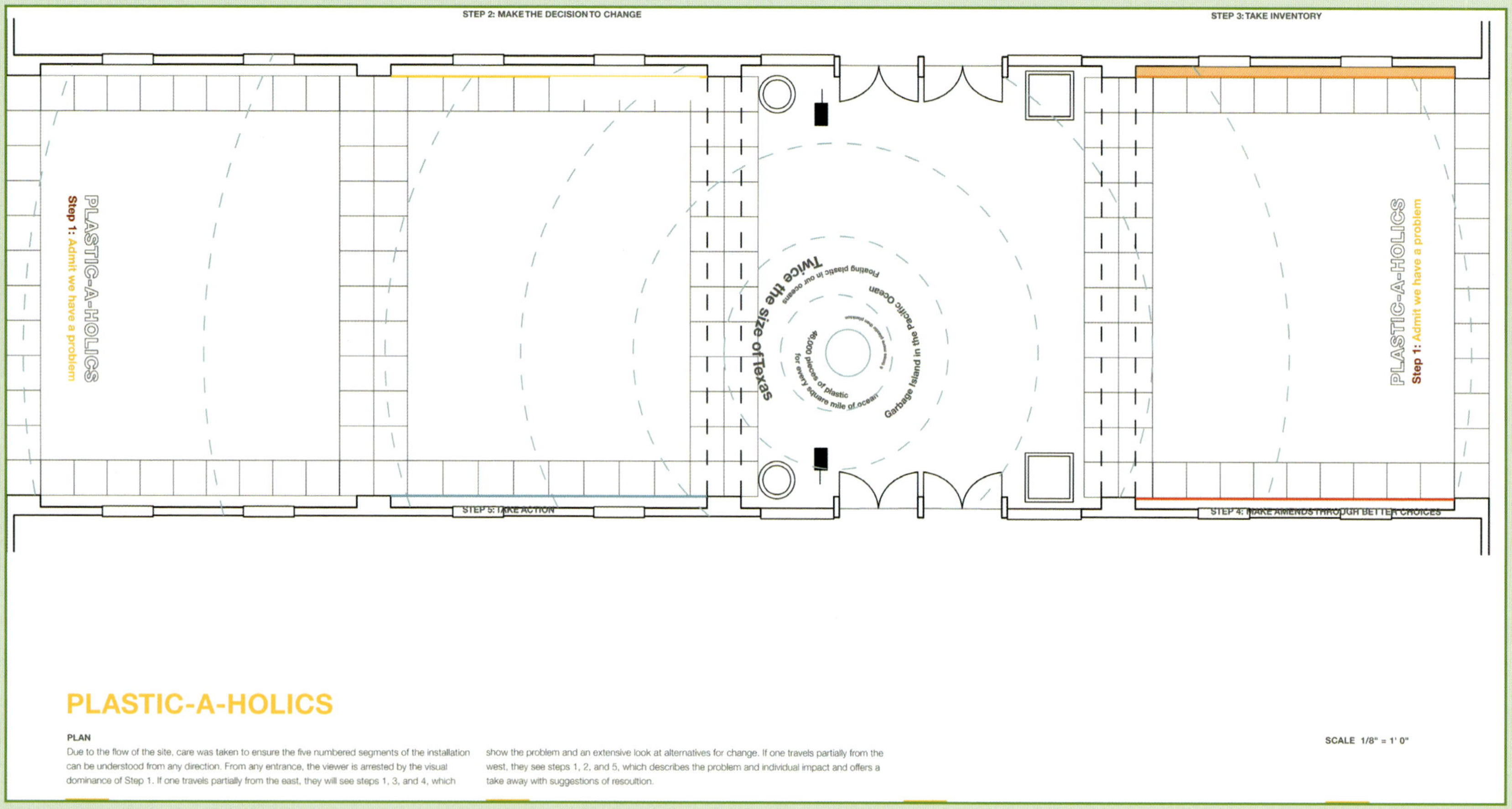

STEP 2: MAKE THE DECISION TO CHANGE

STEP 3: TAKE INVENTORY

PLASTIC-A-HOLICS
Step 1: Admit we have a problem

PLASTIC-A-HOLICS
Step 1: Admit we have a problem

Twice the size of Texas
Floating plastic in our oceans
Pacific Ocean
Garbage Island in the

STEP 5: TAKE ACTION

STEP 4: MAKE AMENDS THROUGH BETTER CHOICES

PLASTIC-A-HOLICS

PLAN

Due to the flow of the site, care was taken to ensure the five numbered segments of the installation can be understood from any direction. From any entrance, the viewer is arrested by the visual dominance of Step 1. If one travels partially from the east, they will see steps 1, 3, and 4, which show the problem and an extensive look at alternatives for change. If one travels partially from the west, they see steps 1, 2, and 5, which describes the problem and individual impact and offers a take away with suggestions of resolution.

SCALE 1/8" = 1' 0"

Figure 87

collaborate whenever we can. Two heads are better than one.

6. **Designing to last:** We want to design things that last by specifying the right material for the job. This avoids the need for replacement (and a double whammy on cost and materials). Lifetime costing makes you look at the big picture.

7. **Staying local, buying ethical:** We work to find good local suppliers for each job, to avoid the extra energy and pollution created by lengthy transport, and to strengthen the local community and economy. When we can't buy locally, we source ethical suppliers.

8. **Supporting what we believe:** We push for agendas we care about: better education, waste reduction, fighting climate change, raising money to make good things happen.

9. **Inspiring, and having fun:** We want to create design that is beautiful, clever, and sustainable all at once. The projects tell their own sustainable story, to encourage

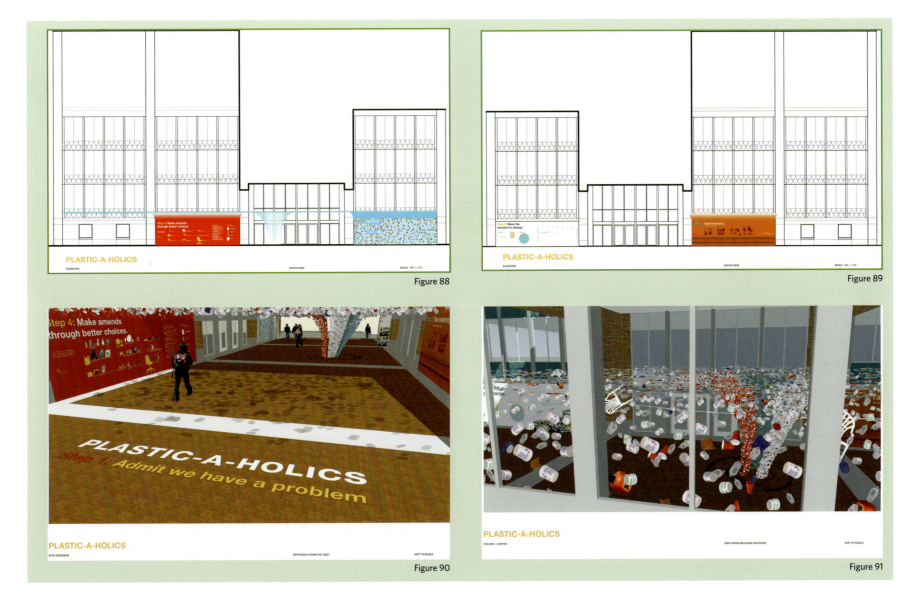

Figure 88

Figure 89

Figure 90

Figure 91

Figure 92

others to get on board. We hope that by having fun, our enthusiasm will be contagious.

10. **Saving money:** We demonstrate to our clients that thinking sustainable can save waste, resources, and money. Making a product work harder is smart.

Objectives

1. Develop a sense for designing in three-dimensional space.
2. Learn about interactivity and engaging an audience (i.e., asking people to do something within the exhibition itself).
3. Collaborate effectively as a group.
4. Push beyond comfort levels, and have a good time doing it.
5. Learn to build sustainability into working methods: using greener materials, doing more with less, experimenting with ways to inspire an audience to make a positive change.
6. Identify a problem and create a call-to-action, to convince your audience to take a particular action in order to help solve a problem or address an issue.
7. The issue you (and your team) choose must allow in-depth research into the subject, and your exhibition must present facts and figures and some background information.
8. The subject is of your choosing, but it must be about something that you feel must change.

Figure 93

Figure 94

Figure 95

Figure 96

Figure 97

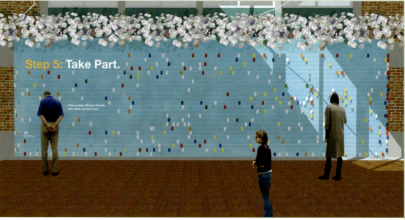

PLASTIC-A-HOLICS

STEP 5: TAKE PART
Illustration of wall progression.

CARD DETAIL

Figure 98

Figures 85–98

To stop the growth of garbage island, *Plastic-a-holics: Addicted to Plastic* is a site-specific installation that asks students, staff, and faculty at the University of Washington campus to take simple steps toward avoiding needless consumption of plastic goods. Borrowing the framework of Alcoholics Anonymous, the first point of contact begins with awareness:
Step 1: Admit we have a problem. Passersby to the site—a covered walkway between two wings of a campus library—walk under an enormous replication of Garbage Island. The floating debris funnels into an unavoidable vortex of plastic products (e.g., bags, bottles, and food packaging). Lining the walls of the walkway, Garbage Island morphs into steps two through five on the road to recovery, laying out the actions passersby can take toward curbing their addiction to plastic.
Step 2: Make the decision to change presents information graphics on US plastic consumption created entirely from plastic items (e.g., milk jug lids, bundles of compacted plastic recyclables, etc.) over a wall of white plastic forks, knives, and spoons.
Step 3: Take inventory, formed from melted orange laundry detergent bottles, asks people to reflect on the myriad, ubiquitous plastic products that are in their lives and provides a bin in which to deposit recyclable plastic, visibly accumulating with mounds of plastic as the installation progresses.
Step 4: Make amends through better choices shows (on a wall of red plastic cups) real alternatives to common plastic packaged products, taking the information to a practical level for everyday shopping.
Step 5: Take part asks people to remove one of hundreds of plastic cards made from recycled plastic shopping bags, printed with additional plastic-curbing steps, strung over a wall of "ocean" (recycled blue plastic), and in doing so, taking home a reminder not to purchase unnecessary plastic while metaphorically cleaning up Garbage Island.

Process

Thoroughly research the subject and develop three-dimensional installation or exhibition concepts based on this research. The exhibition must contain accurate text/image content that presents the case for change. The format and proposed location of the display should be appropriate to the topic.

Components

- **Your message/call-to-action:** What change are you trying to provoke? What action do you want people to take? This should guide all decisions about the design of your project.
- **Audience:** Who are you trying to reach and why? Make your solution appropriate; is it using the right kind of visual language to appeal to that audience? Is it in the right place? Is the message convincing enough to provoke change in that group?
- **Location:** Your exhibition can be located in a traditional interior exhibition space with white walls, if this is appropriate for your subject, or outdoors, in a very specific location, relevant to your audience and your communication objectives.
- **Shape, size, and scale:** Your project should take up a minimum footprint (floor area) of 10 feet by 20 feet and a maximum of 20 feet by 40 feet. Maximum height is 15 feet. Think about how viewers will approach the exhibition, move around and through it. Avoid creating a book on a wall—that is, flat layouts simply hung in a space. Can you take advantage of different viewpoints? Can you use objects or other materials in an unusual way to attract

attention? Is the scale right for the size of the space?
- **Longevity:** The life span of the installation can be anywhere from one day to three months. Think about how long it should exist and why. Is its longevity related to its message?

Develop a Sustainable Solution

Concepts must be designed to be as sustainable as possible. This can be accomplished in a variety of ways through research and a creative approach, for example:

- Using reclaimed or recycled rather than new materials
- Avoiding environmentally damaging materials such as PVC
- Saving energy
- Using materials that are found or produced locally, minimizing transport energy
- Using waste materials in an interesting way

Challenges

1. To reuse existing materials rather than creating new waste
2. Incorporating material objects into the data—in creating information designs
3. Unpredictable group dynamics

Outcomes

1. Development of realistic personal goals that employ design to impact the wider world
2. Realization that seemingly small decisions have a much larger impact on the wider world than previously understood

In this system, personal identity is formed in relationship to nature but apart from others, so that a rupture is created between self and society but in union with nature. With too few individuals opposing development of natural sites that are already in crisis, the status quo works to enforce continual ecological crisis. Personal identity remains in crisis as well, because the boundary between places and people exists in how they see themselves in relation to the human and the natural. Because this system depends on natural capital to grow all things but divorces it from culture and the self, society cannot develop culturally and personally since the self is defined by constant crisis. Environmental and personal crisis are situated along a boundary between designed spaces and the accidental offings of industrial and consumer capitalism.

Mining the Remains

The task of the graphic designer is to mine the remains and define the strata beneath what is typically experienced as natural and cultural. Graphic design is used as a method for creating context in the face of disparate elements. Therefore, cultural meaning is now being brought to bear in defining boundaries as spaces containing rich cultural content and sources for new hybrid spaces. The history of these sometimes underrepresented spaces contains a record of the history of people who defined their relationship to both nature and the machine as adversarial. The brutish forces of both were framed as that which must be contained and set apart from culture.

Beyond the Limits

Always at the frontier of designed space, the individual worked to distance the self and society from the natural world while simultaneously opening up new resources and space for industry and people. Design often posited as a civilizing force rooted in ancient tradition, modern means, and an optimal future served historically to define cultural spaces. The definition of space graphically delineated in and through mapping provided the limits of human culture. These lines defined the frontier of human culture as intrinsically expansive and therefore unlimited. This provided the conceit associated with economic expansion—that unlimited resources exist always just beyond the limit of human expansion into virgin territory. In this view, the limits of human power to dominate nature were defined by paradox and a supposedly unlimited source of material resources.

In the present century, the boundaries of human expansion as a force in opposition to nature are being defined by the material limits they are coming in contact with and the consequences already occurring as that force runs up against limits and turns back against them. Virgin material resources are no longer available or large enough to permit the current growth that has defined the means by which capital has been created, which in reality was depleting natural capital. As we seek to define sustainable design through the built environment, growth will need redefinition as nonexpansive in the physical sense. This will require that designers examine their assumptions about a seemingly limitless supply of land and natural resources defined by expanding boundaries. Otherwise, as boundaries recede and shift, both nature and humanity will fail to be contained; thus crisis both cultural and natural will continue to draw focus away from realistic design solutions. A remapping of the existing spaces must be made in order to redefine design's relationship to the natural environment. This environment's only constant for the foreseeable future is a state of crisis.

The greatest fear and obstacle that presently stymies efforts at redesigning design's relationship to space and nature is a belief in the notion of unlimited supply as real limitations are becoming more difficult to ignore. This is not as might be supposed a reemphasizing of a model of scarcity but rather a redefinition of limits. The shifting meaning of space is the ground on which the graphic designer can work to define new cultural contexts both rhetorically and spatially, bringing the more intangible aspects of culture to bear in defining sites that create new understanding and use-value. Graphic designers working at the edges of the profession work not only to redefine spaces as natural and cultural but also to test the limits of professional practice both through cross-disciplinary and interdisciplinary means. The first is the way that graphic designers work with others who are already closely aligned and in established patterns with the profession; the latter is the creation of

3. Realization that working in a group can be hugely rewarding and that the group can become much more than the sum of its parts

Quotes

"I require LCA (life-cycle analysis) as part of their research and development for their projects. Asking—What will be your project's lifespan? What is its carbon footprint? What happens to it afterward? These kinds of calculations should become as second nature as thinking about height, width, depth, number of pages, etcetera."
—Kristine Matthews

"The project develops in a single term. For my classes, I always introduce sustainability as part of the design discussion and critique. The Smart Matter website (www.smart-matter.com) was developed initially as a learning/inspirational tool for my Exhibition Design course."
—Kristine Matthews

"The project is entitled Make Change, and that is the challenge set to the students, who work in teams of three or four. They are not assigned a topic, but they must reflect on a change they would like to see in the world, and then figure out a way to make that change happen through an interactive installation. They are not required to tackle a topic that is particularly related to sustainability, but they are expected to design their solution using sustainable processes and materials. The intent is to teach students that, as communication designers, they are in a powerful position to change minds and incite positive action."
—Kristine Matthews

"The project encourages a design-as-author approach. If there is a change you want to see in the world, you as a designer have the communication skills (including humor, powerful persuasion, data wrangling, and more) to help make that change happen. Don't always wait for a client; create your own positive agenda."
—Kristine Matthews

"What plastic-a-holics does is visually quantify the amount of plastic we come in contact with daily. Seeing how plastic is integral to our daily life and consumption will hopefully get the viewers to reconsider their responsibility of consumerism and the environment."
—Kristine Matthews

"Students often come into the class feeling that they personally do not have much impact on the wider world. Their own student projects are one-offs, lovingly put together with home equipment and crafted by hand. But then I describe the role they will soon fill: a professional designer specifying materials and processes that will be used for tens of thousands of printed or manufactured goods. They quickly realize that their seemingly small decisions will have a much larger impact on the wider world. In addition, the process of identifying something in the world that they personally want to change—and then strategizing how they can use their skills to make that change happen—can be an eye-opening and empowering experience for a student."
—Kristine Matthews

"For the Make Change project, students design a fictitious installation or exhibition, but they must always site it in a real location of their

new ways of working with other professions, individuals, and organizations as well
as reviving former practices and merging these with new methods, materials, tools,
and technologies.

Graphic designers are already working in new ways, in spaces typically aligned
with other design disciplines and professions, to redefine the spaces between nature
and culture and to create a new language to talk about space. Language, in this case, is
not a metaphor for another system or way of working but quite literally describes what
makes graphic design a culturally relevant practice. The limits of graphic design are
built on a set of assumptions based in the machine age and industrial capitalism and
that overlap with a culture of consumer capitalism. We assume wrongly that graphic
design is limited and sullied by its association with commerce and consumption,
when in fact all modern forms of creative production are defined by contemporary
capitalism and implicated in its workings. All the design professions emerged in their
modern form as products and catalysts of the machine age, so none is able to entirely
unburden itself from that legacy.

We should not limit the profession of graphic design by its negative associations
with the more recent development of design as a commodity in service of consumer
capitalism. Graphic design is different from the other design disciplines because of
the written word. It has been rooted in the book arts since at least Gutenberg's time
and extends further to the ancient guttural markings on rocks and cave walls. With
perhaps the exception of public and monumental architecture of the Classical period,
graphic design as a pursuit has exclusively maintained a tie to written language and
as a result is fundamentally about words but also the application of language skills
across a variety of design disciplines and spaces. Because this legacy persists, graphic
designers should emphasize its power as a record of its positive contribution and
ability to make good on its promise.

Resituating Words

Public spaces are marked by lines but also words—on street signs, emblazoned in
neon, embossed in backlit plastic, adhered in vinyl, and painted on surfaces, all of
which mark off and shape how we think about space. Many of these lines are invisible,
and most accept their directions and directionality without question and underestimate their ideological power. Most, if not all, of the words encountered in the built
environment are related to buying and selling and operate on the surface to simply
attract attention, usually from a moving vehicle, and they are valued almost exclusively for that ability. Even when not directly related to commerce, these words tend
to reinforce the assumption that the material world is defined by costs and therefore
material worth. They are for the most part signs but are not usually considered for
their value and use as signifiers.

When graphic designers resituate words upon spaces and objects thought of
as natural, they begin to understand their place in the way the landscape is read.
The starkest example of the insidious nature of signs and signing upon the landscape and their affect on the public mind are the ways in which they were used in
the segregation of public spaces in the United States, especially in the South. Signs
for "white" and "colored" marked the lines between people, the latter marked as
different and inferior by both signs and inferior spaces (Hale 1998: 3–11, 125–138).
This system was designed to contain the shifting nature of both language and race
by clearly racializing people, words, and spaces. It also sought to naturalize and
make concrete a cultural construct upholding a mythology of racial difference based
ostensibly on color but with whiteness dominating largely through its invisibility.
This record clearly illustrates how designers shouldn't take for granted the power
of words—and therefore the potential power of graphic design—on the landscape
or the ways their placement affects how many people think about both culture
and nature and the human capacity to alter them. Altering landscapes that have
been left fallow, barren, or scarred and that adjoin human settlement traversed
by water, wildlife, and roadways present opportunities to address environmental
issues in situ.

The Forest for the Trees

In the old adage, a tree falling in a forest doesn't exist without human presence to witness it. In this case, the human element is absent, and without it the sound of the tree falling ceases to exist as an index of the tree. The more common index of a tree is the barren stump where the tree has already been felled. The stump is all that remains to indicate not only the recent absence of a single tree but also the collective destruction of forests. In a sense, the tree as a common trope exists only through its evidentiary role in foretelling further ecological devastation—a voice crying in the wilderness. It cannot exist without people in their own relationship as devastator. It warns of the inevitable, where people act as both active agents of destruction and as passive, as unable to act to save it. It also speaks to the many millions of trees already fallen and of those to come, of whole forests felled by the axe.

The forest so well hidden by the trees tells us of a very specific type of forest—a forest not populated by people but by their absence. In their absence, the forest survives as an ideal, an untamed wilderness, but one contained by humans to be preserved in an original state, perhaps an eden, or a new world, or a yet unconquered space at the limit of the frontier. In this state, it remains uncivilized but protected from the animalistic desire also contained within it. Within resides the very source of its destruction—the animal. Along the edges of this space are other indicators of human destruction, not to flora but fauna. Here, always on the edge of destruction, lurk those animals on the endangered species list. They too live only as a sign of what is to come when they will inevitably and forever join their remote ancestors in extinction. They survive only in their status as being in constant danger of disappearing. The inevitability of their demise clings to them.

These common visual devices persist to maintain human dominance of nature, because in each case nature is absent where human culture is present and culture absent where nature is allowed to remain. There is no space between, only a boundary and, like most boundaries, an artificial line drawn on a landscape. This belief in boundaries belies the actual topography of the nature/culture dichotomy. These reductive images, multiplied and distributed, do not accrue meaning as they increase but further simplify

Dis(solve):The Japhet Creek Project

AgriProp: Ecological Propaganda
Cheryl Beckett and Patrick Peters
University of Houston

Students: Arantza Alvarado, Hai Dinh, Miguel Farias Nunez, Marcia Hoang, Zach Kimmel, Jane Nghiem, Anna Reyes, Hector Solis, Joanna Bonner, Megan Conkin, Alison Cheuk, Jennie Macedo, Rachel Outlaw, Ada Pedraza, Josh Robbins, Danny Carter, Kyra Lancon, Jenny Ng, ViVi Vu Nguyen, R-Jay Ruiz, Christopher Steven Pine, Jose Dehuma, Amy Heidbreder, Diana Ngo, Jessica Rios, Haley Ross, Brad Sypniewski, Hai Phan, Anna Dulin, Lindsey Bowsher, Diana Ngo, Tam Truong, Erin Woltz, Aike Jamaluddin, Ramon Arciniega

Goals

1. Deploy in site-specific locations as a strategy to bring environmental messages to an unsuspecting audience.
2. Prompt positive action—citizen art leading to solutions and strategies for ecological improvement.
3. Provide information and plan for making a difference to Houston's environment through action.
4. Merge differing expertise between advanced students in the College of Architecture and graduates in the Graphic Communications Program of the School of Art, Houston, Texas, allowing a fusion of information, message, structure, form, nature, and engineering.

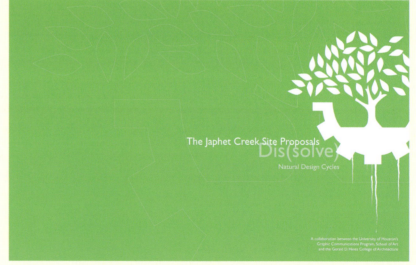

Figure 99

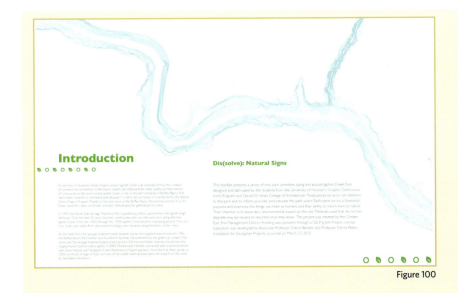

Introduction

As one first of Houston's Green Fingers project, Japhet Creek is an emerald of how the creation of connects or connectivity to the many visitors can improve both water quality and the method of community to the environment Japhet Creek is one of the last tributaries of Buffalo Bayou that hasn't been covered or channeled and, because it is still a natural stream it is protected by the federal Green Fingers Program. Thanks to the hard work of the Buffalo Bayou Partnership and the Trust for Public Lands the main soil stream wild and undeveloped for generations to come.

In 1905 the North Side Sewage Treatment Plant opened two blocks upwind from the Japhet neighborhood. Over the next 30 years factories, warehouses and coal mills were built along and near Japhet Creek. From the 1920s through the 1980s Japhet Creek became a dumping ground. Tires, oil, huts, trash and rubble from demolished buildings were dumped along the bank of the creek.

As the smell from the sewage treatment plant became worse the neighborhood emptied. In 1980s, the Buffalo Bayou Partnership was founded to facilitate improvements to the greenway system. That same year the sewage treatment plant closed and Jim Olmsted and Fraser watchman moved into the original home built to bolster Japhet. In 2004, Olmsted and Hatcher conducted solar local environment. Sabir Smart Hetold, and The Japhet Creek Restoration Project was born. Since the first clean-up day in 2005 hundreds of bags of trash and tons of recyclable materials have been removed from the creek via dedicated volunteers.

Dis(solve): Natural Signs

This booklet presents a series of nine park amenities along and around Japhet Creek Park designed and fabricated by the students from the University of Houston's Graphic Communications Program and Gerald D. Hines College of Architecture. These pieces serve to call attention to the park and to inform, provoke, and educate the park visitor. Each piece serves a functional purpose and examines the things we make as humans and their ability to return back to nature. These intention is to leave zero environmental impact on the site. Materials used that do not bio degrade may be reused or recycled once they leave. The project was initiated by the Greater East End Management District. Funding was provided through a CELP grant. Project concept fabrication was developed by Associate Professor Cheryl Beckett and Professor Patrick Peters. Installation for the Japhet Projects occurred on March 27, 2010.

Figure 100

2 Introduction

3 Site map

Proposals

4 Directional Map

5 Filtration Station

6 Green Bench

7 Green Finger Filter

8 Mudscape

9 Trash Extrication Device

10 Trestle Poetry

11 Tube Identity Fence

12 Waste Oasis

Figure 101

Japhet Park: Dis(solve) Park Amenities

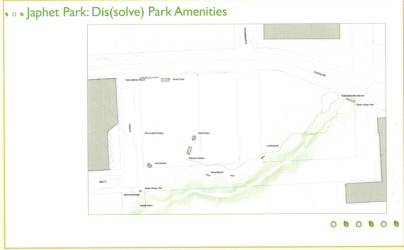

Figure 102

Directional Map

Street Dimensions
Length: 132 ft, 5 in
Width: 23 ft

Proposal

The Directional Map is a functional piece of street art that places emphasis on Japhet Creek as the driver crosses the bridge. It also directs the visitor to other installations in the park including Trestle Poetry and the Green Filter Finger. The map is comprised of iconography drawn from natural elements at Japhet Creek. From the Chinaberry plant to the minnows swimming in the spring, these elements become symbolic guides for visitors.

Material

- Recycled cardboard stencils
- Eco-friendly white paint

designed by: Arenisca Alvarado, Hai Dinh, Miguel Farias, Marcos Huang, Zack Kimmel, Jane Nghiem, Anru Reyes, Hector Solis

Figure 103

Filtration Station

Proposal

The Japhet Creek ceremony and volunteers devote approximately one-third of time and energy into transforming the park into a place free of debris and waste. The Filtration Station meets the needs of these individuals by providing storage for tools, a green roof that doubles as a water filtration system for clean-up, an information center as well as a gathering place after a long day's work.

Material

- Recycled 20' shipping container
- Various lumber
- Recycled 18' x 18' cardboard boxes
- Recycled 4 - 9.5' x 90' plasma-cut steel panels
- 1 - 9.5' x 90' Kalwall printed panel
- 36 gallon rain barrel
- 3 cubic yards dirt and sod
- 90' angular steel and rectangular tubing

designed by Joanna Boehme, Megan Conklin, Alison Cheuck, Jaime Maresko, Rachel Outlaw, Ada Pedraza, and Josh Andrews

Figure 104

Green Finger Filter

Proposal

The Filters promote the vision of the Buffalo Bayou Partnership's Green Finger project. Two Filters are placed at different points of the creek to observe the contamination in the creek and demonstrate the filtering process of the creek.

The text on the Filters reads Japhet Creek cleanses water as it flows downstream where contaminates become trapped in the bottom sediment. Pour water from the creek into the top of the Filter. Observe how the sand and gravel transforms the water as it travels through the Filter.

Material

- Acrylic
- Rope
- Rebar
- Vinyl

designed by Hai Phi Dinh, Ananias Almonds, Marice Huang, Zach Kimmel, Jane Nguyen, Miguel Perez Nunez, Anna Reyes, Hector Solis

Figure 106

Green Benches

Proposal

To create a more attractive and inviting situation for the Japhet Creek visitor, Green Bench offers seating that blends seamlessly into the environment. By using materials that degenerate at different speeds on a titanium structure (metal, wood, plastic, cardboard etc.) and enabling grass to grow in and around it, a powerful allegory can be made about the relationship between nature and future, between the past and the future. This seating option also provides an eye-opening learning experience about materials and the time it takes to decompose.

Material

- Recycled 23.5' x 33' cardboard
- Eco-friendly spray paint
- Plywood
- Recycled political signs
- White vinyl
- Gravel/bromus/ryegrass

designed by Jessica Maresko, Joanna Boehme, Ada Pedraza, Megan Conklin

Figure 105

Modscape

Proposal

Japhet Creek is an area that is being cleaned by volunteers and community to reinforce nature over industry. Modscape benches and planters commingle to create a landscape that reinforces the nurturing process. Transportable and recyclable materials are used to create both benches and planters. The system allows visitors to sit and get an up close look at nature. The system is highly flexible which allows it to be positioned in numerous locations within the park. As it biodegrades, the plant material will begin.

Material

- 18' x 18' x 18' cardboard boxes
- Eco-friendly spray paint
- Plywood
- White vinyl
- Plastic drinking

designed by Danny Carrier, Kyra Larson, Jenny Ng, Viet Vo Nguyen, Bi Jay Patel, Christopher Trevor Pine

Figure 107

₀ₒₒ Trash Extraction Device

Figure 108

₀ₒₒ Trestle Poetry

Figure 109

Process (Eight Weeks)

1. Research
2. Concept/site strategies
3. Scale models/graphic content
4. Fabrication drawings/naming strategies/ information (content development)
5. Fabrication of AgriProp/information distribution methodology
6. Deployment
7. Documentation: visual essay, triptych, PowerPoint, deadline/extended installation schedule

Challenges

1. Schedules: merging teams from Architecture and Graphics meant many hours of meeting outside of class and finding alternative communication links between team members
2. Fabrication/construction challenges that ranged from containing and transporting tons of dirt to keeping plants alive for the broad range of installation situations
3. Deployment location strategies
4. Hauling large-scale AgriProps around the city for multiple installations and deployments

Outcomes

1. Successful deployments of AgriProps in Houston
2. Engaged audience
3. Formal beauty: successful architectural/ structural form conveying information, engaging interaction, and promoting positive action
4. Broadened student awareness of ecological issues and courses of action

5. Placed students in the field, with direct audience interaction
6. Group effort and outcomes taught lessons of working collaboratively
7. Due to the success and publicity of the AgriProps, numerous additional installations (all sanctioned) were added to the agenda.

Project Description

The College of Architecture offers a stand-alone course in sustainability. A vital component of Graphic Communications is reflection on environmental issues and the role design plays in the creation of sustainable solutions. Patrick Peters is the director of the Graduate Design/Build Studio at the College of Architecture for Master's of Architecture students. The pedagogical impact of this opportunity has led to projects such as Dis(solve), a design/build experience at the undergraduate level. This experience, in the form of a collaborative design/build studio with Cheryl Beckett, expands the architectural form into a platform for messages and meaning in a public context.

On a very basic level, the students look at form, function, meaning, and message within a public context. As a collaborative design/build project with a real budget and real deadline, the students were immersed quickly into other fundamental skills, such as:

- Teamwork
- Fabrication
- Budget
- Collaborations across and within disciplines
- Scheduling
- Proposal preparation and presentation
- Working with vendors
- Working to secure donated material

This particular project has its own specific skills in relation to sustainability:

1. Ecological issues, specifically in relation to the bayou system, an integral part of the Houston urban biosphere
2. Industrial and postindustrial site evaluations and their remedial projection into the future
3. Nature in a postindustrial zone
4. The making of a park

Other factors included: The creation of park amenities that enhance the location, relate specifically to the site, serve to inform or educate the public about environmental issues, activate the space, create artifacts that engage the public in a physical and sensory manner, and use reclaimed, natural, or biodegradable materials.

The completed designs inform the public about Japhet Creek/Green Fingers specifically, but also serve as environmental metaphors about ideas and issues that shape our thoughts about nature, water, industry, protection, and people. Each piece functions in a semipermanent manner to merge structure, nature, and environmental impact with regard to Japhet Creek. Going beyond the notion of doing no harm, these statement pieces examine the things we make as humans and their ability to return back to nature. We proposed that the work focus on its own dissolvability, its quality of "accelerated decrepitude" (Bruno 1987) and how the things we make work with nature, and ideally return to nature. Materials within the (Dis)solve proposals strive to leave zero environmental impact on the site. This is especially appropriate given the temporary nature of the installations.

For this project, the assigned reading extended the ideas relevant to a postindustrial

society beyond the Japhet Creek experience. The project introduction reviewed an extensive range of examples that explored concepts related to public spaces and nature as well as a review of the current conditions. The neighborhood community played a vital role in rescuing this parcel of land through cleanup efforts and an awareness campaign. The students witnessed firsthand how the efforts of a few could completely alter and improve a landscape that was overlooked and even more frequently defiled.

The series of amenities are sited to emphasize message placement relative to the surroundings and highlight the assets of the park. Waste Oasis is situated at the bus stop on Clinton Drive. It serves the dual purpose of a place to sit and wait for the bus as well as commentary on a park in relation to industry. The Japhet Creek identity sign, also on Clinton Drive, defines the park as something more than undeveloped land. The Directional Map is painted on the bridge that crosses Japhet Creek. It directs the visitor to a pathway that passes the Green Finger Filter toward the Trestle Poetry at a spring. The largest park amenity, the Filtration Station, is visible from the street and the entrance sign. It serves as the focal point. The Filtration Station describes the entire Japhet Creek project on a city, park, and community level. Text and graphics also define the meaning and goal of the Dis(solve) installation. The location of the Filtration Station designates the trail that follows the creek past other amenities and ends at T.E.D., an end-of-pipe containment system that educates about storm drains and trash as it flows into our bayous.

The detritus of the space and the surrounding industry strongly influenced the material that we used. The park sits at the

Figure 110

Figure 111

edge of one of the largest industrial ferrous scrap metal recycling centers. To witness the operation of numerous giant cranes dumping load upon load from a mountain of household and industrial metal certainly drove home the notion of waste. At the same time, our acquisition of the reclaimed container and waste management dumpster was through the donation and delivery by the same scrap metal company. These two items formed the backbone of the park plan.

The original scope of the project, as defined by the Greater East End Management District, was to design a single temporary sign that described the history of Japhet Creek and its role in the Green Finger initiative. The faculty proposed Dis(solve), a series of park amenities, to create a stronger message about the park in relation to the environment. Without increasing the original budget, the Dis(solve) project provided the original desired signage plus a functional storage shed. More importantly, the installed work sought to create a stronger and more memorable way to bring public awareness to the park and provoke visitors to really think about the human relationship to the environment.

Design plays an interactive role. Structure, message, and environment merged to engage visitors in a more meaningful way of thinking about the relationship of humans to nature. Far from being purely didactic, the information and the environmental issues are presented in a playful manner that encourages visitor interaction. The location of the amenities also promotes discovery and delight. The siting of Japhet Creek Park is at a particularly intense intersection in which industry dominates, yet nature perseveres. The installations ask the visitor, through demonstration, information, and encouragement, to examine the relationship of nature to the immediate environment and beyond.

It is useful to provide students with direct exposure to community involvement and the potential opportunities to contribute through design. Exposure to the passion and efforts of a community is an invaluable lesson. The students witnessed how the efforts of a few people made a big difference in their neighborhood and an impact on the larger environment. Grassroots efforts influenced decisions at a city level. The experience made "what can I do?" a more feasible and significant proposition.

As the first of Houston's Green Fingers project, Japhet Creek is an example of how the creation of corridors of connectivity to the bayou system can improve both water quality and the relationship of the community to the environment. Japhet Creek is one of the last tributaries of Buffalo Bayou that hasn't been covered or channeled, and because it is still a natural stream, it is protected by the federal Green Fingers Program. Thanks to the hard work of the Buffalo Bayou Partnership and the Trust for Public Land, the creek will remain wild and undeveloped for generations to come. In 1909, the North Side Sewage Treatment Plant opened two blocks upwind from the Japhet neighborhood. Over the next 30 years, factories, warehouses, and rice mills were built along and near Japhet Creek. From the 1920s through the 1950s, Japhet Creek became a dumping ground. Tires, rice hulls, trash, and rubble from demolished buildings were dumped along the banks of the creek. As the smell from the sewage treatment plant became worse, the neighborhood emptied. In 1986, the Buffalo Bayou Partnership was founded to facilitate improvements to the greenway system. That same year, the sewage treatment plant closed, and Jim Ohmart and Eileen Hatcher moved into the original home built by Isidore Japhet. In 2004, Ohmart and Hatcher connected with local environmentalist Brian Herod, and The Japhet Creek Restoration Project was born. Since the first clean-up day in 2005, hundreds of bags of trash and tons of recyclable materials have been removed from the creek by dedicated volunteers.

These pieces call attention to the park and inform, provoke, and educate park visitors. Each piece serves a functional purpose and examines the things we make as humans and their ability to return back to nature. Their intention is to leave zero environmental impact on the site. Materials used that do not biodegrade may be reused or recycled once they leave. The Directional Map is a functional piece of street art that places emphasis on Japhet Creek as the driver transverses the bridge. It also directs the visitor to other installations in the park, including Trestle Poetry and the Green Filter Finger. The map consists of iconography drawn from natural elements at Japhet Creek. From the Chinaberry plants to the minnows swimming in the spring, these elements become symbolic guides for visitors.

Materials

- Recycled cardboard stencils
- Eco-friendly white paint

The Japhet Creek community and volunteers devoted exponential time and energy into transforming the park into a place free of debris and waste. The Filtration Station meets the needs of these individuals by providing storage for tools, a green roof that doubles as a water filtration system for clean-up, an information center, and a gathering place after a long day's work.

Materials

- Recycled 20-foot shipping container
- Various lumber
- Recycled cardboard boxes, 18 inches by 18 inches
- Recycled plasma-cut steel panels, 9.5 inches by 90 inches
- Komatex printed panel, 9.5 inches by 90 inches
- 50-gallon rain barrel
- 3 cubic yards dirt and sod
- 80-foot angular steel and rectangular tubing

To create a more attractive and inviting situation for Japhet Creek visitors, Green Bench offers seating that blends seamlessly into the environment. By using materials that degenerate at different speeds on a skeleton structure (metal, wood, plastic, cardboard, etc.), and enabling grass to grow in and around it, a powerful allegory can be made about the relationship between waste and nature, between the past and the future. This seating option also provides an eye-opening learning experience about materials and the time it takes to decompose.

Materials

- Recycled cardboard, 23.5 inches by 33 inches
- Eco-friendly spray paint
- Plywood
- Recycled political signs
- White vinyl
- Gravel/dirt/mulch/grass

the complex relationships between spaces. They further solidify an inevitable divide between those who would otherwise find common ground. As Andrew Kirk argues in *Counterculture Green* in regards to a strict nature/culture dichotomy, "In this ideological tradition, wilderness became the ultimate symbol of environmental purity and abundance, with the polluted technological city its antithesis" (2007: 13).

It is often assumed that these images—because of their rhetorical power to multiply and be consumed—define all space as natural or cultural and that the former must be protected from the latter. Emerging between these spaces are the already denuded and mined landscapes of the postindustrial age. This land was adulterated and made toxic by the human hand and is now unseen as neither nature nor culture, as the absence of both and serving to signify neither. It is in these places that the misuse of natural capital has deposited material as yet fully realized. It has no cachet as either culture or nature but is only waste.

Wasted, Spent, and Drained Spaces

The presence of nature in the city in places where it is unintended take the form of vacant lots and the small strips of land between housing, water, and abutting roads and railways. These places were often once occupied by water and are still providing drainage. These wasted, spent, and drained spaces are being reused in a repurposeful fashion by graphic designers working today to elevate these spaces as sites of leisure, food, and information.

In defining these spaces, the designer creates a truly Postmodern spatiality in a postindustrial world, where Postmodernism's formerly eclectic aestheticism is replaced by a truly pluralistic, physical environment that transcends materiality and ideology. Having been built on the myriad excesses of the industrial and the machined, these spaces provide a mediated but fairly neutral examination of the past and of materially rich detritus in the form of natural and cultural legacies. The designer can return intentionality to these sites that have been rejected because of their proximity to industry. In this case, the designer works at the back end of the design process in attempting an end run around the already systematic wasting of natural resources.

Interlocking Planes

Many of the projects featured in this book treat these sites as texts. By rereading their stories, new ways of visualizing them as valuable and useful are unearthed. Their relationship to the larger natural and human environments punctuate the real meaning of what is usually seen as strictly defined relationships. In calling attention to the unique, local qualities of already used spaces, design refuses to dispose of spaces. These spaces are not defined as wild or sterile but as significant and worthy of recasting as such. These project sites, though meditated, are intended to create multiple interactions between whole systems and whole groups. This creates a place where groups can meet halfway between the built and natural environments. They provide an individualized and reassuring "you are here" quality to a dislocated public that is so inured to a mediated life.

As neighborhoods break down and fall fallow, new urban patterns can develop to confront and critique the ways that places of cultural value are marginalized and eventually succumb to the wasting of spaces that are already defined as urban. The new ways in which they are read and revived as natural is a rejection of the ideal and an embracing of the many ways different people find meaning together in a new shared cosmopolitan sensibility. This effort goes beyond preservation and extends the life of a city by recentering it within a quilt of interlocking planes of meaning, wherein each supports the others. A new aesthetic asserts itself in place of older aesthetic value. Green space can be seen as grayspaces that subvert how planners, developers, and municipalities structure and define how and where people live.

Space in this chapter is defined really by space/s, multiple interlocking spaces that overlap and bleed into each other. These urban spaces intersect with or are conjoined with natural and wasted spaces, those that lie fallow, discarded, and underutilized. In every case, people have made their mark on them. They now may be used, misused, neglected, or potentially valued for what they are. Even in cases where they seem to no longer possess any use-value, designers have something to bring to them. As people have made their mark on them, they are now part of what is made—our built environment. Being built, they are much like any other edifice, either weak or strong but made by people and built in some sense to suit them. They are then not beyond repair and can be remade. In order to understand them, designers need to know themselves and why we all design and build.

Buildings as Signifiers

For the graphic designer, buildings are signifiers. Typically viewed on a screen or page, they have no less potential as representations than the actual site. Something can be known of a building by any number of visual records of it, from sketches, plans, and models to photographs or films. Spaces are not limited to the site on which they rest. They, like all things, also operate visually as symbols of sites both in the specific and in more general terms. When taken in aggregate, they can be rearranged and resituated within both the mind of the individual and of the public. Once recognized as a glossary of what spaces and sites mean, designers can begin to speak with and through them to make sense of what is believed about them and therefore what is desired from them. If designers ignore the rich texts that these spaces are, they will only ever see them for their basic use-value as shelter. Shelter is among the most basic of human needs, but if that is all it is, it cannot explain the rich cultural heritage of cities and buildings. It is not enough to dismiss the kitsch and the shoddy work of the industrial and consumer ages as simply the work of those who prey on the prostrate consumer. A poor-quality building that misuses a site to the detriment of the user is still a vessel that holds some meaning, no matter how debased it might be. To understand the worst strip mall or tract home is to know what is valued or devalued. In knowing this, designers can know at least what is better and work to design what is best.

What Remains

Most of the creative production seen today is poorly made, including most graphic design, most architecture, most contemporary art, most writing, most television, and most of what is consumed as culture. None of these forms stands above the rest in a remove from what is designed for consumption and waste. Designers must redefine

waste in order to understand value. For buildings, that value cannot be limited to a basic function as housing. If the built environment is viewed as performing only the simple task of providing shelter, then why we build at all goes unseen and the knowledge that the real building begins after the tenants move in. Everyone is a tenant, everything is temporary, but human expression in every culture takes a built form. That is what remains.

The Pruitt-Igoe public housing works in St. Louis are an example of structures built only with basic shelter in mind. They proved to be so completely antithetical and destructive to the nuclear family that they were finally destroyed. Often public assistance or welfare was part and parcel of public housing. If a single female was cohabitating with a male, it was assumed he would provide support for her, as any man might as conceived by the nuclear family, and she could lose all public support for her and her children. His absence was the very thing that denied and made impossible one of the assumed purposes of housing as home, a patriarchy. This was in reality made illegal and therefore created both the problems associated by the larger culture with the lack of a paternal figure and a general culture of illegality. This example details the real work of architecture and community as an antithesis to the ideal but being so powerful in its opposition to it that it had to be destroyed. We cannot say that the government did not provide shelter—it did—but it could not fulfill any other cultural expectations of housing or community that is expected from an award-winning architectural firm—or from a simple hut, for that matter. It was so very unsustainable that it literally imploded under its own weight (Freidrichs 2011).

What made the Pruitt-Igoe housing project unsustainable was not the fact that it was part of a city and therefore not part of nature. It is within the natural order of things for people to build. It was unsustainable because it was created and sustained for a time as the antidote to the white, middle-class suburb of the postwar US economy. The former was detailed in journalistic exposés and sensationalist films, surrounded by industry and vice rather than woods and pastures, and the latter was seen in glossy advertisements and were embodied in prepackaged television families. The vices of the city were reinforced by the illegality of any community being established and the threat to women and children living alone in the city. It could not be sustained because it was created through hubris and built on the idea that houses might be conceived as machines, or worse yet, as Frank Lloyd Wright described, as filing cabinets for people. On the other hand, was the suburb built on economic and racial inequality and in part inspired by Wright's own designs?

Voices Across the Landscape

A sustainable approach to signs and signing created by graphic designers and others is therefore not simply a matter of eliminating visual clutter or even of accepting vernacular signage and outdoor advertising at its face value as part and parcel of the contemporary landscape. It is more a matter of recognizing boundaries and limits and then moving across them in order to draw attention to artificiality and to open up a new spatial discourse about sustainability. It is a matter of common sense that this must include a deliberate questioning of the automobile's presence across the entire landscape, both physical and cultural. Such projects would immediately entail an acknowledgment of scale both of systems of design, such as freeways, and navigating these by foot or bicycle. The other immediate constraint that must be acknowledged is the cacophony of voices present on the landscape and intended for drivers and passengers of fast-moving vehicles. This multiplicity of voices was described in *Learning from Las Vegas* as "megatexture" in contrast to the enclosed space of the piazza (Venturi, Brown, & Izenour 1972: 13). Urban spaces normally designed to move people quickly through space and time and which separate them at great distance from each other and require intensive energy and time to traverse must be complemented by a variety of alternate sites. To suggest that these alternate sites create a neutral space would be to enter into the false assumptions associated with the nature/culture dichotomy, suggesting an absence of a subject/object relationship. Rather, these projects speak to a hybrid engagement with space that works to bring a plurality of peoples and places into closer proximity.

In biomimicry, the idea is that technology and nature brought together in hybrid form might eliminate the subject/object relationship. Whether this can be achieved or not is debatable, but at this point it becomes necessary to recognize culture's objectified relationship with nature in order to devise new sustainable design models rather than imagine a place without subjectivity. The role of graphic designers working in space and sites is not to police the visual environment to eliminate visual clutter or litter, as suggested in the racialized words of Massimo Vignelli (Hustwit 2007). This would only perpetuate the notion that only the visible signs of ecological destruction and pollution need be removed and ignores larger systemic problems (Rogers 2005: 141–50).

Summary of Case Studies

Make Change

When Kristine Matthews was studying at the Royal College of Art (RCA) in London, she and her future design partner Sophie Thomas were constantly perplexed by RCA's near-total lack of awareness of its impact on the environment. To convince the RCA to start recycling, they put together an exhibit made from the detritus of the school's everyday life. They collected and hung in the gallery space a week's worth of waste in the form of 5,000 plastic cups and 16,000 cans. The result was a rather beautiful chain of cups and cans that seemed to emulate the strands of DNA that make up all of us. Instead, these chains represented an unbroken process of consumption and contamination, rather than the very material of life. The lesson wasn't lost on the two. By focusing on just one small artifact of everyday life, the one-way drink container, an object designed for mass reproduction and consumption, they had unearthed a fundamental truth.

They revealed the truth that many of the things that we take for granted, often the small and seemingly insignificant things, can add up to a lot of waste. Today, Kristine Matthews teaches environmental design at the University of Washington, working to make sustainability an integral part of the curriculum. She'd like sustainability to be a given in any design process and the very definition of "good" design an integral part of that process. Matthews feels that although it may be necessary at present to provide specific courses on sustainability, the goal must be to "embed it so deeply that we no longer single it out as a separate issue." Additionally, Matthews stresses the importance of not prescribing design solutions in advance, avoiding the assumption that another logo, poster, or package is needed. Her students have really embraced this approach and have taken the challenge personally, because it affects their futures not just as creatives but as citizens and consumers. Because Matthews keeps one foot solidly in the professional world, she can speak directly to the desires of her students, who would like to succeed in the profession while advocating for change. This is where she begins the conversation about sustainable design, at the point of contact with the profession and the demands it places on designers to understand how their concepts get made. Research plays a prominent role in the process. The so-called design problem isn't defined in advance of detailed research anymore than the form it should take. The students are often surprised at the range of information that's available even within the limits of Google. Most students find the process inspiring, and they will compete to see who can find the coolest stuff. Says Matthews, "Research gives the essential raw data to build a compelling story, to grab attention to make a change."

For her project Make Change, Matthews assigns her students to work in teams of four, designing an exhibition or installation. Each group chooses its own subject and frames the problem, determined by something they feel must change. Their objective is to elicit from their audience a specific, positive response to the issue. Collaboration is fundamental to the way Matthews teaches design. Through collaboration, the interdisciplinary nature of the design process becomes apparent to the students. Forming teams engenders healthy competition and is crucial for larger projects. It also facilitates an atmosphere where students can emerge as specialists and discover the range of their talents. Environmental design relocates design away from the screen and emphasizes craft and makes the importance of materials more tangible. As Matthews states:

> [I]f you are creating something with your own two hands (screen-printing, letterpress, and so on), you can't help but be very aware of the materials that you are using; where they are from, how they behave, how they feel. It's something that has been lost in the transition to so much computer-generated design (and the reams and reams of paper that always seem to accompany that process).

Once the students are aware of how things get made, they understand better how specifying is at the heart of the design process.

Before anything gets made, the students create case studies to get them to think about where stuff comes from. As Matthews describes:

> [A]nother really key part of research is into materials, processes and suppliers, sourcing your materials locally whenever possible. I really encourage the students to look into all of the "real world" innovative materials and processes out there, as the materials you choose or the processes you use can sometimes end up forming the backbone of a project.

Through Make Change, Matthews has succeeded in building issues of ethics and responsibility into her coursework as part of the conversation. The result for the students is a very subjective approach to design, where their personal interests and passion are brought to bear in service of important questions. At the same time, their designs demand attention, are smart and aesthetically pleasing; they are design that is to be used, multiplied, and replicated, not design to put under glass or perch on a pedestal. Matthews would argue that good design is sustainable and that neither is mutually exclusive. Matthews anticipates a time when we won't remember what it used to look like, when we won't say "green" anymore, similar to the way the Mac changed everything we do except for the very fundamentals. She sees a time where it won't be a limitation, when it's no longer someone else's job. Today's design students will be the ones who make that happen.

When thinking about what her students will do after leaving school and how they can affect change, Matthews stresses the marketability of design with a sustainable emphasis. Everyone is scrambling to become responsible and transparent; designers can make that real, not just another trivial affectation adopted by the business community. To communicate their skill in doing this, she encourages students to present clients with projects they have self-authored. Everyone is looking for fresh ideas in order to solve a problem in an innovative way. Designers can create ways to partner with clients to meet both of their goals. Matthews hopes that all her students will study or live in another country or culture at some point, because it's the best way for students to understand that not everyone can live the way hers do in North America. It's important to see how others view you and to make tangible how complex systems have been abstracted.

AgriProp and Japhet Creek

The graphic design program at the University of Houston has long stressed student engagement with issues of social responsibility. They take an interdisciplinary approach to design as one aspect of a larger system in which the student participates as both citizen and designer. The goal is to question consumerism as the only basis for defining the design's role and to seek ways to better society through the production of images and objects that create meaning for the communities in which they work. As Cheryl Beckett describes, "Interdisciplinary projects instill awareness that design is not an independent activity but an integral part of a larger system that is linked to a web of social production."

Some of their first efforts involved getting the students out from behind their computers and out of their comfort zones. Initially, this involved trips to other cities like New York. Before long, they realized that the students' disconnect with nature was the issue, and they began to perceive it as something to be overcome. To do this, they typically looked to the human-made environments that surrounded them. Beckett's solution was to make them aware of the natural environment within Houston's beltways. Thus began AgriProp, a site-specific project within the public space along Houston's Bayou and within the urban environment. Several new avenues for developing a more critical context for teaching design emerged through this project. Working on solutions to improve public spaces brought them into direct contact with the public, including community organizations and local government.

The feedback was immediate and specific and brought to light the importance of different perspectives. This highlighted how graphic designers need to collaborate with other specialists to help give their messages legs. Although this was uncomfortable, that unease propelled the students to work harder to make sure they were doing their part in conceiving viable ideas. Beckett saw the students transformed by the immediate demands on their research and design skills and their ability to be flexible. Students were forced to research what materials were compatible with the site in which their work would exist over a long period. As Beckett notes, "Students realize that a designer has the potential to transform and shape an environment as well as create a meaningful place for the surrounding community. . . . The more students are aware of the direct link to what they make and the world they live in, the better."

This is very different from the typical print project and highlights the limitations of educating students to pursue solutions that prescribe certain media or technologies. Actual experience with the people, places, and systems that can be experienced first-hand are emphasized. That said, this does not diminish the latent power of graphic design to persuade, educate, advocate, and move people to take action. This is demonstrated by the AgriProp project's positive and proactive engagement with social issues that seems to transcend politics.

RESPECT

Chapter Five
Social Design

This chapter explores long-term, integrated projects that find graphic designers working directly with communities and social groups on systemic problems to provide concrete and lasting solutions as well as the design processes and tools to sustain them. To say that these projects fall outside of what has been commonly termed graphic design understates the degree to which graphic designers have isolated themselves from the other design disciplines and a variety of other disciplines as well. To say that these projects occur outside of the classroom suggests the manner in which they are redefining design education as wholly interdisciplinary and the classroom as a space beyond institutional and physical limits.

These projects exemplify the ways that graphic design can define broad design problems through its emphasis on language—written, visual, and object oriented. Graphic designers who are trained in a variegated visual literacy bring an organizational power to these projects that may otherwise go unattended. These bold efforts express the optimism the creators have brought to problems where graphic design has not normally been present. Like the projects in chapter two, they challenge the limits of the profession in places even further beyond the comfort zone of most graphic designers. These projects move into areas where it isn't readily clear how the graphic designer can assist in the absence of a well-defined space, blank page, or screen, and in which expertise is required from a variety of disciplines. The issues being dealt with in these places do not occur on a blank page but rather where issues intertwine and must be read one on the other. The ability of graphic designers to contextualize complexity is what defines their role in these spaces.

It may not be apparent to the casual observer the way in which these projects might serve the interests of the market in the form of a service or product. This absence of any noticeable evidence of the work of graphic design assumes its role as subservient to the market and therefore not an autonomous force for positive change. If, in the hierarchy of things bought and sold, design ranks so low, what then of the ordinary and necessary needs of those in developing countries and those living below the poverty line, living perhaps beyond our definition of progress?

The projects discussed here resist the imperatives of what E. F. Schumacher defined as a system in which money is of the highest value—where everything has a price (1973: 46). These projects raise the question of value where often no apparent goods possessing any exchange value exist and where people possess needs that no accounting can calculate. If design only defines things by their exchange value, it will find no value in people without the resources or the ability to produce goods for trade. Designers must, if they are to extend the work of graphic design beyond the theoretical and the purely profitable, see people as the principal resource and their creativity as the energy source for innovations that are profitable beyond a balance sheet. It is simply not enough to conceive of the self as once again in union with nature without also being part of humanity as well, as part and parcel of others. These projects begin this work by defining value through nascent design industries. Through these efforts, the resources and outcomes belong to the people who have worked to define them. Others cannot claim to have discovered the natural and human resources at hand and then exploit them for their own profit and to the detriment of the original owners. This is where we begin, making people indispensable rather than disposable.

Visualizing Rather Than Theorizing

Design is never only theoretical and therefore finite but entails the act of visualizing. The projects in this chapter demonstrate the agency of designers in making under-utilized resources seen and in their latent power to make meaning. Because these projects exist beyond the assumed limits of graphic design, their work lies partly in reassigning boundaries through reassessing aesthetic value and its function. The highly finished quality of much of what is expected from graphic design is often unrealized in the complexity of these projects. The work that these projects inspire must then dispense in part, at least in the beginning, with requiring functionality in

CEDO

Instructor: Ellen McMahon
University of Arizona
Students learn about the rich biodiversity of the Morua Estuary and work on the mural for the Sociedad Cooperativa Única de Mujeres. At the request of CEDO Intercultural and Sociedad Cooperativa Única de Mujeres oyster growers, students from the University of Arizona created a natural history mural and signage for a new restaurant and ecotourism business on the banks of Morua Estuary. The success of the Única de Mujeres mural led to the development of NaturArte, a program to support local people in creating ecotourism operations through grant funding facilitated by CEDO Intercultural and visual communications projects by University of Arizona faculty and students.

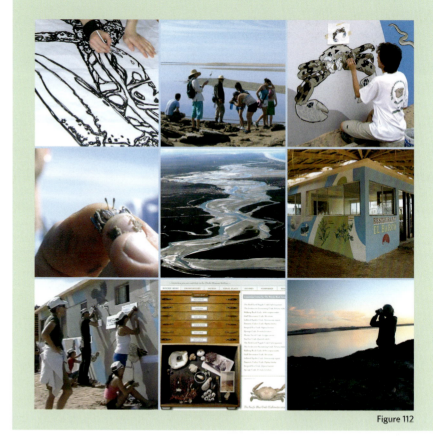

Figure 112

aesthetic terms. To help find small solutions for big problems, they must rely on the process of graphic design that is so widely utilized for big-budget endeavors. Their purpose is to make something out of what was thought to be nothing, at least nothing defined as that which cannot be traded.

Their primary purpose at the start must be to make visible what has been hidden by other concerns, and to consider the majority of people directly affected by systemic problems. These problems are produced by a status quo in which the wealthiest people in the wealthiest nations are considered not by need but by the number of resources they command and use. For graphic designers, the ongoing process of redefining needs occurs in tandem with those they are seeking to help in defining the value of what design can offer. This empathetic engagement with human needs—rather than simply a subjective response to a design problem—is the heart of a new design pedagogy and practice for sustainability. It will sustain students beyond their school years and their primary impetus for pursuing design as a career and as a way of seeing. The ability to visualize rather than simply theorize is critical to this ethos and occurs through making images and objects that offer proofs of good design.

The Notion of Unlimited Supply

Much of what continues to divide the world in the so-called information age is lack of access to what is seen simplistically as "information." Today's truly literate person is one who understands the visual power of design as a means for acquiring accurate and complete information. Information without a critical context will not by its sheer volume inform the viewer or user. It is therefore the work of the graphic designer to not simply inform but to provide a means to see information in a new light. The oversupply of information currently available to those equipped in technological terms should not be conflated with an ability to see and navigate complex and destructive systems. The tendency to overvalue availability of information as being equal with knowledge induces a belief in information's ability to solve on its own problems of both scarcity and abundance that are associated with overconsumption. This notion persists as an illustration of Schumacher's assertion that, "The illusion of unlimited powers, nourished by astonishing scientific and

Design Global Change

Instructor: Natacha Poggio
University of Hartford
Students: Laurie Kovac, Crystal Cote, Jonathan Eckels, Cael Spillane, Josh Parent, Marene Ferguson, Sergio Barrera, Amy Huston, Nikki Lee, Ethan Bodnar, Mullica Zudsiri

Water for India 2009

In January 2009, Hartford Art School Professor Natacha Poggio and a team of five Art and Design students traveled to Abheypur, India, to implement the Water for India sanitation campaign (to partner on the work of the Engineers Without Borders student chapter at the University of Hartford). The campaign originally began as an assignment in the spring of 2008 and was continued after receiving feedback from Abheypur's villagers. Water for India aims to convey the importance of cleanliness, sharing, and respect for water resources. During the January trip,

Figure 114

Figure 113

the team painted a mural at the girls' primary school and distributed coloring books with sanitation tips as well as T-shirts with the campaign logo. For the trip in January 2010, a new team of students worked on expanding the sanitation campaign to provide teaching tools for the primary school teachers and an awareness campaign targeting high school boys to prevent alcohol consumption. At the same time, work began on a gender equality campaign for the girls and young women of Abheypur.

India: Gender Equality Campaign: Bringing Girls into Focus

One of the twenty-seven social change projects selected for Sappi Ideas That Matter grants in 2010 was the Design Global Change proposal Bringing Girls into Focus, a gender equality campaign that raises awareness of women's important roles in rural communities through the use of educational materials. DGC created a set of cards depicting Indian men and women in various roles (e.g., collecting water, farming, selling goods); these cards aimed to trigger conversations about gender issues among high school youth and were accompanied by a teacher's guidebook, which was used to provide educational activities to raise awareness. This project continues the DGC and University of Hartford partnership with Navjyoti India Foundation, a nonprofit organization led by famous female enforcement officer, Dr. Kiran Bedi. Navjyoti serves more than 12,000 people in northern India; their staff distributed the educational cards through their service network, spreading the message of youth empowerment and gender equality.

Figure 116

Kenya: Amaranth Branding

DGC continues the work initiated in 2009 in the Lake Victoria region of Kenya, through *kanga* cloth designs, which promote healthy and safe living within the community, and promotes education about clean water, safety, and amaranth harvesting. This project involves the identity design for a local mill and the packaging for grain amaranth, which will be sold to local schools and hospitals by area farmers from the Alour widows group. University of Hartford faculty (partnering with Brown University, University of Rhode Island, and Mount Holyoke University) are researching and demonstrating that using milled and toasted

Figure 118

Figure 120

Figure 115

Figure 117

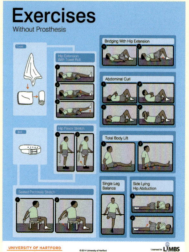

Figure 119

Figure 121

amaranth products promote nutritional absorption, which has improved the immune systems of members of the community who are HIV positive.

DGC continues work in conjunction with LIMBS International, a nonprofit humanitarian organization that designs, creates, and offers low-cost, high-quality prosthetics to amputees worldwide. LIMBS' mission is to transform the lives of patients in developing countries by restoring their ability to walk. LIMBS was founded in 2004 by Dr. Roger Gonzalez—a professor of Mechanical and Biomedical Engineering at the University of Texas at El Paso—who challenged his

students to develop a prosthetic knee that could be affordably produced, highly functional, durable, and locally maintainable. The eventual result of this project is the M3 Relief Knee, which is made from a lightweight plastic, making it waterproof, low-cost, and field repairable. Prosthetic devices are constructed in the United States; the component parts are shipped to clinics in South America, Africa, and India. LIMBS has established eight training centers, trained more than 100 prosthetists, fitted more than 1,000 amputees, and provided some level of programming at more than thirty-five clinics in twenty-two countries.

technological achievements, has produced the concurrent illusion of having solved the problem of production" (1973: 14). This book outlines this conceit as it relates directly to graphic design in four areas.

- The seemingly unlimited supply of knowledge first produced with Gutenberg's application of mechanization to visual and written knowledge and fully realized during the industrial revolution
- The seemingly unlimited supply of virgin land and natural resources existing just beyond the limits of human culture and the frontier
- The seemingly unlimited supply of synthetic materials, known as plastics, used in the design and manufacture of consumables and possessing transformational, almost magical qualities to express and embody modernity
- The seemingly unlimited supply of information technology realized through the digital means of reproduction and dissemination in the late twentieth and early twenty-first centuries

For a paradigm shift to occur in design, assumptions about limitless supplies must be put aside, along with other assumptions about a limited definition of what is environmentally sound. A broad range of thinkers and writers are challenging these notions, but without a background in design, they often lack the necessary insight needed to produce innovation through a sustainable process rather than the perceived value of particular outcomes. One such notion is the ongoing indictment of ordinary consumers in ecological destruction based on consumer desire. Design historians and critics have long understood the value of the subjective position of the consumer as it relates to identity formation rather than as many critics who assess it as simply narcissism. In order to understand how end users will integrate co-designed products with their existing culture, they must fully identify with the end product as being truly connected to who they are. Designers must empathize with users in the intimate ways that designed images and artifacts create meaning. In short, to understand use-value, designers must understand consumption, both for its creative and destructive capabilities. To ignore either would be to forgo assessing the risks when engaging in work outside our normal sphere of influence and skills.

The Value of Design as Thinking

Much of the work shown in this chapter can be defined broadly as sustainable but is more often defined as socially responsible design or social design, work that most often emanates from the fields of architecture and engineering. Designers and often others assume that because these disciplines deal in the concrete rather than the ephemeral, they are best suited for dealing with "real" problems. There may be some temptation to see these attempts as novel or ancillary to actual graphic design practice. Both these assumptions can be overcome through the integration of graphic design methods with design solutions emphasizing invention and tools as the primary method of delivering solutions. The creation of new tools and devices requires explanation of how to use and maintain them.

Although this may seem obvious, it is rarely done well, especially across cultural boundaries, and is often not integrated from inception. If graphic designers partner early in the process with other disciplines, they can drive the process and visually define its goals before, during, and after conception. The more intangible aspects of social design can then serve the more concrete aspects. One of these intangibles is cultural identity and specificity in stating objectives, reaching outcomes, and disseminating the results. For design students, the results not only benefit the users but also teach the students to better appreciate the users in general. This human-centered design is beneficial to all aspects of sustainability, including the economic. What is now termed "design thinking" and was simply, in historical terms, essential design process has now been combined with explicitly creative and strategic language. Design thinking is not simply a novel term used in selling design services. It is a way to recognize the value of design—as thinking. Design thinking provides a critical and creative means to restructure how designers think as they act to innovate.

In-Equal Design

Very little of what is spoken of or written on issues related to socially responsible, green, or sustainable design does not rely to some degree on the work of Victor Papanek. It is difficult to imagine many of the ideas he put forth in *Design for the Real World* (1972) as not having inspired the spate of books being written today on green and sustainable design. Apart from Buckminster Fuller, there is no other figure of equal weight on the subject. All of their ideas were by definition open-source and preceded most other efforts to decentralize knowledge, especially that of design and technology, adapted at a small scale to broad and far-reaching problems. Their role beyond being original thinkers was often as gadfly, making eco-design at least partially and initially a character-driven movement, defined to some degree by the personal limitations of its founders.

The ideas associated with character-driven movements are not without their benefits, but on the whole they are not effective if applied by most people in attempting to cross boundaries of culture and discipline. Both Papanek and Fuller were nomadic and, though associated with many academic institutions, rejected academic structures as defined by the post–Second World War era and then came into vogue as part of the counterculture of the 1960s. In the long term, both their ideas and the institutions they challenged remain, and with each generation both can be equally harnessed to understand and surmount contemporary problems. In-equal design

as a social norm was the chief design problem then and now and as such does not exist solely in a single field of inquiry. The graphic designer can work between and through disparate institutions and structures and the resources and expertise they provide to join common goals.

Surplus Creativity

Today's graphic designer has on hand a surplus of creativity garnered from the labor-saving digital design and publishing tools of the past twenty-five to thirty years. But what has been made of this surplus? Most often it is cycled back into the workflow and spent pursuing the plethora of small novelties associated with digital design skills. Although these skills can then be traded for additional work and shorter turnarounds, they are rarely unique or essential. These discrete skills are not the paradigmatic shifts that were first felt with the initial digitization of basic tools for reproduction but ripples within a larger sea change. The essential skill set that stemmed from the first wave can now be easily acquired and applied without a context and a directive to serve others. New innovations in digital design are now demonstrated in broad convergences, such as the most recent emergence of social media. Today's graphic designer can best serve others not in pursuing the esoteric blind alleys of new digital tricks but by applying surplus creativity to the needs of others.

Social design as seen in this chapter has its origin in Victor Papanek's publication of *Design for the Real World* (1972). He stood alone in declaring the moral imperatives of design, not simply its ability to be good. Without his opening the scope of design to include a moral imperative beyond what he termed "a narrow and parochial view," designers would not now be discussing how to make design simply less bad. He led designers in taking responsibility for what they design. He clearly outlined at that time why we could not continue to expand and export an affluent lifestyle based on racial and class divisions, further alienating and abstracting those outside the pale. He saw clearly that resting on a mountain of waste, perched on the heights, was not a vantage point from which to view the actual situation. The approach he forwarded made clear the false conceit that just because the majority of the world's people did not have the funds to buy the majority of the goods, they were not in fact the minority.

Papanek went as far as to suggest a tithe of our design skills and time. As he said, "ideas are plentiful and cheap" (1972: 16), and therefore open-source design is that which holds the highest value and potential for good. We could, as Firebelly Design does, devote 10 to 15 percent of our billable hours to pro bono work. Victor Papanek went further in suggesting a sabbatical year of time donated to "designing for many instead of designing for money" (1972: 80–81). These ideas reject a model of scarcity in which designers control a society's meager creative capital in reserve for the very fortunate five hundred. Papanek concluded with:

> Even if the corporate greed of many design offices makes this kind of design impossible, students should at least be encouraged to work in this manner. For in showing students new areas of engagement, we may set up alternate patterns of thinking about design problems. We may help them to develop the kind of social and moral responsibility that is needed in design.

Blind Spots

Personality-driven design movements fail in the same respect as any model that elevates particular individuals beyond their capacity to contribute to the whole. This is seen clearly in the blind spots of both Papanek and Fuller and is why we need to model a variety of ways of thinking through making in order to eschew our own personal biases. Fuller's *Operating Manual for Spaceship Earth* (1969), though truly unique, borders at times on the mystical and outside of the context of the counterculture of the 1960s, and it offers little to today's emerging designer. Papanek described design as "the conscious and intuitive effort to impose meaningful order" (1972: 23). Unfortunately, we as designers have not often asked who would, or who *should*, impose that order or what form it should take to serve the most people. People are disposed to centralized and authoritarian systems of all kinds, and they are often unable to recognize their own complicity in these systems. This is true of even our most original design thinkers.

Black Gold Poster Project

Students: Christina Olivas, Leslie Sandoval, Reyna Salinas
Graduate Teaching Assistant, Jacob Munoz
Instructor: Peter Fine
University of Wyoming, USA

Objectives and Outcomes

1. Design a poster to promote a screening of *Black Gold*, a film about fair trade coffee in Africa to coincide with a fair trade sale of goods produced by women from the US–Mexico border region.

Figure 122

Figure 123

2. Provide an outlet for students to leverage their design skills to promote local communities through the design of a limited-edition screen-print poster to be sold at the fair trade sale.
3. Draw attention to underrepresented communities and transnational economic issues through graphic design.

Process

1. Research fair trade goods and coffee.
2. Generate individual and group ideas to design posters.
3. Integrate posters from each of the three students into a single newsprint piece that unfolds to reveal a variety of issues of fair trade coffee.

4. Work with local printers to reproduce multiple issues of the newsprint poster.
5. Combine skills to design and print a limited-edition screen-print poster to be sold at the fair trade sale.

Challenges

1. Interactions with vendors and multiple third parties associated with the event
2. Collaborating to produce a single piece that represents all of the students' ideas
3. Production of quality screen-print for sale
4. Communicating the value of design work as equal to the fair trade goods being sold through the event

To move beyond our current limitations, designers must reject the wrong-headed perception that the feminization and adulteration of design occurs through consumption. As described by Papanek, "Never before in history have grown men sat down and seriously designed electric hairbrushes, rhinestone covered file boxes, and mink carpeting for bathrooms" (1972: 14). Not only is this a clear alignment of the feminine with the trivial and ultimately the useless, but it is also ahistorical in that it genders some artifacts and separates consumption from modernism and perhaps women as well. It is not at all clear how one might design for specific contexts and needs as Papanek demanded if we are to ignore and trivialize the feminine and the presence of women and their needs. It could be argued that these attitudes were a product of his times, but not if we accept the degree to which he rejected and worked against the prevailing notions of his time and hectored students and colleagues to do the same.

Additionally, although Papanek clearly understood the universal value and need for good design in a post-colonial context, his assertion that "symmetrical order is a favorite of children, unusually primitive people and some of the insane" (1972: 24) remains an assumption that began with Adolf Loos's *Ornament and Crime* (1908) and is essentially racist. It seems that if designers are to honestly examine what benefits can be attained through good design, they must be willing to honestly examine the assumptions and intentions of even the most esteemed designers. Clearly, this attitude has no place if, as Papanek describes, design is to reflect its times and conditions and to "fit in with the general human socioeconomic order in which it is to operate" (1972: 34). Bizarrely, he racializes obsolescence as "The miscegenative union between technology and artificially" giving birth "to the dark twins of styling and obsolescence" (1972: 48). His equating of sterility in the form of a "mulatto" with designed obsolescence is perhaps his strangest blind spot. Especially when he immediately follows it with an accurate description of the global haves and have-nots. His insight into the global effects of the "Kleenex culture" (1972: 96–106), which came to dominate design in the twentieth century, as degrading human values to such a degree that entire subcontinents were disposable (1972: 97) speaks more closely to his intent rather than his biases.

Place, Race, and Waste

What Fuller and Papanek understood clearly was the absolute necessity of design in all human endeavors and cultures. Without an understanding of how design can be applied collaboratively in communities in the developing world, it has sometimes been mistaken for a luxury. Some have figured design as post-material, meaning that once Maslov's hierarchy of needs is met, we might expect those in the developing world to be able to appreciate the benefits of quality design and technology. This is directly contradicted by the rich history of art, craft, and design traditions of all kinds in all cultures. A basic understanding of anthropology supports this viewpoint. This makes clear that business sense is not enough and that an understanding of cultural traditions provides the nuance needed to appreciate quality in all its expressions. In fact, good design is apparent in any object that feels right or whole to the user, and this is largely culturally defined. A true understanding of materialism must emerge through an engagement with material culture practices such as design.

It is important to not mistake high-cost or high-end design for good design. Because consumers who can afford the cost of well-designed goods provide the market for most luxury goods, it does not mean that these values cannot be or are not applied equally, especially in spheres outside of the marketplace. Once any luxury good reaches a certain threshold in an economy of scale, it is often made available to larger and more diverse demographics at less cost. Designers must not conceive of anyone being unable to appreciate any basic or universal value related to material culture simply because he or she lives in a context that is largely unknown to the majority.

Some now suggest that place-based environmentalism is limited in its power to affect change if not already expended (Nordhaus and Shellenberger 2007: 89–104). This may be true if one lives in affluence in the Northern Hemisphere within a community or place that is already preserved to support an affluent lifestyle. If all things in all places were equal, that might be a viable position. If, however, one lives somewhere downstream of affluence, the place one lives in does have localized needs that must be addressed. It stands to reason then that place does matter and in fact is the norm, being as most people in the world do not live in places that are already developed to sustain an affluent lifestyle. To deny race as a factor in environmental problems and identity-politics as especially contrary to the goal of sustainability is a failure to recognize racism as just as insidious and often invisible a pollutant culturally as any toxic byproduct of industry. For racism to operate, it need not be intentional. The situating of waste correlates to place and race (Rogers 2005: 165–166), and both must be considered when working in impoverished communities, whether in the global north or around the world. It would perhaps be irrational to base one's politics on race if one is an affluent white who has always been regarded as an individual instead of as part of a racialized group. Otherwise, it is a necessity of context and place.

Self-imposed Ignorance

Designers need to deliberately broaden their perspective to understand their specific role in creating sustainable design. Design has reached the threshold of its own self-imposed ignorance and its significant impact on a continued dependence on increasing consumption. Having already mistaken the role of the consumer for that of citizen in the

The Role of Design in Social Awareness

Instructor: Scott Boylston
Program Coordinator, Design for Sustainability, SCAD
Students: Tiffany Lindeborn, Marina Petrova, Giang, Nguyen Hung, and Forum Shah

Insights

1. Citizen networks do not grow overnight. The key to stewarding such a process through academic classes is for the professor to live the life of what Malcolm Gladwell calls a "connector," in that only through active involvement within the outlying community and a genuine interest in its well-being can a professor link classes to that community in an effective, ongoing manner.

2. Students must have a "safe" place to return to after they've been in the field. Students can afford to stumble in the field as long as they can return to the classroom to learn from those mistakes. Students learn what "freedom to fail" means firsthand, because they get in the habit of correcting their course due to busted assumptions and unexpected feedback, yet the focus remains steadfastly on creative adaptation.

Figure 124

Figure 125

create designs that speak sincerely with members of the community.

7. Students leave these classes both humbled and excited to continue their new form of practice.

Direction A: Pride

This direction is called "Pride," as it focuses on "Proud to be Waters." Throughout the campaign, the people will be featured with their thoughts on Waters Avenue and what makes it so special to them. This engages people and makes it more than just an

information poster. The colorful bands, along with the bright vivid colors of the pictures, reflect the celebratory nature of the campaign. While the colors change per person and picture, the light and dark blue bars of "Proud to be Waters" remain constant, hence giving the campaign a consistent look and identity, while still allowing it to be flexible. The clean and bold type attracts attention and shows the determination of people. Visually, all horizontal panels spell *Waters* to magnify the idea of belonging to Waters and the pride for being a part of Waters Avenue. The design is kept simple and minimal to include as many

3. The cycle of going out into the field and then returning to the classroom should be consistent enough throughout the course to generate iterative learning patterns. In-class readings should be selected to align with the nature of the work. Readings resonate more deeply and insights are more profound when theory and practice weave together.

4. The word *collaboration* is quickly stripped of its veneer, and the students learn how complicated, challenging, and ultimately rewarding collaboration can be. The fact that there is as much collaboration beyond

the classroom walls as there is within them smoothes out differences that otherwise become exaggerated within a closed classroom.

5. The notion of advocacy as a fundamental form of design facilitation is brought to the fore in these courses, and students eventually come to realize that these newly discovered abilities were less hindered by their own practice in the past then by their discipline's expectations.

6. The students do most of their work by listening, and in doing so they are able to

Figure 126

people as possible and to keep the focus on the people.

Direction B: Waters Is...

"Waters is..." is carried on to "I Am Waters" and "We = Waters." Waters is me, you, and us.

Direction C: Wave

The "Wave" concept is about celebrating the people of Waters Avenue. The photographs not only capture the person but what is important to them. For example, Mr. Larry "Gator" Rivers spends his time working with children and teaching them the game of basketball. Mr. Jerome Meadows loves art, and his artwork is captured in his photograph. This direction also shares what the person loves most about Waters, as seen in the first direction, "Pride." This is a very bold direction, with its bright

colors and decorative patterns. The pattern references the residents' African American roots. The wave symbolizes the strength of a wave and the historical connection of Waters Avenue.

The community engagement version is very similar to the individual asset version. There are, however, minor differences. The poster contains a photograph of a person(s) and their name(s), along with one letter from the word "Waters." When the posters are hung next to one another, they spell out "Waters" and form the wave, because each person makes up Waters. Everyone knows as a wave continues, it grows stronger and stronger, eventually becoming so strong that it is unstoppable. This directly relates to the "Wave" direction. As you add more posters to the "wave" or more people become involved with this Waters community, the stronger it becomes. It's about coming together to make a better place.

developed world, it is no wonder that designers are confounded by what they should now do. The crucial subject of waste staring graphic designers in the face is that of e-waste, the detritus of a mediated life essential to the designer in the use of handheld digital devices and the desktop technologies of digital reproduction. This is the very definition of what E. F. Schumacher described as the solution to a problem that creates ten more (1973: 30). Today each new technology seems to increase the amount of new waste tenfold in the form of toxic waste from heavy metals, energy depletion, and lost labor. This also seems to describe what Schumacher saw as an industrial system of cannibalizing the very foundations on which the system rests (1973: 20). The devices that seem to create and reproduce a sense of connectedness may in fact detach people further from humanity and nature.

The principal question is: are the experiences created literally synthetic and therefore similar to what Schumacher described as "the magical effectiveness" of

synthetic materials able to resist degradation by natural forces (1973: 18)? If so, are they further alienating people from nature and therefore increasing a sense that humans are able to conquer natural forces and maintain a lifestyle of privilege through the consumption of artificial experiences? At the very least, attempting to buoy one problem through the creation of another leads to cultural and material imbalances that, if not alleviated, will cause the accumulation of more and more toxicity in all systems both natural and cultural. A dependence on fossil fuels has certainly placed humans in direct opposition to their own best interests. Design's current dependence on digital means of communication and production of knowledge has, as Schumacher described, led to the accumulation of materials that are both equally dangerous and unpredictable (1973: 18).

Schumacher's view was that our position of privilege requires designers to consider what good we can create to counter the excesses of our profession, that it would be better to conserve resources in order to produce new and truly unlimited means of production. As designers who are well placed to influence production and consumption, as well as the users of a variety of digital technologies that produce a significant degree of e-waste, designers should use their position to both reduce waste and to educate others about their use of these technologies. As designers we should not focus too exclusively on graphic design as a discrete skill set applicable to a limited set of solutions but as significant in its ability to influence how and what is produced and consumed, not as Schumacher described, "partial knowledge" (1973: 36), which he forecast correctly as being destructive when applied on a large scale. Designers instead should seek to understand the broad application of design skills to curtailing waste. As Schumacher described, when a system is based on greed, it cannot also exist to meet the needs of humanity but results in failure even when applied to highly successful endeavors (1973: 36).

The Synthetic

The fact that designers are contributing to a synthetic culture equal in its destructive capabilities as any forged in the hearth of the industrial revolution while also being seamlessly beautiful in its aesthetic should give them pause. If this process is being abstracted to such a degree that its fallout is out of sight, are designers being deceived into believing that this system is somehow different from previous industries that produced mind-numbing, stultifying, and toxic-ridden labors? When graphic designers assume that their profession deals only with the surface of the page, package, or screen, they fall into the trap of believing that only the surface matters. Furthermore, they accept at face value the logic of a system that subsumes most facts in service of a few and at the expense of many.

When design becomes a function of simply polishing a surface, it undermines design's creative potential. Designers cannot continue to operate as if only they matter and stop considering the skills they offer in the form of services as only commodities existing equally in relation to all other things on the open market. To continue in this way, designers would have to ignore the costs to themselves as well as others and ultimately undermine the qualities that make themselves creative. What designers do for money is not separate from what they do to enrich themselves creatively and what they can offer to others as not just commodities but also a means of enrichment in terms of social value.

Though designers often deal in abstractions and have a facility for making meaning, people who live downstream of the systems of design in which designers operate are not abstractions. Designers cannot put a price on their own creative potential, much less on the health of others and the planet. In order to operate sustainably as designers, they should seek not only their own creative growth but also how it affects the growth of others. Growth is so often used to describe economic growth alone, rather than expressing organic processes. Designers can seek to grow professionally, but they will not truly succeed if they fail to recognize the ways in which they exist in relationship to humanity and the natural world. What stymies design is both a certain degree of specialization and a myopic view of the process of design. Even though they are generally trained to make connections and create contexts for understanding material things in visual form, designers remain enamored of a mediated workflow and feel they might be immune to its excesses. This is not the case, and the notion reeks of hubris and indifference. Design needs a greater depth of field concerning digital technologies in the same manner as any previous generation of designers to print design, which required not only effective design skill but empathy as well.

Because the technologies designers employ hide both production and consumption beneath a shimmering surface, they can remain forever entranced by what floats above the dingy and dangerous apparatus of production and the rickety scaffolding of consumption. The speed of both production and consumption of digital imagery suggests both an infinite supply but also hides labor and diminishes the value of it all in one click. Though these technologies seem to reduce labor, they only increase the labors of others. This work is not the type that we seek, which is creative and fulfilling but ultimately toxic and debilitating—mentally, physically, and spiritually.

The digital spaces in which designers work only appear neutral and benign. Good design offers proofs of best practices. Design at its best is an antidote to the simplistic worldview where all is reduced to the economics of production and consumption, a view that eliminates both humans and humanity. The designer can employ what Schumacher termed "technology with a human face" (1973: 21, 146–159), which asserts that people are not meta-economic. Technologies that degrade environments also degrade people and are violent in nature to both. Inhuman technologies are not as some might assume metaphorically dehumanizing to an elect class of people whose sensibilities are at risk of being injured. Design is perhaps less than halfway through the digital revolution and has the capacity to reverse the flow and secure and sustain itself.

The Ephemeral and Eternal

The value of designers' creative gifts is not evidenced by the fact that they possess them. They are not really our own but exist only in relation to what we can provide to others. In short, unless we share them, we will never really possess them. The same struggle designers deal with daily—the uneven ground of design where ambiguity is more of a certainty than the concrete—gives designers a great advantage in working toward sustainability. The job of design is now, as it always has been, to make ideas visible. In order to do this, designers must straddle art and commerce, text and image, ephemeral and eternal. They are accustomed to dealing with new subjects in unique contexts. The subject they are now forced to deal with may be unfamiliar, but the activity of it is not. Design is always resisting the mundane to stay on the cutting edge of creative practice. This is not to say designers will always be inventing new forms. Graphic design exists in a relatively closed world of signs and symbols but whose meaning is constantly in play. Just because graphic designers aren't always creating new forms but reusing existing visual language does not mean they are defined by cliché.

The mass culture is at odds with itself, struggling with the cognitive dissonance created by a love of designed artifacts, which is mistaken for a love of consumables and the obvious shortcomings of a throwaway culture. Despite this contradiction, contemporary material culture has sustained value over time despite the advent of consumer capitalism. Mass culture also mistakes the intangible with ephemeral and transient artifacts and experiences. The intangible qualities produced through relationships and attachment to artifacts is derived from their representational power. Design's ability to leverage latent, coded representations should not be underestimated nor misunderstood as trivial. To understand their performative power and profound meaning, designers need only look at their negative inverse in the form of the racialized images discussed in chapter three. The ability of images and words to mold myth and move millions of people has been vividly and systematically reproduced at a dramatic scale.

Design's potential for effecting positive change through myth can only be guessed at, at this point. This can and should be linked to specific ways to change how designers work; this is not to say that a utilitarian emphasis should demand all of design's attention. Designers deal with software and hardware, but what they do is not simply the application of the technological or in the strictest sense a set of tools. This too-narrow focus can lead to a far too prescriptive approach that may exclude the variety of points of view that are needed to reach sustainability. Technology cannot replace the subjective, culturally specific, and meaningful ways of sustaining design. A positivist approach to technological progress has not always maintained truly diverse viewpoints.

The Vernacular

The professionalization of graphic design that occurred in the 1950s and 1960s aligned the profession as it was maturing with a very specific corporate culture and style. This International style proved to be limited in its appeal and effectiveness. What else remains from this confluence of style and power that design should shed? One such area might be its dominance over graphic forms of expressions. The number of nonprofessionals using software designed for professional graphic designers eclipses working designers. Do-it-yourself (DIY) design demonstrates the desire of individuals to assert control over the things they use in addition to how they seek to express themselves. Design should not mistake the ironic, kitschy, and fetishistic quality of some of these goods for simple dilettantism. The success of these modes of making is seen in the fact that professional designers have adopted some of these same vernacular qualities in their own work. It seems clear that even the mere representation of what appears to be an agency of expression in creative production has the power to move designers. The adoption of vernacular forms by professional designers demonstrates the empathetic response needed when designing for subcultures and communities.

Saturation

The current problem with overconsumption cannot be explained away as the result of a materialistic culture built on systematic disposal. If materialism were the problem, mass culture might then overvalue material things. In fact, it undervalues much of the product of human hands and the natural world as well. A materialistic culture implies a care and concern for the material, not only an accumulation of consumer goods. It does though create a situation where that culture both literally and psychically perceives itself as lacking. The feeling of possessing less and less is contradicted by a plethora of goods but reflected in a future in which all our necessary reserves may be depleted. As a culture, we are saturated with the material while also having desaturated our resources. An emphasis on materialism sometimes carries with it a moralistic tone that affects the best of intentions and often colors the discourse on sustainability with an "eat your vegetables" attitude. This attitude is misplaced and based on the idea that being in the right is enough. Holding the moral high ground only leaves design in the position of standing alone and apart from the real needs of others.

Summary of Case Studies

Centro Intercultural de Estudios de Desiertos y Océanos (CEDO)

Ellen McMahon teaches designers to make the world a better place, not with a preconceived agenda, but through close observation and listening, learning about, and understanding the needs of others through collaborative projects. Her background in field biology and scientific illustration has taught her that there is no substitute for firsthand observation and direct experience. Being on site provides the student with a subtle and complex understanding of a place and situation that is not possible to obtain by other means and especially critical when working in economic and cultural situations different from one's own. Traveling is one of the most immediate and effective methods for catalyzing self-examination and questioning. Being in an unfamiliar culture and environment highlights the prejudices, biases, and assumptions that are an unnoticed part of how designers often operate in daily life at home.

The University of Arizona, where McMahon teaches, is located just sixty miles north of the Mexico–US border. University of Arizona faculty and students developed a partnership with the Centro Intercultural de Estudios de Desiertos y Océanos (CEDO Intercultural), a nonprofit binational organization and center of ecological research, environmental education, and conservation in Puerto Peñasco, Mexico. From 2005 to 2010, students in design and illustration classes took frequent three-day trips to stay at CEDO's field station to learn about the culture and environment of the Upper Gulf of California in Sonora, Mexico. Students and faculty stayed at CEDO's field station, which houses CEDO staff and visiting scientists from the United States and Mexico. CEDO staff introduced students and faculty to the oyster growers. All of the projects contributed to unifying CEDO's visual identity and facilitating CEDO's communications with all of its stakeholders.

McMahon's primary goal as an educator is to facilitate the development of all students' visual language and voice through supporting their creative process and increasing their understanding of cultural context. Her goal is for them to ultimately create a niche for themselves within the professional world that is fulfilling and responsible and allows them to keep learning and growing as creative people.

Her main teaching strategy is to listen and look carefully at what each student brings, so she can customize her approach to their interests and learning styles and ultimately bring out their best work. McMahon says, "It's endlessly fascinating for me to witness and participate in the delicate, imprecise, and mysterious process of translation between the non-rational, largely unconscious creative process and the communicative articulation of ideas."

Visual representation is a potent critical activity for both the producer and the receiver as they continuously work to shape an understanding of subjectivity and agency. McMahon takes her students out from behind their computers, out of the classroom, and into the living world. Her academic career started in field biology, moved through scientific illustration, and now encompasses art, design, and writing. Her variegated understanding of the power of all forms of representation to construct meaning and create culture fuels a sense of purpose and responsibility in her teaching and research. This approach to experiential design education grew out of the seminar Critical Issues in Design initiated in 1992 to expose students to the social, cultural, and environmental repercussions of design practice.

The CEDO project was conceived to teach the role of designers and artists in interpreting and communicating about science and the natural world to the unscientific mainstream. This is an increasingly important role for visual communicators as the world gets more technologically and scientifically mediated and complicated. Issues like climate change and human health need to be clarified, explained, and visualized in engaging ways to the general public if design is to reverse the current trend. The project looks at three types of visual practice: (1) the contemporary land art movement, (2) design activism, and (3) new techniques in the visual explanation of scientific information.

One of CEDO's conservation strategies is to support ecologically sustainable micro-businesses in the wetland areas that are most vulnerable to unsustainable tourist development. Única de Mujeres oyster cooperative is a group of women who established the first oyster farm in Sonora and since then have been growing and selling oysters at Morua Estuary since 1982. In 2005, CEDO, together with the Única de Mujeres, supported by the Global Greengrant Fund, constructed a building at the estuary, so they could expand into a restaurant business. When the building was completed, University of Arizona Visual Communication students researched, designed, and painted a natural history mural on all four sides of the building representing the biomes and indigenous flora and fauna of the estuary to serve as an educational tool for ecotourists and other customers and visitors. The project involved several trips to the site, along with ecological, biological, and typographic research. Students made accurate drawings of the plants and animals and designed background forms representing the biomes of the estuary. The mural was composed digitally, and plants, animals, and type were output as line art at actual size. These were perforated with pouncing wheels, transferred onto the wall with bags of chalk dust, and finally painted. The four-sided exterior mural has become a symbol of the potential to protect the ecological integrity and natural beauty of the area through the collaborative creative efforts of local small businesses, the community, CEDO staff, and University of Arizona faculty and students.

These efforts have developed into a conservation and sustainable development initiative called NaturArte, which creates, strengthens, and promotes sustainable ecotourism in Puerto Peñasco's estuaries. Over the last several years, University of Arizona students and faculty have worked with Mexican and US biologists, conservationists, and oyster farmers on the design of interpretive kiosk structures, a bird field guide, identity systems and signage, murals for a restaurant and two ecotour businesses, brochures, and a website. By supporting environmentally sustainable, locally run businesses, NaturArte provides opportunities for the local community and exciting learning experiences for visitors. It was founded on the belief that increasing the economic value of the natural resources to the community improves the chances of them being protected. Students see how their efforts affect policy and public opinion, making it increasingly difficult for highrise tourist developers to approach these ecologically important wetlands as if they were empty lots. The design projects build on each other and add up to an informed and persuasive argument for the value of these estuaries to human and nonhuman communities alike.

It is an ongoing challenge for designers to understand and be responsive to the needs of their collaborators and end users, especially when they are working in economic and cultural situations different from their own. Being there provides a subtle and complex understanding of a place and situation that is not possible to achieve by other means. Design education, like all education, involves raising awareness. By traveling to Mexico, contributing their skills to real-world situations for the long-term care of the planet, students glean new insights into their potential cultural, social, and environmental agency as visual communicators and global citizens. Student trips to Mexico were suspended in 2010 because of increased violence in the border region and the N1H1 influenza outbreak, but projects are ongoing. McMahon received a 2007 Fulbright Scholars Grant to contribute as a designer, writer, and artist to these interdisciplinary-conservation projects in Puerto Peñasco, Sonora, Mexico.

Students improve all of the design and illustration skills they have learned in the classroom as well as new skills required for mural painting and bilingual visual communication. These are applied to projects that raise awareness about sustaining the fragile ecology of the Gulf of California wetlands. The particulars students learn by firsthand observation about the complex interdependencies in the ecology of the estuary can then be applied to natural systems throughout the planet.

Traveling to and working in Mexico is particularly beneficial to this group of students living so close to the US–Mexico border. For the minority of students with Mexican heritage, it means being on familiar ground, surrounded by their first language. They tend to take leadership roles in the group, acting as translators of language and culture. For some of the US students, going to Mexico for the first time is disorienting and frightening, whereas others know the area as a spring break destination. Going in the context of the class allows all of the students to see Mexico, themselves, and each other in a new light. Some of the learning experiences are planned, like the tide pool tours and ecology lectures. Others are not, like the differential treatment students get, based on appearances, at border patrol check points in the United States.

Design Global Change

In 2009, Natacha Poggio began Design Global Change (DGC) through a partnership with the chapter of Engineers Without Borders (EWB) at the University of

Hartford in Connecticut. The project Water for India began in her Issues in Design course. In 2010, she received a Sappi: Ideas That Matter grant to carry out the work in the field.

EWB was already at work in India on the project and needed help with communicating the content to the public it was intended to serve. Poggio and her students coordinated with the engineers to refine the message. Poggio, as a native of Argentina teaching in the United States, was well aware of unseen issues and the need for assessment of the results, through feedback from the users, to determine what if any progress was being made. The design therefore exists not only in the specific artifacts, posters, and murals but also in the process. The process included a series of feedback loops to create an empathetic, context-specific design. The students learned the need to be involved and stay involved over time, rather than simply reacting to an assignment at the eleventh hour. They were able to see how their design skills are applicable not only to specific types of aesthetic problems but to systematic issues as well. Once the skill set is widened to account for end use and for lasting value, this systematic approach can be applied to various specific contexts. Students were tasked not with designing for their aesthetic pleasure or an abstract notion of poverty but for a specific community and out of real necessity. The students then formed their own community in response, made up of themselves, the engineers, and their teachers. The aesthetic value of the work, though important, stems from the research and work done in the field with the intended audience and users. The value of the design was extended through collaboration with other disciplines and as it was adapted to meet the users' needs.

The project helped the students to overcome their assumptions about the value of their design work. The feedback from the children helped them understand that what performs well under certain cultural conditions might not apply to all situations. The process helped them see that what designers sometimes assume to be universal standards of communication are often what people have come to expect in the Western world. Graphic designers schooled in an essentialist approach to design assume that iconographic and pictographic conventions are similar across cultures, as in the case where young girls in the rural Indian village of Abheypur saw in one of the banners depicting the act of hand washing as a worshipful response to water.

The project has now been enlarged through Bringing Girls into Focus, a gender equality campaign raising awareness of women's important roles in rural communities through the use of educational materials. The DGC created a set of cards depicting Indian men and women in various roles (e.g., collecting water, farming, selling goods); these cards aim to trigger conversations about gender issues among high school youth and are accompanied by a teacher's guidebook, which will be used to provide educational activities to raise awareness.

Following the same classroom methodology applied to Water4India—and in collaboration with the Africa Center for Engineering Solutions (ACESS) in the Spring of 2009—Issues in Design students worked on a wellness campaign for Kenya titled Afya Kwanzaa (Wellness First). The campaign uses *kangas* (a traditional cotton garment wore by women in sub-Saharan Africa) to communicate four important topics:

1. Amaranth Promotion: nutrition, planting, harvesting, cooking
2. Safe Water: boiling water, washing hands, washing containers
3. Women's Safety: walking in groups to prevent possible assault
4. Disease Prevention: avoiding stagnant water to prevent malaria

Professor Natacha Poggio traveled to the Rift Valley in Kenya in July 2009 as part of a collaborative team of faculty from the University of Hartford, Brown University, and the University of Rhode Island. She met with farmers and villagers to discuss the different student designs, and the feedback obtained was applied to new kanga designs produced in the summer of 2010.

Poggio has continued her work with LIMBS International, a nonprofit humanitarian organization that designs, creates, and offers low-cost, high-quality prosthetics to amputees worldwide. The collaboration with the College of Education, Nursing and Health Professions aimed to design education materials for patients from different backgrounds, many of whom are illiterate. The purpose of these materials is to facilitate the rehabilitation process and provide comprehensive education for clinicians (local practitioners who fit the prosthetic device or a certified rehabilitation clinician), patients, and their families. Both faculty and their students worked to design posters, brochures, and a clinician's manual to be used worldwide to teach patients how to exercise, climb stairs, use crutches, and generally move safely with their new prosthetic leg. The materials inform users how to care for their amputated limbs and when to go to a health clinic.

It is estimated that somewhere between 3 million and 11 million amputees worldwide are in need of a prosthesis, with approximately 80 percent of those living in low-income countries. These individuals are usually forced to exist as dependents with little hope of a productive role in their society. The highest demand for lower-extremity prostheses exists in areas where extensive walking is a routine part of each day. Unfortunately, these areas are generally located within the poorest countries, where technology is the least advanced and resources are scarce. Even if someone is lucky enough to receive a prosthesis after years of waiting, physical therapists are seldom available to teach patients how to use their new limbs. LIMBS has established eight training centers that serve thirty-five clinics in twenty-two countries. Certified local practitioners assemble, fit, and maintain the prosthetic devices for patients, but the fitting and initial gait training is done by the local practitioner, who has no physical rehabilitation training. Because this one-time session lasts only a few hours, patients often develop inefficient gait patterns after using the prostheses incorrectly.

The Department of Rehabilitation Sciences hired a model with an above-the-knee amputation and fitted him with a LIMBS prosthetic leg. Physical therapy students documented the entire rehabilitation process, photographing the model exercising while sitting and standing, and performing various gait-training activities. DGC faculty and students, realizing that a Caucasian model was not representative of the diverse people LIMBS was seeking to help, turned the photos into illustrations, so that the skin color, facial features, and body type could be altered graphically to better reflect the primary race of a specific region. They then designed concise educational posters and brochures with only minimal headings to facilitate communication for people with limited literacy. With the intent to study the effectiveness of these rehabilitation materials, field testing of the posters (printed in vinyl banners) and take-home brochures was conducted in Peru, Kenya, and Uganda during spring break 2014. The results showed that the materials were effective, although adjustments to the graphics are necessary. Materials need to be converted to reflect the race of not only these countries, but also the other thirty-five clinics worldwide.

Conversations That Change Us: Facilitating Citizen Networks

Building on insightful approaches to community resilience, The Role of Design in Social Awareness is a graduate class taught by Scott Boylston in the graphic design department at the Savannah College of Art and Design (SCAD) that applies human-centered design methodologies and multi-stakeholder engagement tools to help such communities overcome challenges through visual communication tools that empower their residents. In situations where marginalized communities are so battered by vicious cycles of economic and social setbacks, one of the first losses they experience is a sense of efficacy, and specifically, a faith in their own residents to effect positive change.

Through methods that, thankfully, are becoming increasingly common in design and design education, five students taking this Social Awareness class were introduced to one such community in Savannah, Georgia, with only ten weeks to co-create design solutions that were meaningful to that community. The students were beneficiaries of two longer-term initiatives at SCAD intended to facilitate deeper interactions between students and the local population. The social innovation efforts of SCAD's Design Ethos DO-ference in 2012 have continued to provide a more vibrant network of interaction among local communities, professors, students, and classes, while the graduate degree in Design for Sustainability offers ongoing classes in social innovation, which are designed specifically to build off previous work. With these mechanisms providing a more consistent continuum of meaningful interactions, classes such as the one written about here have the means by which their work can more readily connect to the local community. In fact, this case study is an example of one of the foundational efforts within both of the aforementioned initiatives.

The project parameters were straightforward, if anything but simple: create engaging and insightful portraits of residents residing along the Waters Avenue corridor in Savannah as a means of raising the community's awareness of its own human assets and, in doing so, further a conversation of hope and self-reliance. The decision to work with the neighborhoods along Waters Avenue was made, in part, to align with a City of Savannah revitalization initiative that the residents were feeling ambivalent toward. Even as they had hope that the revitalization project would rejuvenate their community, they were distrustful of the city's intentions based on past city-led initiatives that were insensitive to their fundamental needs.

Scott Boylston's project aimed to equip the residents to work more actively and effectively with the city government and to supply them with tools that would prevent similar results, as well as outcomes that would put them at a disadvantage in the face of potential gentrification. The class began with a foundational concept that could be summed up in three words—We Are Waters—which were intended to place emphasis on the fact that the Waters Avenue residents were the most valuable assets they possessed. And the potential deliverables were understood to be visual depictions of ordinary citizens as empowered change agents. The form of these visuals would be dictated through the process of identifying the most effective means of sharing such concepts with the broader community.

Thanks to five previous classes that had worked side by side with the surrounding neighborhoods, this particular class had the ability to introduce themselves to the community through a carefully crafted collaboration with three community keystones, or pillars. This small group embodied the class's focus on *community, culture, and commerce*: a community leader, a public artist, and a business leader. These individuals contributed to the class process in myriad ways. First, through extensive taped interviews conducted by the students during the early weeks of class, they provided a wealth of knowledge about the neighborhood's history and present conditions from an insider's perspective. The weekly interviews were supplemented by home visits, photographic essays, and human-centered design engagement activities, such as shadowing, self-documentation, and self-expression. Second, the pillars introduced the students to other residents who would have otherwise been mistrustful of them, making the deeper transition into the neighborhood more genuine and more effective.

These keystone community members also connected the students further into the neighborhoods through their respective organizations: Jerome Meadows (the public artist) through the Indigo Sky Community Gallery; Freddie Patrick (the community leader) through the Eastside Concerned Citizens; and Sidney J. Johnson (the business leader) through his organization Waters Avenue Business Association (WABA). Each of these locations along Waters Avenue became meeting places for students and the community for countless discussions. In this way, the citizen network that the class relied on to learn about the community grew in depth and breadth. Finally, early interaction with the community pillars helped students gain a level of comfort in a role that had been foreign to them before this class (design facilitator), in a neighborhood that was even more foreign to them. To make this process of immersion even more interesting, the class consisted of only one native US-born English speaker, who was joined by one Indian, one Bulgarian, and two Chinese students.

The nurturing of a citizen network that the students could work with was instrumental for the success of the project. The secondary layer of interaction focused on an array of individuals from three different demographic groups in the neighborhood: high school students, elderly residents, and small business owners. These groups had been identified by a previous class as marginalized, overlooked, or underutilized members of the community. These individuals were interviewed, photographed, and provided the means to self-document their lives through human-centered design tools, much like the pillars before them. In an interesting twist, the students actually facilitated new conversations between neighbors through the development of their citizen network.

It was at this time that the class carried with them large letters spelling out WATERS and strolled through the neighborhoods with members of their citizen network. It was understood that photographs of residents holding individual letters could become a key visualization for a poster campaign, but the initial idea was simply to start a conversation about how residents self-identified with Waters Avenue. Throughout this period of intensive immersion, the students were also developing concepts for their poster campaigns—a format that had risen to the top of the list for class deliverables through conversations with the community at large. The idea was to explore ways to celebrate ordinary residents who possessed the requisite knowledge, vitality, creativity, and compassion to help residents of the neighborhood navigate their shared challenges.

By the third week of the quarter, each member of the SCAD team had designed a rough series of posters based on their experiences with the people of Waters Avenue. Poster designs incorporated photographs of individuals within the citizen network as well as quotes from them that focused on the aspirational aspects of living along Waters Avenue. Traditional critiques had been held within the comfort of the SCAD classroom during the second and third week of the quarter, but they were merely warmups for the big event: a community critique.

During a public meeting held at the Asbury Memorial United Methodist Church, the project scope of the class was shared with the attendees, and the students covered several tables with their initial designs, accompanied by sticky notes, pads and pens for the residents to use. The meeting, which focused primarily on updates to the revitalization initiative, ended with a vibrant discussion of the community's opinion of the poster designs, and every community member was invited to write down his or her reactions. With such a wide array of solutions on display, the residents could plainly see that the SCAD students were earnestly investigating possibilities that resonated with them rather than attempting to dictate a design direction. The positive community response was a testament to the open creative process the class had undertaken.

Before the academic quarter began, outreach to city government agencies that were leading the revitalization effort was essential. This gave the students the opportunity to redesign their solutions with feedback from the residents of Waters Avenue and present their work to the Assistant City Manager's office and the Community Development office the following week. Learning early on in the quarter about this opportunity, the students realized that they could play an essential facilitation role between the city and the community. After all, they had learned so much about Waters Avenue through their citizen network, and an audience with the city administration placed them in a role they had never considered before as graphic designers. Through presentations of their poster designs, they articulated the aspirations and concerns of the citizens of Waters Avenue directly to city representatives. This meeting resulted in a further commitment to support the project on behalf of the city and a powerful sense of agency for the students, who gained a new found appreciation for the power of design as a facilitation tool.

Each of the five students had been developing their own designs with a rich flow of feedback, but there was no longer any way to continue forward with so many different directions. After the Asbury Church critique and the City presentation, the class had to narrow down their design solutions. This task was much less contentious than one might expect, because the patterns of positive responses from the community had been building up consistently. The class narrowed the designs down to the three favorite directions and created teams to refine them.

The next opportunity to present the work to the community cast an even larger net for feedback. The WW Law Center is a community center frequented by every demographic sector along the Waters Avenue corridor. Programs offered by the center range from youth athletics to board games for elderly citizens and everything in between. The three most successful poster sets (each numbering five, with the idea that new residents would be featured on newly printed posters every six to eight months) were hung in the center with prompts for residents to pick their favorites and make suggestions about how to make them better. This display was accompanied by a ballot box and was left up on the walls for two weeks to ensure maximum feedback opportunities.

Throughout the two weeks of final community feedback at the WW Law Center, the graphic design students spent time at the center speaking with individuals who had questions and thoughts about the final solutions. Such interaction at the center had become commonplace over the last few months. After two weeks, votes were tallied and comments were synthesized and analyzed. The written votes and suggestions were tallied, along with responses to the three sets from earlier feedback sessions and feedback received during conversations with residents at the center and the leadership at the center. Two of the three designs received a similar amount of votes, and their strengths and weaknesses were considered through a design principles lens. Furthermore, to close the circle, the final solutions were shared with the community pillars with whom the students had begun the process. Finally, all of this information was shared with the Public Information Office of the City of Savannah, and the city staff had internal discussions.

The final posters have been used within the community as a means to raise awareness of the community's own best assets. The first run of the posters was modest, with digital prints that could easily fit in storefront windows and on community and church bulletin billboards. Plans for printing larger posters as the revitalization continues are underway. A key deliverable beyond the final poster solutions in this and other social innovation courses at SCAD is a Pass it On Document—a comprehensive document that includes thorough process steps, extensive insights, and project contacts—that can be shared with any individual, organization, business, or ensuing class so that they can continue forward progress on the larger vision. These documents have made it much easier to move forward from one quarter to the next on numerous ongoing initiatives with the community, despite the ongoing changes in student participation.

Chapter Six
Teaching Graphic Design at a Human Scale

Graphic design is not a single category describing a vocation but rather a series of activities related to cultural production and the expression of the popular imagination through words and images. It is also not simply a skill set, as multifaceted as it may be, dependent on specific technologies, but is in fact related to the need over time to communicate through those words and images. If designers imagine that it is a skill set learned in trade schools, colleges, and universities to serve industry alone, then they will isolate the profession and educate students who are dependent on perfecting a skill set that may cease to exist before they can realize its value. If graphic design continues to be taught in this manner, this will at best maintain an institutionalized method for teaching design, keep pace with industry standards, and reflect the public's desire to see their thoughts and feelings in print. At worst it is unsustainable, if seen simply as an agent of consumption.

If designers imagine that the teaching of graphic design exists only as an extension of the marketplace and only in service to its needs, then they will continue to overlook the discipline's basis for existing. Graphic design studies cannot simply be an extension of industry, because in most cases a design education precedes practice. If designers assume that the market's role is to draw students from graphic design programs, then they forget that the average university student exists already as part of a social class prepared to enter higher education regardless of the promise of paid work in a specific profession. Even in the absence of the promise of a career or at least a first job in graphic design, a college-age student will still enter college.

Art schools provided much of the labor force that served the graphic design field in the first three-quarters of the twentieth century with little or no specific instruction in graphic design. The training was often almost completely divorced from the modern experience, especially in the United States, where sources as divergent as the Bauhaus and the Beaux Arts provided individuals who were capable of basic hand skills and had a background in the history of art and art forms. Graphic design education has been theoretically based on what is believed to be formal instruction in basic design principles but what is in reality an expression of an ideology of design. This ideology developed in part as a curious strain and a sometimes conservative reaction to Modernism. This ideology persisted in art and design schools beyond the point at which it was largely rejected by many artists and designers as being a product of large institutions and centralized power—as being authoritarian.

This manner of teaching, presented as basic design principles, existed along with many more experimental forms of teaching, learning, and designing, although in most cases these existed theoretically as the antidote to the other. Great designers and teachers of design were seen as possessing both formal and informal design attributes and skills. This paradox was sometimes used to explain how they could also exist in the world of professional design without formal training in design while still representing its essential qualities. This too was mirrored in a designer's ability to conduct the business of design with one foot in the art world. A manifestation of concerns about feminized art spaces versus the "real world" of business and industry inflected the perspective as well. In the more experimental, informal methods of teaching, spaces were created to consider design methodologies that questioned design forms and systems of design but also offered the opportunity to reject the prevailing ideology of design: that is, a graphical representation of the modern world that was centralized and dependent on maintaining large systems.

The Ideology of the Ideal

This formalist representation of design was an effort to codify design pedagogy but resulted in its reification as an ideal. Its representation as the ideal rather than as

the ideological was perpetuated, because it was located as the theoretical basis for future design practice in an ideal world where design would serve a permanent and substantial role. It was not truly forward thinking but was a static representation of the machine aesthetic, one that was already being replaced or perhaps transgressed to some extent by new popular forms such as television. Television was, in fact, an expression of a new industrial revolution of moving images, which created the seedbed for Postmodernism. Design education emerging in the postwar period was ineffective in transforming design to tackle problems of sustainability that in a postindustrial design context would seem to suddenly appear as being far beyond the reach of the profession.

What did emerge and did impact design practice and pedagogy was a tsunami of digital design and reproduction technology across creative practice in the late twentieth and early twenty-first centuries. The development of the Mac and postscript printing was in keeping with the attitudes and applied thinking of many of those influenced by Buckminster Fuller and as represented in *The Whole Earth Catalog* (1969). Once adopted, these technologies also led to the absorption of the pragmatic countercultural bent of the catalog's creator, Stewart Brand, as described by Kirk in *Counterculture Green* (2007: 1–12). This was an easy leap for designers who were already engaged in commerce through graphic design practice and the complexity of navigating consumption, technology, and aesthetics. In addition, the Mac as the ideal form of the personal computer reflected the desire of most graphic designers to work beyond larger institutional models, and at once also seemed to personify this desire in a Lacanian dialogue with technology as image-making. The speed at which this paradigm shift occurred in graphic design clearly describes the creative impulses of the designer as in tandem with technology and commerce.

It also fit nicely with E. F. Schumacher's description of sustainable technologies that were at small scale, compatible with "man's creativity" (1973: 36), and in this case relatively cheap, at least to the creative professionals who were already engaged in designing. Ironically, design as a practice was challenged in the convergence created by desktop publishing. The rapidly ensuing reality of the total means of production, easily obtained and utilized, led designers to question their role as mediators between people and ideas, essentially the fear that machines could replace them. Schumacher also expressed this fear as common to the era in which he wrote, when technology was a suspected threat to humanity on an individual and titanic scale. What wasn't yet appreciated was the degree to which the mediated life would dominate culture and would cause the machine to become nearly invisible, except as a canvas on which to explore ideas.

The notion that technology could both capture and transcend mediation was not in keeping with the ideologically based Swiss style of design that influenced so many designers in the postwar period. McLuhan (1964) had of course anticipated this convergence of self and technology through consumption but as "media" not as "design." That designers would design the ways in which others mediate and therefore design their own experience is fraught with ambivalence resulting from the role of consumption in contemporary life and its material and spiritual fallout.

Style and the Vernacular

This material and spiritual fallout was further complicated by the sudden emergence of vernacular design forms in the 1980s and 1990s, in what is sometimes referred to as grunge. This vernacular aesthetic followed the rapid rise of the personal computer. The old design guard assumed that distressed type and disjointed grids were a manifestation of digital technology, as style, applied to graphic design. As David Carson asserts, it was not his intention to bring down established forms, but rather his naiveté and good timing that led to his meteoric rise (Hustwit 2007). His imitators made good on the threat to the Swiss style in their application of digital technology in mimicking vernacular forms. The emergence of grunge as a stylistic trope named for a musical genre from the Northwest United States is likely not accidental. It served as both an antidote to conventionality and an embracing of the "authentic" at a time when alternative or countercultural lifestyles were entering the mainstream in a diversity of forms. The eclecticism of grunge further supports it as a defining aesthetic of the alternative in a space and time where interest in alternative lifestyles was emerging in a myriad of forms and from sources that were not always originally aligned with activist-based environmentalism.

Musical style and the detritus of consumption as primary source material for a creative lifestyle makes clear the generational shift, as described by Richard Florida

in *The Rise of the Creative Class* (2002: 85–101). An emerging generation of digital natives reflected the principles of individual agency and autonomy expressed in *The Whole Earth Catalog* and began to influence the cultural landscape. The development of a new aesthetic in the Northwest United States, as part of a leisure-based lifestyle in an urban environment enclosed—perhaps even preserved—by water, trees, mountains, and sky is indicative of what Kirk described as reconciling the "contradictory connections between consumption, leisure, technology and nature" (2007: 13). But what does all of this have to do with graphic design education and sustainability?

Human-Centered Pedagogies

In teaching design, most instructors and teachers are influenced first by the pragmatic. Their chief concern being to prepare students to work in the field or at least to prepare them to enter and then learn through professional practice. In application, this pedagogy is often subsumed by a desire to make immediate and meaningful connections with individual students. In the space between the individual and teacher, larger concerns collapse into a concern for that individual. The classroom is a space where one learner and one teacher can share in growth and discovery and engage the student's potential to exceed the teacher and the often increasingly limited scope of a teacher's direct professional experience.

In graphic design, it's typical to insist that the teacher possess direct and perhaps extensive professional experience. It is right to assume the teacher understands in practice the ways that design and commerce are products of each other and the manner in which each is constrained by the other. What is overlooked is that experience, no matter how extensive, is always limited. Therefore, experience cannot teach everything if we are to depend on teachers. Teaching is not simply the job of instructing a group but is instead about the activity of learning and based in an ethos innate to the teacher. The teacher has a keen awareness upon first entering the classroom that he or she possesses a great quantity of hard-won experience but also lacks much of what is needed to teach design. It is simply too broad a field. By walking into a classroom, the teacher embodies the future hopes of the students and all the shortcomings of any predecessors.

Although limited by experience, the teacher is tasked with enlarging the students' knowledge base beyond what can be learned alone in either the classroom or the marketplace. If the teacher is successful, students will be educated in how to educate themselves. In the area of sustainability, this is crucial. The design students who learn to think through the act of designing and who are exposed to concepts related to sustainability are well positioned to tackle problems and solutions for sustainability in ways that are inaccessible to those trained in other fields. The ways in which sustainability might be taught should be grounded in a pedagogy that is personal and therefore sustainable at a scale that is human. Human scale begins in the space between two people, where the personal space of the two is delicately breached, in this case between one student and one teacher. Following that, a set of criteria for modeling learning should incorporate elements of the noninstitutional learning, professional practice, or direct application and play.

Nonprescriptive learning produces outcomes with varying degrees of specificity. The design teacher must be grounded in a discipline and research area to learn with confidence along with the students. The teacher's own research guides the methodology wherein the teacher teaches to his or her strengths, even if it reveals weaknesses. This creates a space wherein experimentation and often failure is also allowed. Success is achieved through one's ability to continue a line of thinking beyond conventional outcomes. The proper relationship between teacher and students is one in which trust rather than power is the basis. This strategy undermines the teacher's inclination to teach to dogma. If designers reject typical design pedagogy as ideology, then they will likely eschew dogma as impractical and unsustainable. A continual requestioning of the goals of the learning process must be applied if the design students are allowed to work in defining the question of what is to be designed. This method teaches the students to find connections rather than follow a path of study and to design their own education.

A human-centered approach should focus on raising expectations. Raising the teacher's expectations of the students raises the students' expectations of themselves. Teaching at a human scale involves, by necessity, collaboration among students and teachers. The inclusion of other players from outside the students' comfort area adds an interdisciplinary dynamic, an essential aspect of sustainable design thinking. This dynamic is defined not simply by collaboration with others but as a breaking down of disciplines as defined by market-driven career paths. Small groups working in parallel rather than strictly in competition allow groups to cross-pollinate ideas and techniques. Small groups can learn to manage themselves to avoid having to dictate too much to too many people.

Many of these ideas relate directly to ideas and practices that emerged through the appropriate technology movement of the 1960s and 1970s. In this milieu, decentralized technology was rejected in favor of localized, vernacular, and small-scale approaches to design. This design movement focused on tool-making, invention, and hands-on learning by nonexperts. It possessed little in the way of aesthetic sensibility except in its lack of polish. It did have parallels in the alternative and underground press movement and in the revival of graphic forms from the Arts and Crafts and Art Nouveau movements, along with vernacular imagery from the Victorian era, as well as the revival of craft traditions. Archaic or recently sidelined technologies, such as the letterpress, a quickly diminishing form in the 1960s among printers, were revitalized during this time. Poster workshops associated with civil rights and other social justice movements, along with alternative papers and magazines, facilitated a more pluralistic society that emerged through old technologies to embrace difference as an aesthetic.

Design as antidote to technocracy and expert knowledge funneled progressive impulses toward what today is referred to as do-it-yourself (DIY). Both then and now, there exists a desire through these practices to simplify and reestablish the designer's relationship to authentic or original work as well as to technology. Design is able to constantly resuscitate its relationship to technology and consumption in the complicated and ambivalent relationship of design to nature, as expressed in preserving archaic or authentic ways of making. Today, DIY production and consumption is being transformed not as transgressive to nature but in close association with small-scale, local, and creative forms of commodity design. The boutique quality of these forms is rapidly influencing designers and nondesigners alike in an effort to assert personal identity in the face of corporate consolidation of cultural production.

Any effort to teach human-centered design to those who would seek to practice it should make the design students first aware of their relationship to designed images and artifacts and then nurture them in defining and giving voice to who they are in service to their primary identity in a life that feels eclipsed by institutional identities. If per chance the design students quit practicing design past graduation, they will have learned to form their self in relationship, not to brands, but as a product of their own making through design. This mode of individual agency is in keeping with many of the goals of a wide range of the countercultural subgroups of the 1960s. These movements' broader goals of collective action across a wide spectrum of smaller groups anchored by inspired individuals and leaders who lived their lives as activists and often as artists and designers points the way for establishing a human-centered design education.

This history marks a method of teaching where individuals reach their maximum performance level prepared to design as well for themselves as they might for others. This personal approach to design teaching is quite appealing to the pragmatic student personalities that populate design programs, wherein individual creativity is seen largely as an apolitical act. In the present political milieu, the conceit that the political has outgrown a complicated contemporary context is appealing to young people. They believe that politics rather than consumption is spiritually and materially polluting. This marks the end of the age during which baby boomers saw themselves as antithetical to commodity culture. The current emphasis on DIY cultural production lovingly nurtures an ironic and eclectic expression of consumption in a way that reframes personal identity, transcending sacred cows of the 1960s and 1970s such as race, feminism, and sexuality.

The Politics of Design

Common among the current generation of design students in the United States is a general belief that the middle has moved to the right politically, and therefore the content of reactionary right-wing politics positioned against environmentalism is in itself not political but drained—like so many wetlands—of its political content, its -ism. The position of many students is that to be an environmental activist is to simply oppose the status quo in ways that are outdated and perhaps destructive. Design education can overcome the ambivalent and sometimes cynical disposition of today's students by employing them in directing and defining their own creative energy toward pragmatic and scalable design learning. Through projects that engage students with real problems and possess a one-to-one relationship to their own role as consumers and designers, they can quickly come to terms with their impacts and their real abilities as designers to make a difference. Students may remain ambivalent about the politics of sustainability, but their pessimism can be dislodged in favor of design as a solution to nearly any problem and as a means to question dominant societal narratives. Design's broad application across a wide variety of localized issues reinforces both its personal, small-scale, and nonspecific power, contradicting its large-scale, specialized, technological imperatives.

Material and Materialism

Design's power as a way of visualizing thinking in action rather than a purely theoretical exercise for the classroom is manifested when students work in small groups and on small projects with a large potential to affect production and consumption. The insight gained from this experience is that individuals working in small groups over time can produce exponentially positive change. What is especially useful to students is an intimate engagement with processes and materials. The material nature of design in dealing with production and consumption can lead to a serious and specific interrogation of not only the practical concerns surrounding how to pick and choose the best materials but also with materialism itself. Through careful consideration of what materials are best suited for each application, students come to understand how efficiency and reduction of waste are vital to what they do. This ongoing research process insinuates itself into the ways students act to change their own consumption. The result is the application of creativity to everyday choices and a concrete way to consider what is bought and used and wasted every day.

A serious and specific discussion of materialism as a lifestyle based on systematic obsolescence has been needed in design education since at least the 1950s. An education in design as a component of general education for all students could very well provide that solution. Because design is not just about objects but also ideas, it can help make sense of how things are made and why.

Design also demonstrates that people are neither separate from nature nor from technology. The ground designers occupy is inherently ambiguous and therefore changing. It is furthermore not pure, nor is it sullied by its interaction with so many of the problems of contemporary life. Pure design, or so-called good design, does not need to be defined; rather it should be diagnosed as a problem that must first be overcome before we can actually set about securing solutions to real problems that must be faced. There is no ideologically pure design. It cannot be reduced to pill form. By seeking to create and then hold to a pure design, designers give up their strength as creators and make themselves irrelevant by ceding that strength to others.

Today, more designers are graduating from a variety of schools, but what are they being trained to do? There is an overabundance of people trained as designers, but their talent and training often goes unused. The issue of what resources we have or do not have is central to the debate on sustainability. What is valued is used well; what is not tends to be wasted. Where there exists a lack of resources or access to them, this forms or reinforces a worldview based on scarcity, on the absence of resources, and one in which many people are likely to seek to preserve what little remains rather than risk losing it. But how do designers help in using what exists, make more and better use of it, and continue to generate new resources?

The resources possessed in design education are principally time, students, and teachers, but also the intellectual pursuits and process of discovery that generate the experience of a design education. When a feeling of scarcity pervades in design schools, it can lead to many students overlooking what is truly vital to learning. It is not simply a matter of making do with what little is at hand but of using it well and not overlooking what is possessed in terms of students and teachers. These are design's two most important resources. The third—and at heart the principal resource in all of this—is creativity itself.

Incubators of Critical Exploration

A centralized, hierarchical, specialized, formalist, and siloed system of teaching and thinking have led to an impasse in the teaching of design. This impasse can be broken by recentering design education on collaborative learning among teachers, students, and communities through interdisciplinary projects that engage the diversity of issues associated with sustainability. What, if anything, should university teachers and students be working on but creating new ways to research how design can effect positive change? What else should classrooms be utilized as but incubators of critical design exploration? This would avoid morally bankrupt methods of teaching that treat the students as consumable—a resource to be used and then discarded with each new batch. Simply preparing design students to enter the field ready to exchange their creative labors for a paycheck does not reflect a university or college's mission.

Teachers and students as the two primary resources in making positive change can be defined as capital. In *Natural Capitalism* (1999: 4), Paul Hawken describes four types of capital that are necessary to an economy. He defines the first type, human capital, as capital in the form of intelligence, culture, and organization (he then goes on to describe financial, manufactured, and natural capital). Certainly, design and education both fall under this definition of human capital. None of the latter forms of capital can exist without the first being supported and maintained.

Describing what designers create as capital helps define the value of both design and an education in design. If they can work within this sphere to both maintain design practice and its positive effects on natural capital beyond simply containing present impacts, then they'll begin to define what sustainable design is. As Hawken describes, industrialization devalued and marginalized natural and human capital in favor of output. If design is to be taught sustainably, then designers will need to work holistically and collaboratively to reemphasize the value of cultural production. It seems logical to conclude that the same forces that are currently depleting natural capital are depleting human capital.

An example of this subject lies in the fallow fields of landfills and is described by Heather Rogers in her book *Gone Tomorrow: The Hidden Life of Garbage* (2005: 204). Rogers relates the narrow focus on waste disposal to a trust in technology and experts as losing sight of what is most important, an abundance of natural resources in the form of waste, which are largely exported. In the present, designers have lost sight of human capital as it relates to teaching design in favor of digital technologies that seem to expand the designers' vision but in fact narrow their field. Mistaking digital proficiency for design aptitude causes designers to enter into a whole series of mistaken assumptions about what it means to both teach and learn design. In untangling this view, designers may be able to come to terms with their own complicity in facilitating the overproduction and overconsumption of designed images and artifacts built into systems of waste that design also works to abstract.

Greening the Graphic Design Education

What is relevant to the teaching of graphic design in a future where material limitations and the virtual design experience threaten to dominate? A graphic design education emphasizing sustainability offers much in terms of securing the role of the designer in commerce as well as contemporary culture.

Several important themes emerge when we look at the efforts of individual design professors and instructors infusing the present design curriculum with classes and projects that address systematic environmental problems and the impact design can have on them. What tends to emerge first is an increased appreciation of a holistic approach to the teaching of graphic design, which includes the study of a variety of visual artifacts, the larger built environment, and the ordinary products of consumption. This interdisciplinary model tends to diminish the insularity of graphic design education while still emphasizing the basics of graphic design that we have come to accept and expect. The recent renewal and rapid increase in the appreciation of the severity of environmental problems within popular culture has certainly provided much of the impetus for this change, but design educators are also sincerely interested in making the consequences of design real to their students and demonstrating design's importance to the broader culture that is often, but not always, manifest.

The timeliness of the subject increases with the obvious connection between design and consumption, as well as the need to emphasize design as a process apart from commerce that can exist to serve the greater good. Design education, it would seem, is always in need of ways to make clear to students the creative potential of design. It may seem obvious that increased creativity among design educators and students is emerging in response to environmental problems, but because it is not a value common to other fields and has only recently been adopted

as a management tactic, its importance cannot be overstated. The means by which ideas occur and the methods for increasing and maintaining the development of new ideas must come from design in order to solve systemic environmental problems. It's difficult to isolate themes in sustainable design education given that a holistic approach is necessary and desired. That said, the following topics are offered to those seeking to make change within design education to further effect change across society.

Research

More than anything else, intensive research is cited as necessary to a sustainable design curriculum. Projects should ask students to uncover and make sense of complex issues and how they exist as part of the systems of design largely outside the control of the graphic designer. In addition, students should be tasked with investigating how the graphic designer plays a role in the structure or workings of these systems and can as a result create strategies to effect change. Designing for complex information requires advanced instruction in typography and, by extension, information design. These skills are essential. Furthermore, students should investigate whether information can be sustainably archived, accessed, and communicated. Most important to this process is the search, not for solutions to well-known problems and immediately available answers, but a quest for the right *questions*. Assumptions should be laid aside, especially those that imply the need for a product, as well as questions that marketers find useful in evaluating how consumers can be made aware of a product or service. The first question that should be asked is whether the artifact is truly needed. That in turn will determine a whole set of questions related to production and consumption.

Nonprescriptive

The laying aside of assumptions leads to the next theme, which is to avoid prescribing design solutions. This method rejects the notion that it is enough for the graphic designer to learn the forms regarded as common to the field. For instance, the assumption that what is needed is another logo, a poster, or a website. The highly reductive nature of many of these forms is often useful in making known a basic concept or an emotion, but these forms are not universal, as is commonly supposed. This strictly Western view is not only exclusive, but it cannot accommodate the complex realities of a postindustrial society. Every fall, design education begins once again at ground zero seeking to emulate the creative outburst and convulsions of post-European Modernism following the First World War that initially included several contradictory impulses, much of which encouraged experimentation in the face of a near-total lack of financial and civil authority. Today, designers face the possibility of total environmental chaos and/or at the very least a society that no longer needs or values design's contributions.

The Modernist's impulse to seek universal solutions through mechanical reproduction proved to be something of a red herring. They were constrained in their search by the absence of practical solutions that are in fact applicable to all. The particular strain of Modernism long associated with the formal training in graphic design conceived at the Bauhaus, codified through the Swiss style, and reiterated nearly everywhere that graphic design has been taught, holds both the promise of progress and the baggage of dogma. This formalist approach to teaching design seems to divorce form from content, glossing over all the imperfections and fissures in the geometric modernism of the Bauhaus and its antecedents. A return to a looser, more experimental, and more inclusive design methodology is necessary for stimulating new thinking, as well as dealing with new forms that are now available and that reflect a more pluralistic society.

Outside

Building on the theme of less prescriptive assignments is the need to go outside. This means both literally exiting the classroom, the lab, and the building, as well as engaging in any activity that is outside of the students' comfort zone. Assignments should challenge the students' assumptions and expectations about the limits of the profession. Self-authored projects that address topical concerns regarding not only the environment but also questions of ethics have tended to lie outside the comfort zone of most students. Environmental design and projects that veer into the territory of installation and public art offer a way for audiences to interact with student work in the context of the built environment. Specific connections can be offered up about the ways consumption occurs and the ways the larger built environment affects the health of everyone and everything, rather than attempting to simply illustrate them. Site-specific work created for the public in shared spaces at the intersection of the built and natural environments provides unique opportunities for students to interact with public entities and communities.

These interactions illustrate the autonomous function of design when the work-for-hire model is subverted by the designer's response to the needs of a community. Situating work outside the class makes tangible not only immediate environmental concerns but also the traditional strength of design, one that connects design with people and places. Virtual experience should exist to supplement our understanding of the natural world; stepping back from the desktop or laptop may be necessary. Technologies can elicit certain responses that are in themselves prescriptive. Stepping back might include stepping out. Field trips may seem hackneyed, but a trip can be used to bring new ideas back to the classroom through a visit to a local materials recycling facility (MRF), retail environment, community meeting, farmer's market, or local ecological niche.

Materials

The unique position the designer occupies between production and consumption places materials at the center of any discussion of sustainable design. Specifying materials and processes helps immensely in demystifying design as it is practiced outside of the classroom. This dynamic existed long before the increased attention to the damaging effects of consumer waste. Traditionally, classes in pre-press and reproduction helped to reduce student anxiety over the unknown, often abstract process by which ideas take form. Today, this same dynamic exists but is compounded by the need to address how the materials and processes designers use to make ideas visible have been largely hidden from view. In the past, most of the waste designers produced simply "went away," but the distance between here and away has closed.

Even the aesthetic quality of work graphic designers produce has sought to make clean the work of large institutions such as corporations and governments and the economics of both.

Designers have been complicit in this practice, but their power to effect change as mediators should be leveraged to alter past practices. Assignments should seek to foreground materials by addressing how they are sourced, made available, and affect consumption. Victor Papanek proposed that the package is the product. This aligned the ethical dimension of design and sustainability with Marshall McLuhan's declaration that the medium is the message (1964). In today's context, the material can exist as the idea, because it is sustaining, depleting, or perhaps wasted. The question of whether something is truly necessary now can enter the discussion. Can another material be specified? Does this material need to be used at all? Will another material be better, somewhat better, or not better at all? Anchoring a project to materials revitalizes the designer's interest in craft. Just as at the Bauhaus, where students moved through different workshops devoted to various materials such as wood, textiles, or metal, this renewed emphasis on materials recalls why the designer should care. Isn't it better to make material choices not because they look good but because the material makes better all of design's relationships to people and the places called "the environment"?

Ethics

Good design has been attributed at various times to different things. In the 1930s, Raymond Lowey referred to good design as "an upward sales curve." Although that description is not entirely inaccurate, it limits the reach of design to do good to how it can affect sales. The Museum of Modern Art traded on the phrase "good design" to market designed objects and affect taste in postwar America. Unfortunately, the objects, although highly desirable, were unattainable to most people. Both definitions implicate good design in consumption and by extension waste. As discussed, the design professions began with reform as an integral part of their practice. It was only later that designers came to accept their primary mission as being one with commerce and consumption.

Many students assume that their role as designers is to sell or market something. The reform of society by design implies that ethics are central to design practice. Reforming or addressing the pressing environmental concerns is only one aspect of how design education should and can address ethical questions in the broader sense—and that includes environmental ethics. In the present, this extends into nearly every aspect of everyday life, from economics, health, and climate change to food, clothing, and shelter. In other words, design's impact is more pronounced today because of the scale at which environmental issues are affecting nearly every aspect of life. Future design education must address these issues by seeking solutions that are relevant to the ways design contributes to these problems and the ways it can address and/or redress them.

Personal

When discussing ethics, it is essential that designers understand themselves and their intended audience or users. The reasons why people identify with designed objects and images are highly personal and, though complex, they can be appreciated to a large degree. Empathy is the primary tool in the exchange between the design experience and the user's desire to make change. It has been said that global environmental problems cannot be solved through shopping, but that does not diminish the impact of design on the things people buy and sell. The consumer, or perhaps the more apt term is the user, must identify positively with an object in order to change buying patterns. This is true whether the consumer simply switches to a better product and continues to consume at the same rate or attempts to significantly reduce consumption.

Whatever the case, the choice is personal. The user must be afforded the opportunity to identify as an ethical person in order to bond with a designed object, image, or experience. The average person believes him- or herself to be good; it is in everyone's best interest that this feeling be supported by the ways in which the average person consumes. Different audiences and users will walk away with different conclusions based on their specific backgrounds. Much of this is relative to the community in which they were raised and the way that they identify. The relationship of the single individual to the whole is important in understanding how individuals and groups respond to different designs. This is vital to the designer's grasp of how to ideate for a variety of nuanced approaches to a design solution. The designer as a single entity acting alone to produce heroic or epic works is not a realistic approach. The designer must understand how each unique viewpoint is relevant to a solution, including his or her own. Until the public at large is made more aware of its impacts individually and as a whole, it will continue to act in its own self-interest. Self-interest is not all bad, as it may motivate people to act to preserve their own health, as well as the health of the environment. Empathizing with individuals and appreciating their self-interest and appealing to it can hasten an awareness of sustainable design.

Collaboration

The designer's ability to empathize is important in collaboration because of the relationship of design to all human activity. Design education will require a renewed emphasis on work among groups of students to address environmental concerns. The term *group* is used here instead of *team* in order to deemphasize the pervasive language of competition in contemporary culture. The ridiculous degree to which competition is modeled on reality television has had a destructive influence on student perceptions of small-group dynamics. Nonetheless, some sense of the relevance of competition and small-group dynamics remains critical. The ability to work in groups with a variety of creative professionals is an increasing asset that every student must carry into professional practice. Furthermore, graphic design especially must engage with other design disciplines to affect how things get made, so that messages designers create can help shape production and consumption. Within academia, graphic design education must work across disciplines. Business, engineering, natural and social sciences, and the humanities should be investigated as potential collaborators in the creation of innovative ways to integrate sustainability with design education.

Communication

Ultimately, the question of what the graphic designer can bring to any collaboration must be answered. How can design help initiate and shape the discussion? Creativity is an obvious answer, but it is quite broad and perhaps does not state specifically what the graphic designer offers that is different from other design professions and players in finding sustainable solutions. The intersection of text and image in graphic design is what distinguishes the practice from other design disciplines. What occurs at this junction connects graphic design with written language and all the fields that base their primary research on texts, as well as the history of art and image making of all kinds. The plethora of new media that is predicated more on seeing than reading justifies a response from graphic design that seeks to understand all of what has come to be deemed visual culture. Fields that are based in the written word all now include the reading of images as part of their work.

Graphic design's practice in the production of images and words for reproduction gives the designer unique insights into how meaning is created. Thinking critically through the integration of word and image as it occurs is graphic design's unique contribution. This production of meaning, designed typically for mass consumption, drives at the heart of what production and consumption means to our culture. No other discipline can speak with the same authority to and with the ubiquity of words and images that currently surround us. Training in graphic design offers the most advanced study of what it means to be visually literate. Graphic design grounds the individual in a process of contemplation that exceeds any other in the nuances of visual culture and by extension most of what defines contemporary society. Student projects that leverage the power of graphic design to advocate, educate, build awareness, and persuade the public to act are what will demonstrate the role of graphic design and guarantee its future relevance.

Self-Conscious

Sustainable design teaching focuses on Design: Past, Present, and Future, the integration of history, theory, and criticism with the teaching of studio practice in design. Contemporary design is taught with an understanding of how the discipline evolved as a particular strain of Modernism, which matured in the context of consumer capitalism, and with an interest in defining future design practice and education. This includes a particular interest in the ways individuals, institutions, and nations have evolved their identities through the consumption of artifacts. Ultimately, it centers on what happens to design in the hands of the users, through consumption.

Several of the outcomes sought are derived from the design methodology first pioneered by Ellen Lupton and J. Abbott Miller and outlined in their book *Design, Writing, Research*. Rick Poynor, writing in the introduction, stated that this emphasis is "nourished by an unusual degree by the processes of critical reflection encouraged by writing and research." They sought to bridge theory and practice, as well as to bring the verbal and the visual into closer relationship and to shape content as "self-conscious authors" (1999: viii–x).

Self-consciousness is at the heart of what sustainable design education proposes now in answer to what graphic designers must become if they are to act confidently to help solve the ongoing environmental crisis. First, students must know the history of their practice and how theories of design motivated and defined the intent of designers and provided much of their inspiration. Design criticism then takes stock of what has occurred, including the environmental consequences. At this point, students can respond through their work to what has come before in anticipation of the ways future design practice is being redefined in the present and how it will continue to evolve in reaction to the limitations of a linear model of consumption and waste.

There is already a model for addressing design's negative effect on the environment. As recently as the 1960s and 1970s, design was engaged critically with its past and its effect on the natural environment in what was termed *outlaw design*, which coincided with the ecology movement. The technologies and forms that most interested these designers and technologists were those that seemed to reproduce design practices similar to cottage industries of the past and that most emulated Morris's vision of a return to the craft skills of the guilds. This movement helped revive interest in an eclectic array of past styles that included Arts and Crafts and in turn repeated the romantic alignment of the natural with the feminine. These tropes reentered popular culture and entertainment, which they were ostensibly opposed to as products of consumerism. It is clear that outlaw design carried forward much of the baggage associated with previous critical assessments of both industrialization and consumerism. The movement was, in the end, unable to unburden itself of

Modernism and create a contemporary popular aesthetic that might transcend old ways of making. The failure ultimately was its inability to conceive of an aesthetic that both questioned power as visualized in very concrete form through the International style and to envision a common ground between environmentalism and capitalism.

The threat of the movement being co-opted through popular forms of expression was very real, yet the popular media of advertising design as described by Thomas Frank in *The Conquest of Cool* helped engender the counterculture of the 1960s and of which the design outlaws played a role. Frank asserts that the advertising of the 1960s acknowledged and sympathized with the mass society critique, what he calls "anti-advertising: a style, which harnessed public mistrust of consumerism" (1997: 55). For the outlaw designers, it was the built environment, which they most vehemently opposed in the form of the International style of architecture more commonly referred to as the Swiss style among graphic designers. The architecture, which was originally conceived at the Bauhaus as worker housing, reached its apex in the form of corporate office buildings, which Wright referred to as "filing cabinets for people" and which Tom Wolfe satirized in *From Bauhaus to Our House* (1981).

In part, the design outlaws sought the absence of style, not in the exclusion of ornament or decoration but in the absence of brute force as typified by the application of more corporate power in the name of progress. They were right in their equation of style with power, and they were right to stand suspiciously apart from it. What the design outlaws might have looked to in answer to corporate hegemony was the nascent consumerism described by Susan Strasser in *Waste and Want: A Social History of Trash*, where she convincingly demonstrates the recycling, remaking, and reuse of waste products as inherent to the development of early consumerism in the nineteenth-century United States until, as she describes it, "disposal became separated from production, consumption and use" (1999: 15).

The limitations of the outlaw design movement began with their view of technology in the form of the opposition between nature and technology; in this case, specifically the modern technology of industrial capitalism as well as the mainstream media, consumerism, and popular culture. A dichotomous approach to practice and criticism is common to Modernism. The notion that nature and technology are in opposition to one another is not very different from the Victorian view of nature/

culture in which humans apart from nature must dominate, tame, or control their environment. Oddly, the oppositional basis of outlaw design seemed to contradict their espoused approach to holistic living with nature in a modern society.

"I don't think our work is about reaching goals. It's about proposing intelligent and responsible solutions to our clients. It's not a matter of achievement but values."

—Audrey Blouin | student
University of Quebec at Montreal

"The present worldwide concern for the environment cannot now be dismissed as a fashion, as it was during the early 1970s, nor as pure panic over the sustainability of life on earth. I believe that it is rather a great spiritual reawakening, a desire to reestablish closer links between nature and humankind."

—Victor Papanek
The Green Imperative:
Natural Design for the Real World

"Design, by its nature, is an interdisciplinary area, this is clearly a strength. The complex or 'wicked' nature of the environmental problems we now face require flexibility, interdisciplinary collaboration, and creative thinking."

—Emily Wright | Professor
University of Swinburne, Australia

References

Adamson, Glen (2003), *Industrial Strength Design: How Brook Stevens Shaped Your World*, Cambridge, MA: MIT Press.

Barthes, Roland (1957), *Mythologies*, New York: Random House.

Bruno, Giuliana (1987), "Ramble City: Postmodernism and Blade Runner," *October*, 41: 61–74. Accessed at: http://web.stanford.edu/dept/HPS/Bruno/bladerunner.html

Buell, Lawrence (1995), *The Environmental Imagination: Thoreau, Nature Writing, and the Formation of American Culture*, Cambridge, MA: Harvard University Press.

Drucker, Johanna, and Emily McVarish (2009), *Graphic Design History: A Critical Guide*, New York: Pearson Education.

Ewen, Stuart (1988), *All Consuming Images: The Politics of Style in Contemporary Culture*, New York: Basic Books.

Florida, Richard (2002), *The Rise of the Creative Class*, New York: Basic Books.

Frank, Thomas (1997), *The Conquest of Cool: Business Culture, Counterculture, and the Rise of Hip Consumerism,* Chicago: University of Chicago Press.

Freidrichs, Chad (2011), *The Pruitt-Igoe Myth* (DVD), First Run Features.

Freinkel, Susan (2011), *Plastic: A Toxic Love Story*, New York: Houghton Mifflin Harcourt.

Fuller, Buckminster (1969), *Operating Manual for Spaceship Earth: A Bold Blueprint for Survival That Diagnoses the Causes of the Environmental Crisis,* Carbondale, IL: Southern Illinois University Press.

Garreau, Joel (1992), *Edge Cities: Life on the New Frontier*, New York: Anchor Books.

Hale, Grace Elizabeth (1998), *Making Whiteness: The Culture of Segregation in the South, 1890–1940*, New York: Vintage Books.

Hawken, Paul, Amory Lovins, and L. Hunter Lovins (1999), *Natural Capitalism: Creating the Next Industrial Revolution*, New York: Little Brown.

Hine, Thomas (1995), *The Total Package: The Secret History and Hidden Meanings of Boxes, Bottles, Cans and Other Persuasive Containers*, New York: Little Brown.

Holmes, Oliver Wendell (1859), "The Stereoscope and the Stereograph," *The Atlantic Monthly*, June. Accessed at: http://www.theatlantic.com/magazine/archive/1859/06/the-stereoscope-and-the-stereograph/303361/

Hustwit, Gary (2007), *Helvetica* (DVD), Swiss Dots.

Imhoff, Dan (1999), *The Simple Life Guide to Tree-Free and Certified Papers*, Simple Life.

Kirk, Andrew (2007), *Counterculture Green: The Whole Earth Catalog and American Environmentalism*, Lawrence: University Press of Kansas.

Klein, Naomi (2000), *No Logo*, New York: Picador Books.

Loos, Adolf (1908/1997), *Ornament and Crime: Selected Essays*, Riverside, CA: Ariadne Press.

Lupton, Ellen, and J. Abbott Miller (1999), *Design, Writing, Research: Writing on Graphic Design*, London, UK: Phaidon Press.

McLuhan, Marshall (1964), *Understanding Media: The Extensions of Man*, New York: Signet Books.

Nordhaus, Ted, and Michael Shellenberger (2007), *Breakthrough: From the Death of Environmentalism to the Politics of Possibility*, New York: Houghton Mifflin.

Packard, Vance (1960), *The Waste Makers*, New York: Simon and Schuster.

Papanek, Victor (1972), *Design for the Real World: Human Ecology and Social Change*, New York: Thames and Hudson.

Papanek, Victor (1995), *The Green Imperative: Natural Design for the Real World*, New York: Random House.

Rogers, Heather (2005), *Gone Tomorrow: The Hidden Life of Garbage*, New York: The New Press.

Roszak, Theodore (1969). *The Making of a Counter Culture: Reflections on the Technocratic Society and Its Youthful Opposition*, New York: Anchor Books.

Schumacher, E. F. (1973), *Small Is Beautiful: Economics As If People Mattered*, New York: Harper and Row.

Smith, Cynthia E. (2007), *Design for the Other 90%*, New York: Cooper-Hewitt Smithsonian Design Museum.

Sparke, Penny (1995), *As Long As It's Pink: The Sexual Politics of Taste*, New York: Harper Collins.

Strasser, Susan (1999), *Waste and Want: A Social History of Trash*, New York: Henry Holt.

Venturi, Robert, Denise Scott Brown, and Steven Izenour (1972), *Learning from Las Vegas: The Forgotten Symbolism of Architectural Form*, Cambridge, MA: MIT Press.

Walker, Stuart (2006), *Sustainable by Design: Exploration in Theory and Practice*, Oxford, UK: Earthscan.

Wolfe, Thomas (1981), *From Bauhaus to Our House,* New York: Picador.

Wurman, Richard Saul (1989), *Information Anxiety*, New York: Bantam.

Wurman, Richard Saul (1997), *Information Architects,* New York: Graphis.

Zelov, Chris, and Phil Cousineau, (1997), *Design Outlaws on the Ecological Frontier*, Hellertown, PA: The Knossus Project.

Illustrations Credits

Figure 70, author image, courtesy of Michelle Rivera

Figure 71, author image, courtesy of Michelle Rivera

Figure 72, author image, courtesy of Michelle Rivera

Figure 73, author image, courtesy of Michelle Rivera

Figure 74, author image, courtesy of Michelle Rivera

Figure 75, author image, courtesy of Michelle Rivera

Figure 76, author image, courtesy of Michelle Rivera

Figure 77, author image, courtesy of Michelle Rivera

Figure 78, author image, courtesy of Michelle Rivera

Figure 79, author image, courtesy of Michelle Rivera

Figure 80, author image, courtesy of Michelle Rivera

Figure 81, author image, courtesy of Michelle Rivera

Figure 82, author image, courtesy of Darold Ross, Candace Barnett, Joel Zamora, and Fangshu Zhu

Figure 83, author image, courtesy of Carmela Martinez, Danielle Garcia, Matt Ortiz

Figure 84, author image, courtesy of Carmela Martinez, Danielle Garcia, Matt Ortiz

Chapter Four

Figure 85, courtesy of Kristine Matthews

Figure 86, courtesy of Kristine Matthews

Figure 87, courtesy of Kristine Matthews

Figure 88, courtesy of Kristine Matthews

Figure 89, courtesy of Kristine Matthews

Figure 90, courtesy of Kristine Matthews

Figure 91, courtesy of Kristine Matthews

Figure 92, courtesy of Kristine Matthews

Figure 93, courtesy of Kristine Matthews

Figure 94, courtesy of Kristine Matthews

Figure 95, courtesy of Kristine Matthews

Figure 96, courtesy of Kristine Matthews

Figure 97, courtesy of Kristine Matthews

Figure 98, courtesy of Cheryl Beckett and Patrick Peters

Figure 99, courtesy of Cheryl Beckett and Patrick Peters

Figure 100, courtesy of Cheryl Beckett and Patrick Peters

Figure 101, courtesy of Cheryl Beckett and Patrick Peters

Figure 102, courtesy of Cheryl Beckett and Patrick Peters

Figure 103, courtesy of Cheryl Beckett and Patrick Peters

Figure 104, courtesy of Cheryl Beckett and Patrick Peters

Figure 105, courtesy of Cheryl Beckett and Patrick Peters

Figure 106, courtesy of Cheryl Beckett and Patrick Peters

Figure 107, courtesy of Cheryl Beckett and Patrick Peters

Figure 108, courtesy of Cheryl Beckett and Patrick Peters

Figure 109, courtesy of Cheryl Beckett and Patrick Peters

Figure 110, courtesy of Cheryl Beckett and Patrick Peters

Figure 111, courtesy of Ellen McMahon

Chapter Five

Figure 112, courtesy of Natacha Poggio

Figure 113, courtesy of Natacha Poggio

Figure 114, courtesy of Natacha Poggio

Figure 115, courtesy of Natacha Poggio

Figure 116, courtesy of Natacha Poggio

Figure 117, courtesy of Natacha Poggio

Figure 118, courtesy of Natacha Poggio

Figure 119, courtesy of Natacha Poggio

Figure 120, courtesy of Natacha Poggio

Figure 121, author image, courtesy of Leslie Sandoval, Reyna Salinas, and Christina Olivas

Figure 122, author image, courtesy of Leslie Sandoval, Reyna Salinas, and Christina Olivas

Figure 123, courtesy of Scott Boylston, Tiffany Lindeborn, Marina Petrova, Giang, Nguyen Hung, and Forum Shah

Figure 124, courtesy of Scott Boylston, Tiffany Lindeborn, Marina Petrova, Giang, Nguyen Hung, and Forum Shah

Figure 125, courtesy of Scott Boylston, Tiffany Lindeborn, Marina Petrova, Giang, Nguyen Hung, and Forum Shah

Chapter Six

Chapter opener photo, courtesy of Peter Claver Fine

Index

A

Abdullah, Nida, 9, 10
Abheypur (Indian village), 87, 100
ability, x, 37, 53, 56, 78, 79, 86, 97
    and analysis/synthesis, 7, 108
    of designers, 14, 16, 21, 27, 30, 36,
        73, 84, 85, 95, 106, 114
    and digital design, 12, 25, 26
    and digital technology, 5, 31
    and visualization, 25, 87
absence, 18, 74, 80, 81, 85, 106, 110, 112, 115
absorption, 106
abstract/abstracted/abstraction, xiv, 12,
        46–47, 53, 57, 63, 84, 96, 111, 112
abundance, 53, 55, 80, 87, 110
academia, 114
access, 5, 8, 13, 15, 58, 87, 110
accident/accidental, 6, 54, 71, 107
accounting, 6, 86
acculturation, xiii, 58
accumulation, 95, 97

acquisition, 30, 79
activism/activists, 97, 107, 109
activities, xviii, 14, 17
Adamson, Glen, xvii
AdBusters, 3, 17, 18
adopted/adopters/adoption, 25, 31, 33,
        37, 55, 83, 97, 106, 111
adulterated/adulteration, xviii, 80, 92
advertisement, 2, 3, 5, 10, 18, 19, 81
Advertising Federation, 18
advocacy, 2, 5, 11, 31, 41, 83, 84, 94
      for consumers, xii, 50, 58, 114
      for sustainability, 5, 20, 37
aesthetics/aestheticism, xiv, 6, 106
affluence, 15, 93
Africa, 89, 91
African Americans, 95
African Center for Engineering
        Solutions (ACESS), 100
Africans, 51, 52
Afya Kwanzaa (Wellness First), 100
agency, xii, 17, 19, 46, 47, 56, 86, 98, 103, 107, 109

AgriProp, 74, 77, 84
Alcoholics Anonymous, 70
alienation, xviii
alignment, 92, 115
Allard, Sylvain, 42, 45, 56, 57
altruism, 38
Alvarado, Arantza, 74
Alway-Rosenstock, Sara, 27, 36
amaranth promotion/branding, 88, 89, 100
ambiguity/ambiguousness, xii, 3, 18, 22, 96, 110
anthropology, 92
antithesis/antithetical, 80, 81, 109
appeal, 46, 71, 97, 109, 114
archaic technology, 108
architects/architecture, 14, 28, 29, 37, 73,
        81, 89, 115
Arciniega, Ramon, 74
Argentina, 100
argument, 3, 15, 31, 36, 37, 59, 99
art nouveau, xvi, 108
artifice/artificiality, 55, 82
ASCII, 12